Beginning Game Development with Godot

Learn to Create and Publish Your First 2D Platform Game

Maithili Dhule

Apress®

Beginning Game Development with Godot: Learn to Create and Publish Your First 2D Platform Game

Maithili Dhule
Singapore, Singapore

ISBN-13 (pbk): 978-1-4842-7454-5   ISBN-13 (electronic): 978-1-4842-7455-2
https://doi.org/10.1007/978-1-4842-7455-2

Managing Director, Apress Media LLC: Welmoed Spahr
Acquisitions Editor: Spandana Chatterjee
Development Editor: Laura Berendson
Coordinating Editor: Divya Modi
Copyeditor: Kim Wimpsett

Cover designed by eStudioCalamar

Cover image designed by Maithili Dhule

Distributed to the book trade worldwide by Springer Science+Business Media New York, 1 New York Plaza, Suite 4600, New York, NY 10004-1562, USA. Phone 1-800-SPRINGER, fax (201) 348-4505, e-mail orders-ny@springer-sbm.com, or visit www.springeronline.com. Apress Media, LLC is a California LLC and the sole member (owner) is Springer Science + Business Media Finance Inc (SSBM Finance Inc). SSBM Finance Inc is a **Delaware** corporation.

For information on translations, please e-mail booktranslations@springernature.com; for reprint, paperback, or audio rights, please e-mail bookpermissions@springernature.com.

Apress titles may be purchased in bulk for academic, corporate, or promotional use. eBook versions and licenses are also available for most titles. For more information, reference our Print and eBook Bulk Sales web page at www.apress.com/bulk-sales.

Any source code or other supplementary material referenced by the author in this book is available to readers on GitHub via the book's product page, located at www.apress.com/978-1-4842-7454-5. For more detailed information, please visit www.apress.com/source-code.

Printed on acid-free paper

Dedicated to all aspiring game developers!

Table of Contents

About the Author

Maithili Dhule is an Electronics engineer by profession, and holds a Master's degree in Integrated Circuit Design. She is a writer by choice, and an aspiring game developer. After coming across the art of creating games, she quickly realized it was one of her passions. During her free time, she can be found experimenting with different game engines or being immersed in one of her favorite games. She also enjoys trying out new restaurants, sketching portraits, writing poetry, and going for runs while listening to a good music playlist. She has developed a browser-based game called Dragon's Flight, which is playable on the website Itch.io. You can reach out to her at `mathletmakesgames@gmail.com`.

About the Technical Reviewer

John Wigg is a computational and data science student. He holds a bachelor's degree in physics, and his interests include computer graphics, game development, and open source. In the past, he has worked as a technical assistant for many of his university's working groups. As a fan of the Godot game engine, he likes to release open source projects and tools for it as well as participate in game jams. In the future, he hopes to draw from his scientific background to explore a career in computer graphics and visualization.

Acknowledgments

"If I have seen further than others, it is by standing on the shoulders of giants."

—Sir Isaac Newton

Here I am today, the author of a book on a topic I enjoy immensely—game development. There are quite a lot of people I am grateful for, for helping make this book come to fruition.

I would like to thank my family for being supportive and patient and for motivating me while I spent back-breaking hours working on the manuscript.

I am grateful for my friends (all around the world!) for making me laugh and smile and for always believing in me.

I feel lucky to have been taught by so many wonderful teachers over the years. Thank you for teaching me, inspiring me, and making me capable to enough to write a book!

I am also immensely grateful to my acquisition editor, Spandana Chatterjee, for giving me this opportunity to combine my passion for writing and making games. I would also like to thank my technical editor, John Wigg, for taking the effort to go through the entire book and suggesting valuable feedback. Moreover, I am thankful to Divya Modi, Laura Berendson, and the rest of the Apress team for your collaboration and help.

Thank you all for making my dream a reality!

Introduction

Game development is a journey of discovery and creation—it's an art, really. With the right tools and knowledge, we can all be artists. What makes it remarkable is that it welcomes people with all kinds of talents; you can be a coder who makes the program work, you can be a designer who creates game characters and builds the game world, you can be a musician who adds music and sound effects, or you can be someone who does all of that! It gives you the chance to either work independently (earning the cool title of indie game developer!) or collaborate with other talented individuals.

Surprisingly, some of the very best games out there start with small teams or are created by just a single person. But this has the incredible advantage of giving you the opportunity to learn more. This is where books and resources on game development, such as this one, come into the picture.

I would like to take a moment to thank you, reader, for picking up this book. We'll begin our learning journey together. While some of us may be just starting out in game development, some among us may be seasoned programmers who want to get a solid understanding of the basics of making 2D games with Godot. Here's a glimpse into what comes next:

We'll …

- **Briefly talk** about some design principles that are used by famous games to make them fun to play. We'll discuss game engines and what makes Godot a great one for beginners and experts alike.

- **Get comfortable** with navigating around the Godot interface, and brush over the basics of GDScript, the main scripting language used in Godot.

- **Play around** with game physics and use the related concepts to animate and control our game character.

- **Design** the entire 2D game world, adding different collectibles that the player can collect and introduce enemies that the player can defeat.

- **Create** a simple system to keep track of the player's score and lives, and create a mechanism to reload a scene if a player falls off a cliff or to load the Game Over scene if the player loses the game.

- **Add** some cool music and sound effects to our game, and design the GUI for various game screens such as the title screen.

- **Export** our games to various platforms such as mobile (Android), PC (Windows), and the browser.

- **Learn** ways to publish and monetize our game.

Now, let's dive right into making our first 2D platformer in Godot!

PART I

The Art of Creating Games

CHAPTER 1

Introduction

In this chapter, we'll talk briefly about early games and the rise of the gaming industry. We'll take a look at the basic principles of game design and the secrets behind making a game exciting to play. We'll also learn about the concept of a game engine, how to choose one, and some compelling reasons to pick Godot.

The Birth of Video Games

The origins of video game development date back to the 1950s, a time when a computer was a gigantic piece of machinery that took up the whole room. It was unimaginable to use such a huge machine for the purpose of entertainment, let alone gaming.

This changed in 1958, when Tennis for Two was created to attract guests to an exhibition and demonstrate advances in technology. This game simulated an actual tennis match between two players, giving each player the ability to hit the on-screen ball using simple handheld controllers. Two perpendicular lines formed the ground and the net, while the ball was just a simple green dot on the screen that changed its trajectory every time a player pressed a button on the controller.

A decade later, a group of students designed the game Spacewar! at the Massachusetts Institute of Technology. In this space-themed combat game, two players tried to destroy each other's spaceship through strategic shooting and maneuvering through a star system that was on the verge of collapse. There were no winners or losers, and the game simply restarted once one of the spaceships was hit. Deemed as one of the first video games playable on multiple computers, it paved the way for the future of game development.

© Maithili Dhule 2022
M. Dhule, *Beginning Game Development with Godot*, https://doi.org/10.1007/978-1-4842-7455-2_1

The years following the 1970s saw the rise of arcade machines and gaming consoles, with companies such as Atari, Magnavox, Nintendo, and Sega dominating the gaming industry. Gaming consoles such as the Magnavox Odyssey and Atari 2600 became popular among the public.

A number of timeless pieces were soon created, such as:

- *Pong*: A two-dimensional predecessor of the modern-day air hockey.

- *Space Invaders*: A space shooter where you have to defeat multiple rows of incoming aliens by firing at them with the help of a laser cannon.

- *PAC-MAN*: A game where you play as a hungry, yellow character that has to munch through all the dots in a maze while picking up fruit and powerups, all while avoiding colorful ghosts.

- *Donkey Kong*: An action platformer in which you play as Jumpman, attempting to climb ladders and avoiding the barrels and fireballs thrown at you by an evil monkey.

- *Super Mario Bros.*: A 2D side-scroller in which you play as Mario or Luigi to try to save Princess Toadstool from the boss turtle Bowser while fighting evil mushrooms (Goombas) and turtles (Koopa Troopas).

- *Ultima*: A series of open-world, fantasy-themed games where the player can customize their character, upgrade its skills, and explore the fantasy realm of Britannia.

Today, the gaming industry is worth hundreds of billions of dollars and continues to grow with advances in technology. We can take our pick from tons of gaming consoles such as Xbox Series X, Sony PlayStation, and the Nintendo Switch and Wii, or choose to play on our PC or smartphone. In fact, many games, such as Fortnite and Minecraft, are now playable on multiple platforms.

Game graphics have evolved from being simple, pixel-based to incredibly lifelike and hyper-realistic. Half-Life: Alyx, Assassin's Creed, The Outer Worlds, and Far Cry are some of the best examples of games that have worked painstakingly to create a gaming experience that closely mirrors real-life objects, people, and places. The game graphics, storyline, and characters of modern games have become so advanced that they put the player right in the middle of the game, blurring the lines between reality and fiction.

Principles of Game Design

A game needs a sense of accomplishment. And you have to have a sense that you have done something so that you get that sense of satisfaction of completing something.

—*Shigeru Miyamoto, designer of Super Mario*

As a game designer, you hold the power to create a fantastic experience for the player. What makes games great to play isn't just complex mechanics and beautiful graphics; often, the simplest of games can turn out to be quite fun and exciting. Let's learn about the fundamental principles that are used to design popular games.

Game Progression

The trick to make your game more interesting lies in challenging the player to overcome difficult yet achievable scenarios while providing rewards for successful attempts. This can be done through the progression of gameplay. The game's initial levels should introduce the player to the gaming controls and the game's objectives, characters, enemies, and possible rewards.

The game difficulty should increase gradually to avoid overwhelming the player. With every next level, you can introduce different elements of game mechanics such as new weapons, abilities, powerups, and locations. You can choose to give the player various missions or tasks to complete within a level, such as collecting a certain number of coins or defeating all the enemies in that level. You can also keep certain levels locked until the player completes some of these tasks.

The game Temple Run is an excellent example of game progression. The player starts out by running slowly and is introduced to the mobile tilt-controlled style of gameplay. As time passes, the speed of the endless runner keeps increasing until the player runs into an obstacle. The challenge to run as far as possible and collect as many coins as possible, all while a monster chases you, makes the game fast-paced and exciting.

Put the Player in Control

In a management-style game like Roller Coaster Tycoon (RCT), Planet Zoo, and the Age of Empires, everything that happens in the game world is in your hands. In such games, you often start out with limited resources and work your way up to the top. The game then simulates conditions that test your skills, which leads to either success or disaster in the game. For example, in RCT, you are the boss of an amusement park. You can control the smallest of things—the price of the park ticket, the number and type of staff you want to hire, how many scary or gentle rides your park will have, and even the landscape in and around the park. Based on these factors, the game will create random events that may happen in the case of an actual theme park. The number of guests that come to your park, their opinion about each ride, and the amount of profit you will make will depend on how well you design the park. Having total control over a virtual world in games like these can keep you engaged for hours on end.

Give the Player Choices

According to modern-day psychology, when you are given choices, it makes you feel powerful. In the game Life is Strange, you play as Max, a character with the ability to reverse time. By making specific choices at different points in the game, you control the game's narrative. If the story doesn't play out the way you wanted it to, you can always go back and change your decision and see a different version of the game storyline. This game mechanic is widely used in the choose-your-own-adventure genre.

The act of being able to make a choice that directly impacts a game can be pretty meaningful for a player. A lot of role-playing games are designed using this idea. For example, almost all RPGs give you the ability to customize your character at the beginning of the game; you can pick everything from the character's looks to its special skills and abilities. This helps create a unique experience for the player by helping them connect emotionally to the characters and makes the game interesting and playable multiple times.

Create Immersive Scenarios

Massively multiplayer online role-playing games (MMORPGs) such as the World of Warcraft and Runescape and strategic Life simulation games such as those in the Sims franchise let you customize your character and explore an open world filled with endless possibilities. Such games tend to be highly immersive as they have activities that mimic real life, such as fishing, woodcutting, and trading. They often contain elements of fantasy and science-fiction, which tickle the player's imagination. The thrill of virtually walking through dangerous and harsh terrain, battling mythical monsters, and being the hero and saving the day can be highly enticing. This element of escapism makes the game incredibly satisfying and addictive for the player.

Have a Creative Vision

What do Lara Croft, Mario, Max Payne, Sonic the Hedgehog, and Princess Zelda have in common? They are all memorable video game characters that are known and loved by fans all over the world. In fact, they are as famous as the game they star in! The credit to their fame goes to the fact that they have been meticulously designed according to the game's theme and storyline.

If you want to create a game that will stand out, you need to think about a couple of things:

- The game type, e.g., platformer, MMORPG, puzzle

- The game genre, e.g., horror, fantasy, science-fiction, action-adventure

- The story you want to tell through your game

- Whether your game is going to be two-dimensional or three-dimensional

- Whether you want to include super-realistic characters and places or cartoon-style, two-dimensional ones

Once you decide your game's overall look and feel, you need to pick a game engine to start creating it. In the next section, we'll explore what exactly a game engine is and how to choose one.

What Is a Game Engine?

Say you want to bake a cake. All you need to do is to gather all the ingredients, mix them in a bowl, and put them in the oven to bake. Now imagine trying to build the oven from scratch! Luckily, you don't need to do that. There are dozens of different ovens available in the market that you can purchase, each with a different set of features.

A game engine is like an oven that you can use right out of the box. It is a collection of audio, visual, and technical tools that form the basic framework needed to create any game. These reusable software tools make it easy to pick and choose the components you need while designing your game. Most engines are packed with various features such as:

- 2D and 3D graphics rendering engines that support animation

- A physics engine for handling rigid body collisions and interaction

- An audio engine for adding music and sound effects

- Support for different programming languages such as GDScript, C#, C, and Java

- Integration of technologies such as artificial intelligence, virtual reality, and augmented reality

- Support for publishing the game to various platforms such as mobile, PC, console, and the Web

To truly build a game from scratch, you would have to first create the game engine by yourself, a task that could take months, if not years. With the use of ready-made tools provided by game engines, you can focus on the process of creating the game instead of trying to reinvent the wheel!

If you are just getting started with game development, game engines can help you quickly create a prototype of your game while learning key concepts without going too deep into the technical details. If you make a game for one specific platform, you can use the same engine to generate another build for a different platform without redesigning the entire game.

With the availability of popular game engines such as Godot, Unity, and Unreal, it has become easier than ever to jump right into creating games today. Figure 1-1 shows the interface of the Unity game engine, which shows a sample game scene. Let's take a look at some of the factors we need to consider while choosing a game engine.

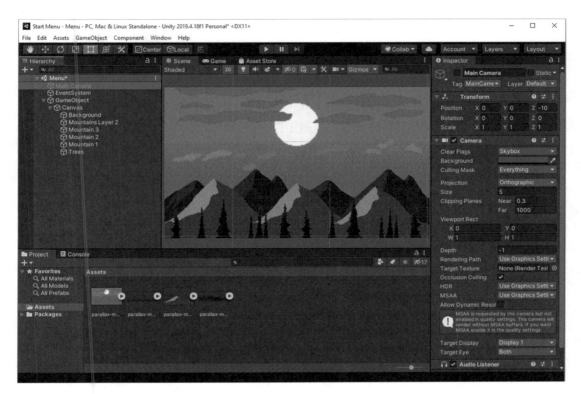

Figure 1-1. *A game scene created using Unity, a popular game engine*

How Do We Choose a Game Engine?

Some of the most popular game engines on the market that exist today include Godot, Unreal Engine, Unity, CryEngine, GameMaker Studio, AppGameKit, and RPGMaker. With such a daunting number of choices available, which one should you pick?

Several factors can help you decide:

- The kind of game you're trying to make, indie or AAA?

- Your team size and budget

- The tools and features that are necessary to build your game

- The platform you want to release your game to, PC, mobile, and/or console?

- The engine interface you prefer

- The programming languages that you are comfortable with

Independent or indie games are usually created by an individual or a small team. Celeste, Stardew Valley, Super Meat Boy, and Hollow Knight are some famous examples. They typically have a smaller budget and are less taxing on the hardware when played. If you're aiming to create an indie-style game, you may not need a fancy engine with lots of features you won't use.

On the other hand, AAA games are the golden eggs of the gaming industry and are developed by huge teams over a long period. Bethesda Game Studios, known for developing the Elder Scrolls series, and Square Enix, known for creating the Final Fantasy series, are examples of AAA studios. These companies invest millions of dollars to make these popular titles, often using their own in-house game engines. They generally have significantly higher budgets as they need advanced tools for creating highly immersive, hyper-realistic characters and worlds.

Every game engine has a unique interface, with its own set of pros and cons. You should try playing around with different ones until you find one that you're comfortable with. Engines like Unity and Unreal are free for personal use, as long as the revenue you earn on your game doesn't cross a certain threshold. Advanced versions of such engines offer more extensive features and more technical support but may set you back a few thousand dollars a year. Godot, Spring Engine, and Panda 3D are examples of open source software, which means that you don't need to pay a single cent to use them for creating and selling your game.

You also need to consider the level of programming that you are most comfortable with. C++, C#, and Java are some of the most commonly used languages used in game development. Game engines usually support multiple languages but may be associated with one or two predominant ones. For example, Unity natively supports scripting in C#. On the other hand, many game engines, such as Godot, CryEngine, and Unreal, support visual scripting as well. This lets you focus on the flow of the logic without concentrating too much on writing technical code.

Chances are, since you've picked up this guide, you are just starting out with game development and might be considering beginning with a simple 2D game. If this is the case, you may not want to spend a lot of time and money on creating your first game. It's best to stick with beginner-friendly engines that have good documentation and community support. Let's take a look at some of the reasons why Godot might be a great choice.

Why Choose Godot?

Here's what makes Godot an excellent choice as a game engine.

The Graphics Engines Are Amazing

Godot has dedicated 2D and 3D graphics engines that are packed with valuable features. The 2D engine, which uses pixel coordinates, allows you to animate just about anything with its straightforward, keyframe-based animation player. A flexible kinematic controller enables you to implement rigid body interaction with ease. A tilemap editor lets you paint the game world with auto-tiling and create beautiful parallax backgrounds. 3D lighting and shadow effects, camera-perspective control, and the ability to create a procedural sky are just some of the features you can use to enhance your game.

It's Easy on the Eyes

A dark blue screen with neatly arranged docks, buttons, and shortcuts make up the beautiful, uncluttered UI of the Godot Engine. The interface is intuitive and straightforward and doesn't confuse the user with too much information. You can easily switch between the 2D and 3D editors, the Scripting window, and the Assets library, all with the click of a button.

It's Open Source

This means that Godot is completely free for anyone to download and use. You hold the copyright to every game you create with this engine and don't have to pay its developers a single cent for doing so. Released under the MIT license, it gives you the ability to sell the game for profit without paying any royalties.

It Can Be Run on Multiple Platforms

Godot works on Windows, Linux, and macOS, available in both the 32-bit and 64-bit versions. You can readily deploy your games to various desktop and mobile platforms, as well as to the Web. You can export the game to different gaming consoles such as Nintendo Switch and Xbox One using third-party applications (usually at a certain extra cost).

It Supports Live Editing

You can modify your game even while it's running! You don't have to worry about losing any changes if you accidentally close your project; the changes are always saved by default.

It Has Its Own Scripting Language

Godot game code is generally written in GDScript, a simple, easy-to-learn scripting language similar to Python. You can directly type your code in the editor using Godot's scripting interface. Programming languages such as C++, C#, and Visual Scripting are officially supported as well.

There Is a Vast Community Support

Godot has active community support such as groups and channels on Discord, Facebook, Reddit, Twitter, Steam, and YouTube. There is a dedicated GitHub repository of engine-related codes that are accessible to all. You can use the Godot Forum to ask the other users for help if you get stuck while creating your game and read about issues that others may have faced. What's more, there are user groups hosted by Godot community members in many parts of the world.

The Documentation Is Extensive

Docs.godotengine.org is the official website that contains the Godot API and step-by-step manual for getting started in Godot. There are tons of tutorials and resources available online, which discuss topics such as creating canvas layers, learning the basics of game-related math and physics, accessing the asset library, and creating multiplayer games. You can even access the built-in references to the documentation from within the UI itself.

You Can Tinker with It

Godot is community-driven, with hundreds of contributors working on improving it. As a user, you can play around with its source code, modify it, and even distribute it to other users. You can even create your own custom tools and add them to the visual editor.

Teamwork Is a Breeze

Using Godot's filesystem makes it easy to collaborate and practice version control when working on a project with a team. Moreover, you can create instances of every game scene, allowing each team member to independently work on different aspects of the game. For example, if one person is working on making the character, another can work on level design simultaneously. Files can then be shared between team members on GitHub.

It's "MegaByte"-Sized

The fact that the download size is a meager 60 MB or less means that it doesn't waste space on your system. This lightweight nature makes it highly portable.

Key Takeaways

In this chapter, we learned about the advent of video games and how they led to the creation of timeless classics like Super Mario, Donkey Kong, and PAC-MAN. We were introduced to various game design principles and learned how strategies like game progression, giving the player control and choices over the game narrative, and introducing immersive scenarios can make the game more enjoyable. We discussed how it is essential to have a creative vision for our game and think about its type, genre, and characters. We took a look at what a game engine is and were given pointers on how to choose one. Lastly, we found out some of the compelling reasons to work with Godot. Now, let's get started with the Godot Engine!

PART II

Starting Out with Godot

CHAPTER 2

Getting Started with Godot

In this chapter, we'll learn how to download Godot and get started with creating a new project. We'll also explore the engine interface while learning about its essential components.

Downloading the Engine

As we learned in the previous chapter, Godot has many advantages. One of the best ones is that it is open source, making it completely free to use. What's more, you can download this tiny, megabyte-sized file, unzip it, and use it right out of the folder without the hassle of installation. First, download the latest version of the engine from either the Steam store or Godot's official website, `https://godotengine.org/download/`. Godot is also available for download on Itch.io, a website that hosts and sells indie games and game assets (`https://godotengine.itch.io/godot`).

You can download the Godot engine for Linux, Windows, macOS, and the Linux server, as shown in Figure 2-1. The standard version for Windows, which is available in both 64-bit and 32-bit options, supports Godot's own scripting language, GDScript. This is the one that we will be using in this book. There is another version available called Mono, which supports the C# programming language. You can determine whether your operating system is 64-bit or 32-bit by heading to System Settings ➤ About My PC on your computer.

© Maithili Dhule 2022
M. Dhule, *Beginning Game Development with Godot*, https://doi.org/10.1007/978-1-4842-7455-2_2

Note   This book assumes you're using either version 3.2.3 or version 3.3 of Godot. Keep in mind that the projects that you work on using older versions of Godot can be opened with and generally work fine in newer versions of the engine, but the opposite may not true.

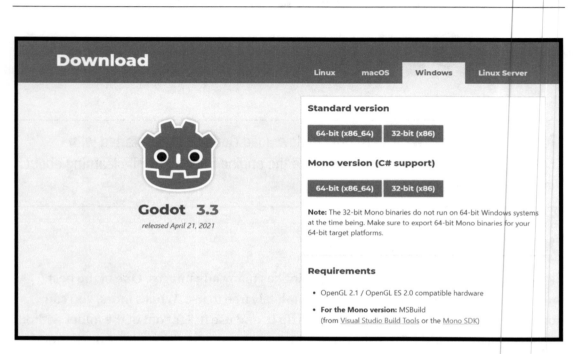

Figure 2-1. *Different versions of the Godot Engine are available for download*

After unzipping the downloaded folder, you'll find an executable file (.exe) named according to the version of Godot you're using, for example, Godot_v3.3-stable_win64. You can run this file from anywhere on your computer by copying it to that location and double-clicking it. Once Godot launches, two windows will pop up: a black-colored command prompt console, as shown in Figure 2-2, and the Project Manager window, as shown in Figure 2-3. It's okay to minimize the command prompt window, but don't close it; otherwise, the Godot application will quit as well. This window usually displays error messages for issues that may occur while you're using the engine.

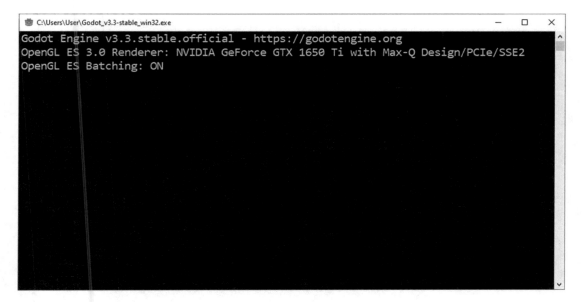

Figure 2-2. *The Godot command prompt console window*

Creating a New Project

The Project Manager window allows you to create, import, and run projects. The first time you launch Godot, the Project Manager will give you the option to open the asset library, as shown in Figure 2-3. This library is basically a collection of user-developed tools, templates, plugins, and game demos that you can download and run in Godot. They are all created and published by its community members and are completely free to use. For now, you can choose to click Cancel; you can always access the library on the Templates tab in the Project Manager window.

Figure 2-3. *The Godot Project Manager*

Next, click the New Project button in the panel on the right, and a window will pop up, as shown in Figure 2-4. Here, you can type the name of your game in the Project Name field and click the Browse button to select a project path to save your project. A green tick next to the Browse button indicates that the folder under the specified path is empty, while a red cross means it isn't. Godot needs an empty folder for storing your project files, so make sure to choose a path that points to one.

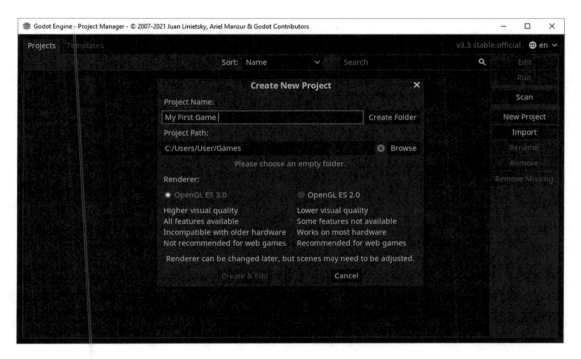

Figure 2-4. *When creating a new project, make sure to select an empty folder*

There are two options for the renderer that you can select: OpenGL ES 3.0 and OpenGL ES 2.0. Version 3.0 results in higher-quality rendering and provides more features but may not be compatible with older hardware. On the other hand, 2.0 is lower in quality but may work on older and newer hardware. We're going to stick to 3.0 in this book. Once you select the renderer version, click the Create & Edit button at the bottom of the Project Manager window to create your project. See Figure 2-5.

TRY IT!

Creating Your First Project

1. Download the latest version of Godot, unzip and extract the application (`.exe`) file, and double-click to launch it.

2. Create a new project, and give it the name of your game, for example, **Jump N Run**.

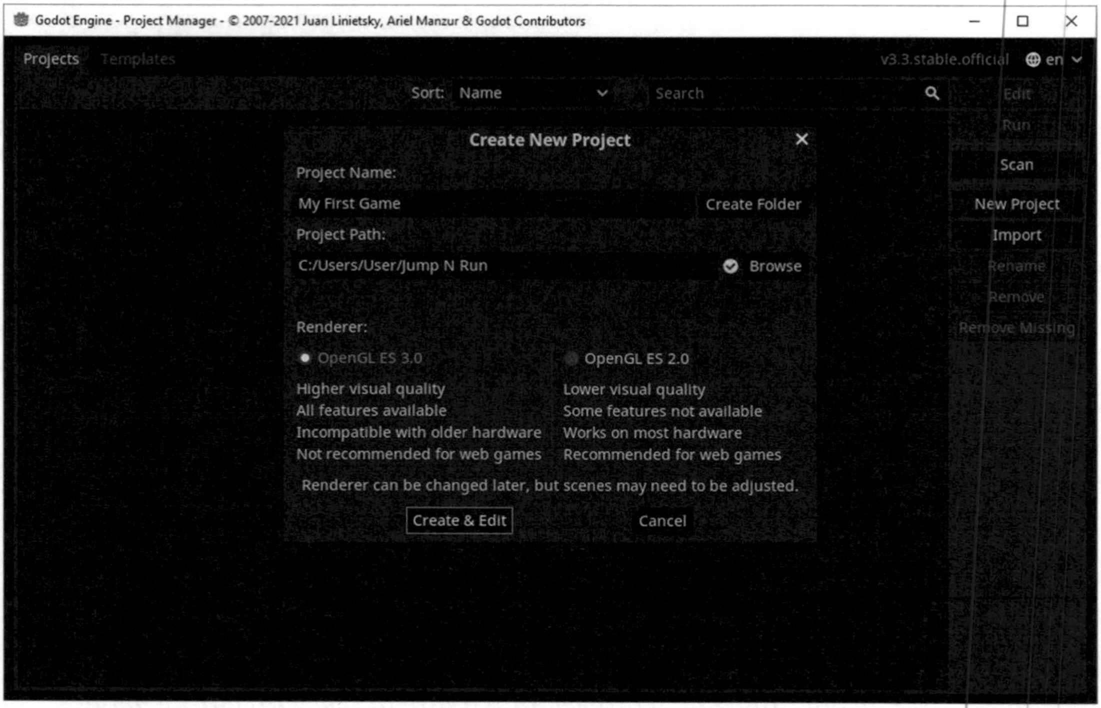

Figure 2-5. *Creating a new project with the OpenGL ES 3.0 renderer*

Exploring the Engine Interface

The Godot interface consists of key components, such as:

- FileSystem dock

- Scene dock

- Inspector dock

- 2D and 3D workspaces

- Output, Debugger, Audio, and Animation panels

- 2D and 3D toolbars

- Playtest buttons

Let's take a look at each of them. See Figure 2-6.

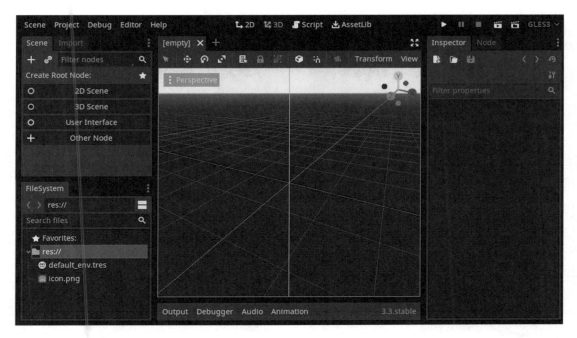

Figure 2-6. *The Godot interface*

FileSystem

The FileSystem dock is a window that displays all the files and game assets in your project. By default, it contains a resource file called default_env.tres, and the PNG image of the Godot logo, as shown in Figure 2-7 (a). This resource file contains settings for designing the game environment when working with the 3D editor. In this dock, you can create folders and add files such as images of different characters for animation, such as for running and walking, as shown in Figure 2-7 (b).

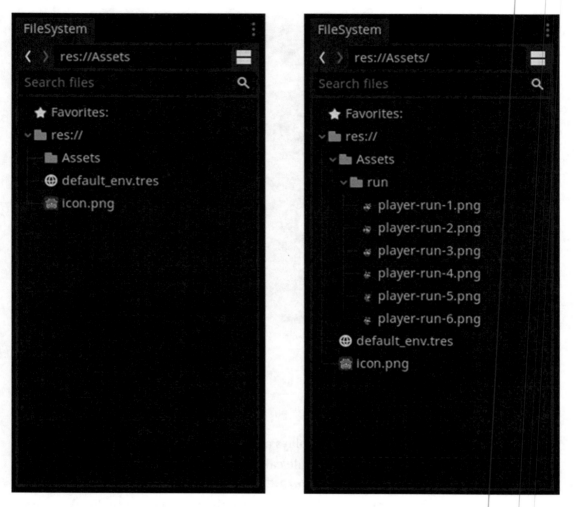

Figure 2-7. (a) The default FileSystem dock, (b) FileSystem dock showing the game assets and game scene

Scene Dock

Every scene has a set of nodes associated with it, as we'll see later in the book. This dock shows the hierarchy of nodes in a particular scene. You can also create the instance of a scene using the icon ⬚ and attach a script to a node using the ⬚ icon. Figure 2-8 (a) shows the default view of the Scene dock, while Figure 2-8 (b) shows an example of a hierarchy of nodes used to create a game character. You can create a new node by clicking the ⊞ icon and searching for and choosing the node type, as shown in Figure 2-9.

Here, KinematicBody2D is the root node, while the Sprite and CollisonShape2D nodes are its children. We will play around with this dock a lot when creating characters and designing the game world.

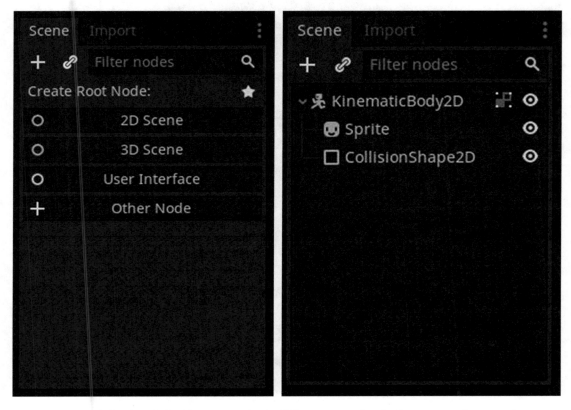

Figure 2-8. *(a) The default Scene dock, (b) a Scene dock showing a hierarchy of nodes*

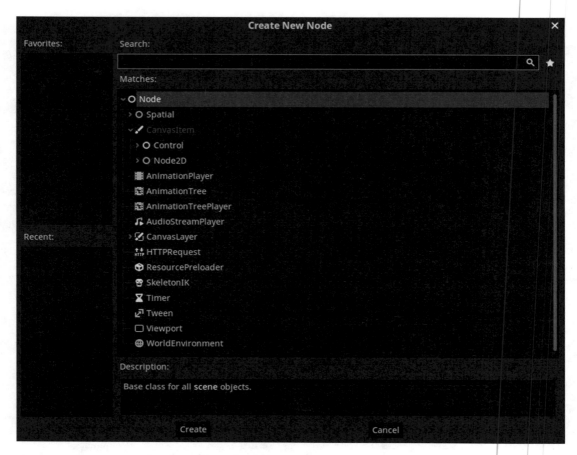

Figure 2-9. Nodes can be added to the Scene dock by picking them from the list or manually typing their names in the search box

Inspector Dock

The Inspector shows you information related to a selected node in a scene.

For example, the Inspector dock shown in Figure 2-10 (a) shows the properties related to the current node that is selected in the Scene dock, a Node2D. Properties related to this node, such as its Position (relative to the parent node), Rotation in degrees, and Scale can be seen and changed in the Inspector. The Node tab next to the Inspector displays different signals related to the selected node, as shown in Figure 2-10 (b). Signals are messages that are emitted by a node when an event occurs. For example, when we click the Play button on the Title screen, we can tell Godot to start playing the game scene using a certain built-in signal. We'll take a look at signals in later chapters.

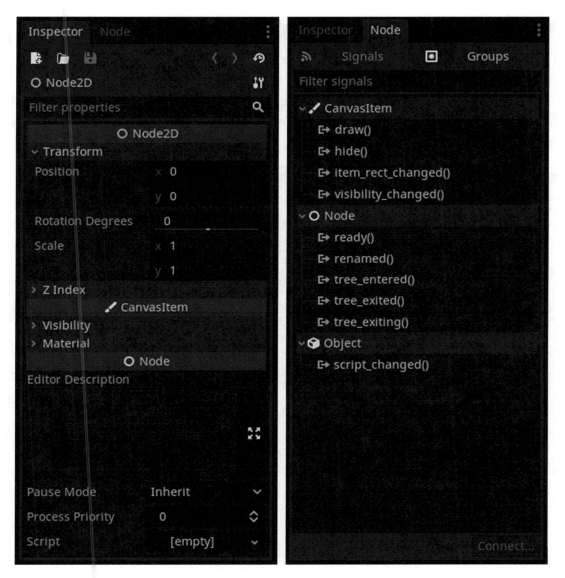

Figure 2-10. *(a) The Inspector dock displays properties related to a selected node, (b) the Node dock displays the signals related to a selected node*

Workspaces

Godot has both 2D and 3D workspaces for creating two-dimensional and three-dimensional game scenes, respectively. Figure 2-11 shows the 2D workspace. You can easily switch between the workspaces by clicking the 2D and 3D buttons. The Script and AssetLib buttons next to them can be used to write the script for objects in your workspace and access the Asset library, respectively.

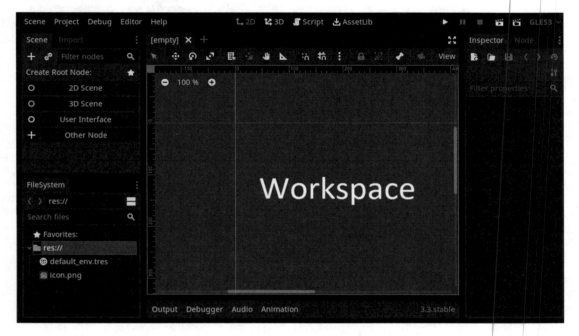

Figure 2-11. *2D workspace*

We will be working on the 2D workspace in this book. This workspace will be your playground, where you'll design characters and enemies and paint your game world using tilesets, as we'll see in later chapters. You can use your mouse scroll button to zoom in and out, and you can move around the workspace by holding down the right-click button while moving the mouse.

Animation Panel

The Animation panel is present at the bottom of the workspace. It's used for animating AnimationPlayer nodes. For example, as shown in Figure 2-12, we can create an animation of a rotating coin using this panel.

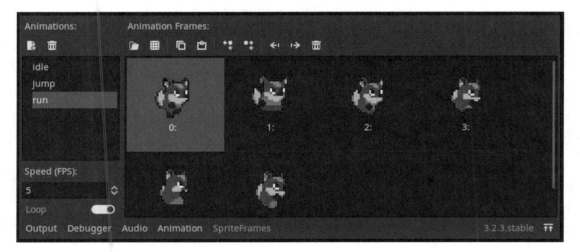

Figure 2-12. *The Animation panel*

SpriteFrames Panel

The SpriteFrames panel is used to create 2D sprite animations using individual images. It shows up only at the bottom of the workspace, next to the Animation panel, when a SpriteFrames resource is loaded in the Frames field (in the Inspector dock) of an animated sprite. We'll see more about this when we work on player animation later. You can create various types of animations using distinct images, called *frames*, of the character you want to animate. You can make your character do various actions such as climbing, running, sliding, walking, or staying idle in the game. For example, Figure 2-13 uses six-character frames, which form a running animation when played in a loop.

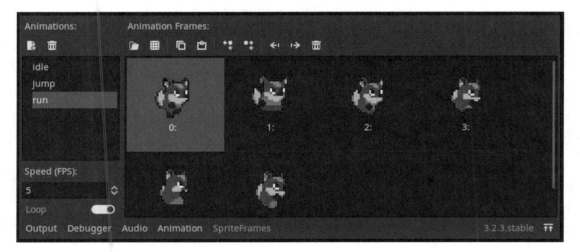

Figure 2-13. *The SpriteFrames panel*

Output Panel

The Output panel lists all the changes you make in the interface, including the workspace. It also displays the game output, warnings, and errors when a scene is run from the editor. For example, Figure 2-14 shows that an object called CanvasItem was moved twice in the workspace, and the position of a node was set to a particular value. Note that if you face issues with your Output Panel, navigate to Editor ➤ Editor Settings ➤ Network ➤ Debug and change the Remote Port number, then re-run the project.

Figure 2-14. *The Output panel*

Debugger Panel

The Debugger panel, or the Debugger, as shown in Figure 2-15, is a powerful tool that catches bugs and runtime errors in your game and has tools for measuring game performance. A red dot next to the Debugger indicates that there is an error that needs to be fixed.

```
Debugger    ● Errors (1)   Profiler   Network Profiler   Monitors   Video RAM   Misc
Expand All   Collapse All                                                                Clear
✓● 0:00:00.552      get_node: (Node not found: "InterfaceLayer/PauseMenu" (relative to "/root/Game").)
    <C++ Error>     Condition "!node" is true. Returned: __null
    <C++ Source>    scene/main/node.cpp:1371 @ get_node()
    <Stack Trace>   Game.gd:8 @ _ready()


Output    ● Debugger (1)   Audio   Animation                                     3.3.stable ††
```

Figure 2-15. *The Debugger showing runtime error messages*

Audio Panel

The Audio panel, shown in Figure 2-16, is part of Godot's audio engine and helps you create audio buses to add music and sound effects to your game.

Figure 2-16. *The Audio panel*

2D Toolbar

A 2D toolbar, shown in Figure 2-17, is present just above the 2D workspace. It has various tools to manipulate objects placed in the workspace, such as moving, rotating, or scaling an object, or making sure an object's children are not selectable. The view button lets you add grids and rulers to your workspace. The 3D toolbar offers slightly different tools for use with the 3D workspace.

Figure 2-17. *The 2D toolbar has tools for manipulating objects in the workspace*

Playtest Buttons

These buttons are used for playing, pausing, and stopping various game scenes. This is shown in Figure 2-18. GLES3 indicates that the OpenGL ES 3.0 back end is being used in this case.

Figure 2-18. *The Playtest buttons*

Tips and Shortcuts

Here are some tips and shortcuts:

- The Dock sizes can be changed by dragging their edges left and right or up and down.

- The + and **x** buttons at the top of the workspace can help you instantly create or close a scene, respectively.

- By toggling the 👁 button next to a node in the Scene dock, you can turn off the visibility of that node in the workspace.

- You can drag and drop game assets directly into the FileSystem dock.

- The buttons on the top left of the interface let you create and save scenes and access the project and editor settings. The online documentation can be accessed via the Help menu (at the top left of the interface), by clicking the 🔗Online Docs button. The offline documentation can be accessed via the same Help menu, by clicking the 🔍Search Help button. This button is also available on the Scripts tab.

- You can download tools and plugins for your game via the ⬇AssetLib button at the top of the workspace.

- You can also download other game demos and templates by accessing the Asset Library from the Templates tab in the Project Manager.

```
TRY IT!
```

Play Around with the Interface

1. Add different nodes to the Scene dock, and tinker with their properties in the Inspector dock.

2. Create a folder called Assets in the FileSystem dock and add some images to it from your computer.

3. Download a game demo or template of your choice from the AssetLib (on the Templates tab in the Project Manager), and save it to a new project folder. Open the project and see it in action.

Key Takeaways

In this chapter, you learned how to download and launch Godot and created your first project. You also got your first look at the engine's essential components such as the FileSystem, Scene, and Inspector docks, the workspaces, and various buttons and panels. You learned how to access the online and offline Godot documentation and were introduced to a few tips and shortcuts related to the interface.

CHAPTER 3

GDScript in a Nutshell

In this chapter, we'll cover the basics of GDScript, the official scripting language of Godot. We'll learn about important programming concepts such as variables, data types, operators, functions, dictionaries, and looping. If you want to jump right into game creation, feel free to skip this chapter.

What Is GDScript?

Behind every game, there is a programming language that powers it. GDScript is the one that's custom-made for Godot. It is simple, clutter-free, and tightly integrated with the engine, with its creators deeming it easy for beginners to learn. It was created with the intent of helping users focus on the engine rather than on spending time learning how to integrate code written in other languages. It also enables developers to easily get rid of bugs in the engine code and effortlessly introduce new features. That being said, Godot also has support for other languages such as C++ and C#, among others, which are primarily supported by the Godot community.

We'll be using GDScript in this book to add life to our game by animating characters and making them interact with the game world. If you prefer to learn as you practice, feel free to skip this chapter and go on to the next one. Do note that the concepts you'll learn in the following pages are common to most programming languages, with the only difference being in the syntax. Now, let's dive into the basics of GDScript.

© Maithili Dhule 2022
M. Dhule, *Beginning Game Development with Godot*, https://doi.org/10.1007/978-1-4842-7455-2_3

Scripting

In GDScript, you add a script to a node to control its behavior. To start scripting and trying out the examples given in this chapter, you will need to create a new project, add a node to the scene, and attach a script to that node. Once you do that, you can start scripting in Godot. For details of how to create a new project, you can refer to the previous chapter. Now, let's take a look at the other steps:

(1).   **Adding a Node to the Scene**

In the 2D workspace of your project window, go to the Scene dock and click the █ 2D Scene █ button under Create Root Node. This will create a node called Node2D. Then, save the scene by clicking Save Scene As (Shortcut: Control + Shift + S) under the Scene tab at the top-left corner of the engine window. The scene name should be in the format SceneName.tscn (e.g., Node2D.tscn).

(2).   **Attaching a Script to the Node**

With the newly created Node2D being selected, click the ▣ button to attach a script to this node. This will open a prompt called Attach Node Script. Click the Create button. (The default path of the script will be `res://Node2D.gd`, with `Node2D.gd` being the script name.) This opens the scripting workspace, as shown in Figure 3-1. You can type your code in this space and click the play button at the top-right corner of the engine window to run your code. You can click the stop button to stop running your script. To view the output, click on the Output button present at the bottom of the engine window, as shown in Figure 3-2.

(3).   **Defining the Main Scene**

After typing your script and clicking the play button to run it for the first time, you'll be prompted to define the main scene. Click the Select button, and another prompt called Pick a Main Scene will pop up. Here, you should select the scene you saved in the first step, e.g., Node2D.tscn, and click Open.

Now you're all set to start writing and running some code!

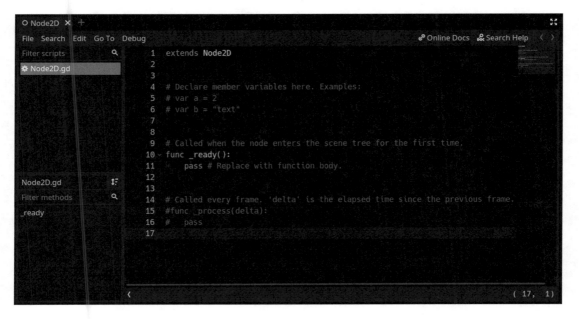

Figure 3-1. *The Scripting dock*

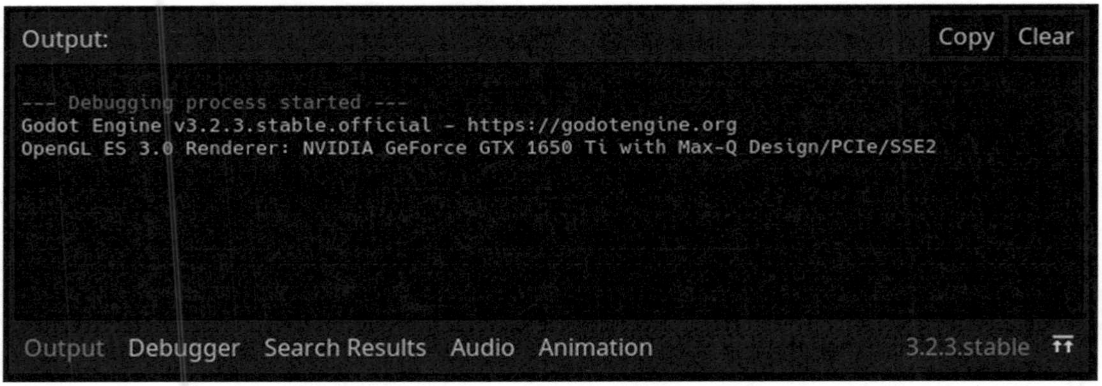

Figure 3-2. *The Output panel*

Variables and Data Types

A variable is an entity that can store data values. In Godot, it is represented by the keyword var. Every variable is associated with a data type that tells us the nature of the stored value. Different data types include integer, float, Boolean, and string. Let's take a look at them.

Integer

- An integer is a whole number and can be positive, negative, or zero.
- It is represented by the keyword int.
- Examples: 5, 12, 1000, -25, 0 , -500

Float

- A float is a fractional number that includes a decimal point.
- It is represented by the keyword float.
- Examples: 5.0, 12.4, 0.0002

Boolean

- Boolean represents two conditions: true and false.
- It is represented by the keyword bool.

String

- A string represents a word, sentence, or continuous series of characters or numbers enclosed within quotes ("").
- Examples: "M", "ABCD", "1234", "This is a string"

Declaring a Variable

Variables are used to store values that may change throughout your code. You can use them to store data related to your game, such as a player's score, the current game level, and the speed of an object. To declare a variable, write the keyword var, followed by an identifier, that is, the name you want to give the variable. You can choose to assign a value to the identifier either during variable declaration, or in some other part of the code.

In GDScript, identifiers can include any combination of uppercase and lowercase alphabets, an underscore (_), and the digits 0 to 9. Identifiers cannot start with a digit and are case-sensitive. This means you can call a variable Emily1234 but not 1234Emily. Also, emily and Emily are considered to be two different string values. Here are some examples of variable declarations:

```
(1) var player_name = "Eva"
(2) var score = 150
(3) var player_on_ground = true
(4) var distance = 10.5
(5) var total
```

Explicit and Inferred Typing

When declaring a variable, you can choose to specify its type optionally.

Here are some examples:

```
(1) var fruit: String = "Pineapple"
(2) var fruit = "Pineapple"
```

In each of these cases, you store a string called Pineapple in the variable fruit. But in the first case, you directly state that the value you are storing is a string, while in the second case, this is inferred. The first method is called *explicit* typing, while the second is called *inferred* typing.

Constants

Constants are values that don't change when you run a game. When you declare a variable as a constant, its value stays the same throughout the code, and it can't be assigned any other value.

Here's an example:

```
const LENGTH = 10
const SPEED: int = 100
```

Enums

An *enum* is a group of constants and can be useful when you want each constant to be associated with a consecutive integer. An enum can be written in multiple ways. Here are some examples:

1.
```
const CIRCLE = 0
const SQUARE = 1
const RECTANGLE = 2
const TRIANGLE = 3
```

   Can also be written as:

   ```
   enum Shapes = {CIRCLE, SQUARE, RECTANGLE, TRIANGLE}
   ```

2.
```
const Player = {IDLE = 0 , RUN = 3, JUMP = 4}
```

   Can also be written as:

   ```
   enum Player {IDLE, RUN = 3, JUMP}
   ```

   Values can be accessed by Player.IDLE, Player.RUN, Player.JUMP

Note   Godot 3.1 and newer versions do not register keys in an enum as global constants. You should access a key in an enum in the format Name.KEY, where Name is the enum's name.

Keywords

Every programming language has specific words called *keywords* that are reserved. These should not be used as identifiers, as they hold a special meaning to the compiler. The following are some of the popular keywords of GDScript:

if	elif	else	for
while	match	break	continue
pass	return	class_name	extends
var	const	enum	func
static	onready	export	signal
is	as	self	tool

For the complete list of keywords, you can check out the official GDScript documentation at: https://docs.godotengine.org/en/stable/getting_started/scripting/gdscript/gdscript_basics.html#keywords.

Comments

When you want to add comments in your code, you can do so by writing # followed by the comment. These are ignored by the engine.

```
#This is an example of a comment
```

Output

When you want to display a message or a variable value in the output, you can use the print statement. You have to specify the text to be displayed within the quotation marks and the variable value to be displayed after a comma. Examples include the following:

```
1.  print("This is being displayed at the output!")
2.  print("The total Sum= ",sum)
3.  print(my_variable)
```

Note   Remember to use "straight" and not "curly" quotation marks in your print statements; otherwise, it might cause an error!

Functions

A *function* is an organized block of code that groups together related actions or tasks. It helps make the code more readable by avoiding writing the same code in multiple places. For example, you might have a function to calculate and display the total points a player earns in a game. Since these points will keep changing throughout the game, we can use this function every time we want to update the score.

The function _ready() is an important GDScript function that is called every time a node is created in the Scene tree. Another important function is called _process (_delta), which is executed for every frame in the game. Here, delta represents the total time between each frame. These two built-in functions can be changed according to our programming needs. We can also create our own functions for different tasks, such as creating a coin-collection system, spawning enemies, and calculating player health.

Every function starts with the keyword func and can *return* a value that we can use somewhere else in our code. You can also choose to pass values, called *arguments*, to a function if you need to use them there.

In the first example given in the "Snippets of Syntax" on the next page, we declare a function for printing a user's name. This function, called print_my_name, has an input parameter called my_name. We pass the string "Lisa" as an input to this function when we call it in the _ready() function. In this way, the variable my_name stores the string "Lisa", and the sentence "Hi, my name is Lisa" is printed at the output.

In the second example , we have a function called add that takes two numbers, num1 and num2, as input, prints each of them, and returns their sum to the _ready() function. In _ready(), we declare a variable called my_sum and pass the values 5 and 6 to num1 and num2, respectively. When we print the variable my_sum, the sum of these two numbers, i.e., 11, is displayed at the output.

SNIPPETS OF SYNTAX

1. Passing and Printing a Name

```
func print_my_name(my_name):
    print("Hi, my name is ",my_name)

func _ready():
    print_my_name("Lisa")
```

Output

```
Hi, my name is Lisa
```

2. Passing Numbers to a Function and Adding Them Together

```
func add(num1, num2):
    print("num1 = ",num1)
    print("num2 = ",num2)
    return num1 + num2

func_ready():
    var my_sum = add(5, 6)
    print(my_sum)
```

Output

```
num1 = 5
num2 = 6
11
```

You can declare variables either locally (inside a function) or globally (outside of any function). A local variable is visible only in the function in which it is declared, while a global variable is visible to all the functions in the code. In the example shown earlier, the variable my_sum is local to the _ready() function.

TRY IT!

Creating Your First Function

1. Create a function called all_about_me, and pass your name, age, height, and weight to it from _ready().

2. Using print statements, display this information at the output.

Array

An *array* is a data type that stores a set of variables at different index positions. You can think of it as a set of address locations, with each location holding a different value or variable. Each stored item is called an *element* and can be accessed using its index, starting from index 0. In the following diagram, Variable 1 is stored at index 0, Variable 2 at index 1, Variable 3 at index 2, and so on.

Variable 1	Variable 2	Variable 3	Variable 4	Variable 5
[0]	[1]	[2]	[3]	[4]

Here's an example of an array called Games, which stores the names of four different video games:

```
var Games = ["Mario", "Donkey Kong", "Pac-man", "Breakout"]

func _ready():
    print(Games[0])
    print(Games[1])
    print(Games[2])
    print(Games[3])
```

Output:
```
Mario
Donkey Kong
Pac-man
Breakout
```

As we see at the output, Mario is stored at index 0, Donkey Kong at index 1, Pac-man at index 2, and Breakout at index 3. Taking this Games array as an example, let's look at some typical array functions.

1. Count the number of elements, using `size()`

    ```
    var num_elements = Games.size()
    print(num_elements)
    ```

    Output

    ```
    4
    ```

    Since Games has four different items, the output will be 4.

2. Check whether it contains a specific element, using `find()`

    ```
    print(Games.find("Pac-man"))
    #Checks whether Pac-man appears in Games and returns the
    index if found
    ```

    Output

    ```
    2
    ```

    ```
    print(Games.find("Ms. Pac-man"))
    #Checks whether Ms. Pac-man appears in Games
    ```

    Output

    ```
    -1
    ```

Since Pac-man is present at the index number 2 in Games, the output is 2 for this case. On the other hand, since "Ms. Pac-man" is not part of Games, we get a value of -1 at the output.

3. Check the number of times an element occurs, using `count()`

    ```
    var count_element = Games.count("Breakout")
    print(count_element)
    ```

    Output

    ```
    1
    ```

    As "Breakout" appears only once in Games, the output is 1.

4. Add an item at the end of the array, using append()

```
Games.append("Tron")
print(Games)
```

Output

```
[Mario, Donkey Kong, Pac-man, Breakout, Tron]
```

In the previous example, we added Tron to Games.

5. Shuffle the order of the items using shuffle()

```
randomize()
Games.shuffle()
print(Games)
```

Output

```
[Donkey_Kong, Tron, Breakout, Mario, Pac-man]
```

Random Number Generation

There are tons of uses for a random number when you're making a game:

- Spawning a random number of enemies during a game level

- Creating a luck-based computer card game

- Randomly generating elements in the game world, such as the map

- Spawning a random collectible or drop when the player beats an enemy

In GDScript, you can generate random numbers using built-in functions that are based on the concept of pseudorandomness. This means that a number is generated using an algorithm and is thus not truly random. You can easily predict the number if you're familiar with the algorithm, but this is unlikely. To get a random number, we first need to use the predefined function, randomize(), along with another function specific to the type of random number we want. Let's take a look at how this works.

1. **Random Integer Generation**

```
func _ready():
    randomize()
    var random_int = randi()
    print (random_int)
```

Output

3252001091

The function randi() generates a random integer in the range of 0 to 4,294,967,295. If we want to specify our own range, we can do so in the following way:

```
var rand_generator = RandomNumberGenerator.new()

func _ready():
    rand_generator.randomize()
    var random_int = rand_generator.randi_range(30,40)
    print (random_int)
```

Output

36

We first have to declare a new random number generator, e.g., rand_generator, and randomize it using the syntax shown earlier. Then, we can use the randi_range() function to specify the range of possible values for our random number. In the case shown earlier, a random integer between 30 and 40 is generated.

2. **Random Float Generation**

```
func _ready():
    randomize()
    var random_float = randf()
    print (random_float)
```

Output

0.278825

The randf() function generates a random float between 0 and 1. If we want to specify the range of values, we can do it as follows:

```
var rand_generator = RandomNumberGenerator.new()

func _ready():
    rand_generator.randomize()
    var random_float = rand_generator.randf_range(-1.5,5.0)
    print (random_float)
```

Output

```
4.950228
```

Here, we use randf_range() to specify our possible range of float values. The example shown earlier generates a random float value between -1.5 and 5.0.

Operators and Computation

Mathematics and logic are the two most essential ingredients of a code written in any programming language. Godot uses simple mathematical, comparison, and logical operators to perform calculations on variables. Let's take a look at each of them.

Mathematical Operators

Mathematical operators are used for simple calculations between two or more variables.

Table 2-1. *Mathematical Operators*

Operator	Symbol	Example
Addition	+	var Sum = A + B
Subtraction	-	var Difference = A - B
Multiplication	*	var Multiply = A * B
Division	/	var Divide = A / B
Modulo (Remainder)	%	var Remainder = A % B
Squareroot	sqrt	var Squareroot_A =sqrt(A)

Note   The / operator calculates the quotient after division, while the % operator calculates the remainder.

Comparison and Logical Operators

Comparison operators compare the values between two variables, while logical operators evaluate an expression based on certain logical conditions.

Table 2-2. *Comparison and Logical Operators*

Operator	Symbol	Condition	Description
Equal To	==	A == B	True if A is equal to B.
Not Equal To	!=	A ! = B	True if A is not equal to B.
Less Than	<	A < B	True if A is less than B.
Greater Than	>	A > B	True if A is greater than B.
Less Than or Equal to	<=	A < = B	True if A is either less than B **OR** equal to B.
Greater Than or Equal to	>=	A > = B	True if A is either greater than B **OR** equal to B.
And	&&	A && B	True if both A and B are true.
Or	||	A || B	True if either A **OR** B is true.
Not	!	!A	If A is false, then return true. If A is true, then return false.

SNIPPETS OF SYNTAX

Mathematical Calculations Between Two Variables a and b

```
extends Node2D
var a = 50
var b = 20
var sum
var difference
```

```
var multiplication
var division
var remainder
var squareroot_a
var squareroot_b

func _ready():
      print("a = ", a)                #Printing the value of a
      print("b = ", b)                #Printing the value of b

      sum = a + b
      print("sum= ", sum)

      difference = a - b
      print("difference= ", difference)

      multiplication = a * b
      print("multiplication = ", multiplication)

      division = a / b              #a is divided by b
      print("division = ", division)

      remainder = a % b            #Remainder when a is divided by b
      print("remainder = ", remainder)

      squareroot_a = sqrt(a)
      print("squareroot of a= ", squareroot_a)

      squareroot_b = sqrt(b)
      print("squareroot of b= ", squareroot_b)
```

Output

```
a = 50
b = 20
sum = 70
difference = 30
multiplication = 1000
division = 2
remainder = 10
squareroot of a = 7.071068
squareroot of b = 4.472136
```

if-else Statements

Whenever we want to set certain conditions before executing a block of code, we can write if-else statements. We use these statements when we want to tell the computer, "If something happens, then do this; else do something else." The keyword if checks whether a certain condition is true and executes a certain portion of code if it is. If it's not, then we can check whether other conditions are true using elif statements and specify the corresponding blocks of code that need to be executed for each particular case. If none of the conditions is true, the code specified under the else condition is executed.

SNIPPETS OF SYNTAX

Let's take a gaming scenario to see this logic in action:

If a player's health is below or equal to 10%, the player needs to collect one healing powerup to increase health to 50% and two healing powerups to increase health to 100% to continue playing the game. But if the player doesn't collect any powerups and the player's health falls to 0, the game is over.

This can be represented by the following code:

```
extends Node2D
var health = 100 #Initial value that will change in the game
var powerup

func _ready():
    if health <= 10:  #Check if Player's health is below or equal to 10 %
        if powerup == 1:
            print("You got one power-up! Health= 50%")
        elif powerup == 2:
            print("You got two power-ups! Health= 100%")
        else:
            print("Gameover!!")
    else:
        print("Health is more than 10%, you're safe")
```

Note   Indentation is important in GDScript! Make sure to press the Tab key every time you write a new line of code inside a function and when you want to include certain lines within an `if`, `elif`, or `else` statement.

┌──┐
│   **TRY IT!**   │
└──┘

if-elif-else Statements

1. Write the previous code in your Godot editor.

2. Assign the variable health any value between 0 and 100, and assign the variable powerup any value between 0, 1, and 2.

3. Run the code for different values of health and powerup.

Dictionaries

In GDScript, a dictionary can be thought of as a container that stores unique keys, as well as different values associated with each of them. It's similar to an array, but the stored values do not have a corresponding index. Instead, you can look up a particular value by searching for its key.

Let's create a dictionary that holds information about the attributes of a game character by storing key-value pairs in a variable called Player. Note that the dictionary definition can be declared either inside a function (e.g. func _ready) or outside any of the functions in the script. The print statements should be included within a function.

```
var Player = {"Type": "Wizard", "Age" : "500", "Strength" : "Magic",
"Weakness" : "Silver"}
print(Player.Type)
print(Player.Age)
print(Player.Strength)
print(Player.Weakness)
```

Output
```
Wizard
500
Magic
Silver
```

In this example,

- Type is the key, Wizard is the value.

- Age is the key, 500 is the value.

- Strength is the key, Magic is the value.

- Weakness is the key, Silver is the value.

As shown in the example, we can print every element of the dictionary by accessing it using dictionary_name.key and replacing dictionary_name with the name of the dictionary and key with the name of the key linked to the particular element we want to access.

For instance, we can use Player.Strength to get the value Magic. We get the same result if we use Player ["Strength"].

Let's look at some of the things we can do with dictionaries. Note that the code shown in the following examples (1 to 5) should be included within a function (e.g. func _ready), and properly indented.

1. Check if it's completely empty.

```
if Player.empty():
        print("The dictionary is empty!")
else:
        print("It's not empty")
```

Output
```
It's not empty
```

2. Check the number of elements.

```
var num_elements = Player.size()
print(num_elements) #displays the number of values stored
```

Output

4

3. Check if it contains a particular key.

```
if Player.has("Hobby"):
        print("The key called Hobby exists")
else:
        print("No such key exits in this dictionary")
```

Output

No such key exists in this dictionary.

4. Print all the keys.

```
var all_keys = Player.keys() #keys() returns all the keys
print(all_keys)
```

Output

[Type, Age, Strength, Weakness]

5. Print all elements.

```
var elements = Player.values()
print(elements)
```

Output

[Wizard, 500, Magic, Silver]

6. Add items.

```
func new_item (key,element_value):
        Player[key] = element_value
        print("The added key is: ",key)
        print("The added value is: ",Player[key])
        print("Updated dictionary: ",Player)
```

```
func _ready():
        new_item("Fav_Food", "pizza")
```

Output

```
The added key is: Fav_Food
The added value is: pizza
Updated dictionary: {Age:500, Fav_Food:pizza,
Strength:Magic, Type:Wizard, Weakness:Silver}
```

Fav_Food is the key, and pizza is the value that is passed to new_item() from _ready().

Looping

When we want to execute some part of the code multiple times, we use an important programming concept called *looping*. There are two types of loops in GDScript: for loops and while loops. Let's explore each of them with examples.

for Loop

Let's look at an example of an array that holds the player's score during each game level, for a total of four levels. This means that the array stores the player's level 1 score at index 0, level 2 score at index 1, level 3 score at index 2, and level 4 score at index 3. We can use a for loop for iterating through each of these values.

To access every item in the array, we define our own variable name that points to the current item. Every time the code inside the loop is executed, this variable then points to the next item in the array. In this way, we can access each of the array elements.

```
extends Node2D
var Level_Score = [0,10,40,60]
var Total_Score = 0
func _ready():
    for current_score in Level_Score:
        Total_Score = current_score + Total_Score
    print("Total score = ", Total_Score)
```

In the example given earlier, we first define an array called Level_Score to store the player's points during each level. We also declare a variable called Total_Score for storing the result of the addition of all the elements in this array. Next, use a for loop with an iterative variable called current_score, which loops through all the array elements, starting from the element at index 0. After a cumulative addition of all the points inside the for loop, we display the result at the output. We can also use for loops for looping through numerical ranges, strings, and even dictionaries.

Some other examples of for loops include the following:

1.   Print all the characters in a string.

```
func _ready():
    for ch in "GODOT":
        print(ch)
```

Output

G

O

D

O

T

2.   Iterate over values from num = 0 to 4.

```
func _ready():
    for n in 5:
        print(n)
```

Output

0

1

2

3

4

3. Iterate over a range of n = 10 to 15.

```
func _ready():
        for n in range(10,15):
                print(n)
```

Output

```
10
11
12
13
14
```

4. Skip certain numbers in an iteration.

```
func _ready():
        for n in range(10,20):
                if(n<=14):
                        continue #values below 15 are not printed
                if(n==18):
                        break #values after 18 are not printed
                print(n)
```

Output

```
15
16
17
```

Note   The continue keyword is used to skip a certain iteration of a loop and to continue with the next iteration. The break keyword is used to skip all the remaining iterations and break out of the loop.

---

5. Iterate over a dictionary and print all the values.

```
func _ready():
        var player_points = {"P1":10, "P2":50, "P3":80}
        print("Leaderboard: ")
        for key in player_points:
                print(key, " = ", player_points[key], " points")
```

Output

```
Leaderboard:
P1 = 10 points
P2 = 50 points
P3 = 80 points
```

while Loop

We can use while loops in cases where we have to continuously execute some code until a certain condition is reached. Let's see an example:

```
extends Node2D
var points = 10
var total_score = 0
func _ready():
      while (total_score <= 200):
              total_score = total_score + points
              print("Total score so far = ", total_score)

              if(total_score == 100):
                      print("You got 100 points! You won!")
                      break
```

In the above example, we have written a while loop for updating the total_score continuously by cumulatively adding 10 points to it, until total_score reaches a value of 200. The current value of total_score is displayed every time 10 more points are added to it. But once the total_score reaches a value of 100, the break statement causes the while loop to end, and the statement, "You got 100 points! You won!" is displayed in the output.

```
TRY IT!
```

Dictionaries and Loops

1. Create a GDScript dictionary of five of your favorite movies, assigning a different key to each of them.

2. Write a script for checking whether the dictionary is empty and for checking whether a certain key exists. Print all the keys and values in the dictionary.

3. Write a `for` loop to display each of the items in your dictionary at the output.

Key Takeaways

In this chapter, we took a brief look at the basic concepts related to GDScript. We first looked at how to start scripting with Godot's IDE. Then, we learned about different kinds of variables and data types, keywords, constants, and enums. We also explored how different mathematical operators, functions, arrays, dictionaries, and looping are used in GDScript through examples. In addition, we found out how to randomize different types of variables and use them in our code.

CHAPTER 4

Exploring Game Physics

In this chapter, you'll learn about concepts related to game physics and get introduced to the concept of collision bodies. The chapter also talks about how various bodies interact with each other through the introduction of forces such as gravity. We'll create rigid bodies and static bodies in our first game scene and play the scene to watch them in action.

Collision Objects

When you develop a game, you'll want to control what happens when certain objects in a scene come into contact with each other. For example, when the player jumps onto a springboard, you want the player to jump to a certain height. If the player falls into a pit full of spikes, you want to detect this and declare "Game Over!" for the player. This is where the concept of collision bodies comes into the picture.

In terms of game development, a collision body is an object with a definite shape whose behavior is controlled by in-game physics. You can decide what happens when these collision bodies interact with each other. You might want them to bounce back when they collide or even allow one to pass through the other. For example, when we're making a platformer, we want our character to stay on the ground and not fall through it. In this case, the platformer and the ground are both collision bodies that do not merge into each other when coming into contact.

© Maithili Dhule 2022
M. Dhule, *Beginning Game Development with Godot*, https://doi.org/10.1007/978-1-4842-7455-2_4

In Godot, there are different types of collision bodies:

- *RigidBody2D*: Detects collisions, is affected by forces such as gravity that are applied to it, and acts according to game physics.

- *StaticBody2D*: Detects collisions but stays in one place even after collision.

- *KinematicBody2D*: Detects collisions but is not affected by game physics; instead, its behavior is controlled by the user's code.

In addition, there is one more type of physics body:

- *Area2D*: Detects when particular objects come into contact and when they enter or leave a specific area. An Area2D is not affected by other bodies in the same way as the other three physics bodies given in the previous list.

In this chapter, we'll create rigid bodies and static bodies in our game scene and observe what happens when they collide with each other. But first, let's learn more about Godot's node-scene architecture.

The Node-Scene Architecture

Godot's creators describe the engine as your kitchen, where you, the chef (game developer), get to create new recipes (games) using different ingredients (nodes and scenes). In fact, *nodes* are the basic building blocks of your game, while a *scene* is what the player sees when the game is playing. As you saw in Chapter 2, every scene in Godot is associated with a set of nodes. You can choose from tons of different nodes to add to your game scene, such as nodes for displaying images, nodes for creating collision bodies, or even nodes for game animations and music. A scene consists of one or more nodes arranged hierarchically (like a tree).

You can assign a node to be the child of another node, with the only requirement being that the children of a particular parent node should all have unique names. Figure 4-1 shows an example of a parent-child node hierarchy. Here, MyGame is the main or root node of the scene, with Player and Player2 being its child nodes. Each of these child nodes, in turn, has two children each, called CollisionShape2D and Sprite.

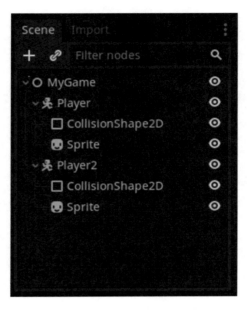

Figure 4-1. *An example of a parent-child node hierarchy*

Every game can have multiple scenes that can be saved and loaded back later. For example, every game level can be a different scene, and each of them can be loaded according to how the game progresses. So after a player finishes the first level, the scene for Level 2 can be loaded. If the player loses the game at any point, the scene that shows the "Game Over" message can be loaded. We'll look at this in later chapters. For now, let's take a look at how to create nodes for collision bodies and add them to our scene.

Adding Nodes to the Scene

Nodes can be created via the Scene dock located on the top-left side of the engine interface. There are options for adding different types of nodes such as 2D, 3D, and control nodes (User Interface nodes). Since we are working in 2D, we will add only 2D nodes. To add the first node to a Scene go to the Scene dock, and click the 2D Scene button under Create Root Node, as shown in Figure 4-2. This creates a node called Node2D, which will be the main parent node, called the *root node* of our scene.

To rename a node, right-click it and choose the Rename option from the menu that pops up, as shown in Figure 4-3 (a). Then, type in the new name of your choice. An easier alternative is to double-click the node to rename it or to use the keyboard shortcut F2. Let's rename our root node to GameLevel, as shown in Figure 4-3 (b).

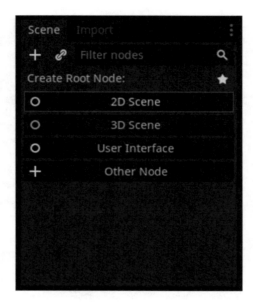

Figure 4-2. *Adding a root node to the scene*

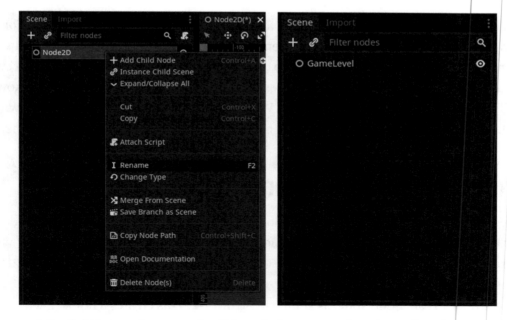

Figure 4-3. *(a) Renaming a node, (b) node is renamed to GameLevel*

Creating a Rigid Body

Now, let's add a rigid body (represented by the node RigidBody2D) as a child of GameLevel by clicking the ➕ button in the Scene dock. We can also do this by right-clicking GameLevel and selecting the Add Child Node option. A window pops up, and we are presented with a list of all possible nodes we can add to the scene. We can do either of the following:

- Enter the name of the type of node we are looking for in the search box.

- Navigate the path pointing to the node by expanding the tree structure. Click the small arrow on the left of a node to see its expanded list. As shown in Figure 4-4, RigidBody2D can be found under this path:

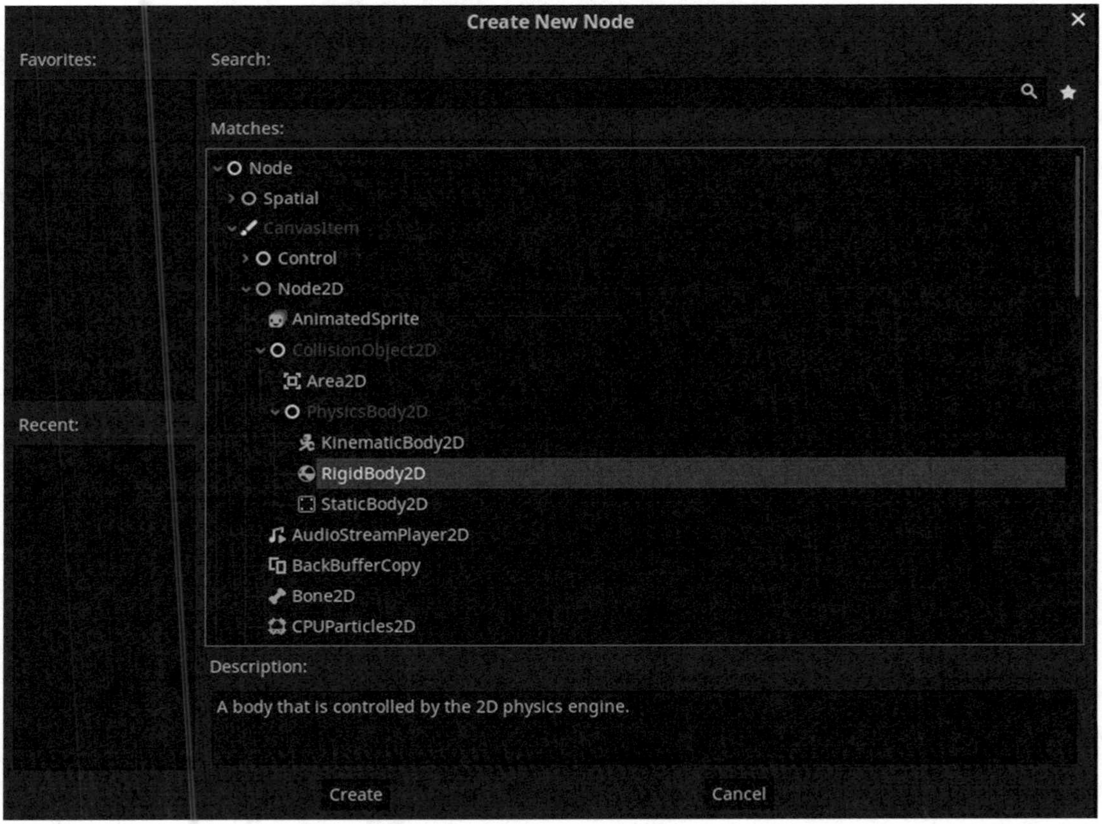

Figure 4-4. *Path to RigidBody2D in the Create New Node window*

Node ➤ CanvasItem ➤ Node2D ➤ CollisionObject2D ➤ PhysicsBody2D ➤ RigidBody2D

Note   RigidBody2D, StaticBody2D, and KinematicBody2D are nodes that
represent physics bodies. They are children of the parent node PhysicsBody2D,
which, in turn, is a child of the CollisionObject2D node.

Under PhysicsBody2D, select the node called RigidBody2D, and click the Create
button. This node will automatically be created as a child of our root node, GameLevel,
as shown in Figure 4-5. Don't worry about the yellow icon that shows up next to
RigidBody2D; we'll see how to get rid of it a little later.

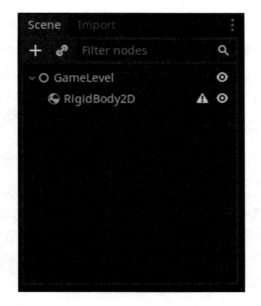

Figure 4-5. *Creating RigidBody2D as a child node of GameLevel*

Adding a Sprite Node

RigidBody2D represents our first collison body, that is, a rigid body that we want to add
to the scene. But we can't see anything yet on the editor screen! We first need to add a
node called a *sprite* as its child. Click the RigidBody2D node in the Scene dock to select
it, and then click the ➕ button to add a Sprite node 🙂 Sprite as its child. Just like we did

before, to add the Sprite node, either type **Sprite** in the search box of the Create New Node window, or navigate to it using the following path:

Node ➤ CanvasItem ➤ Node2D ➤ Sprite

Once you click the Create button, a Sprite node is created as a child of RigidBody2D. When you do so, your node hierarchy should look something like Figure 4-6 (a), *not* like Figure 4-6 (b).

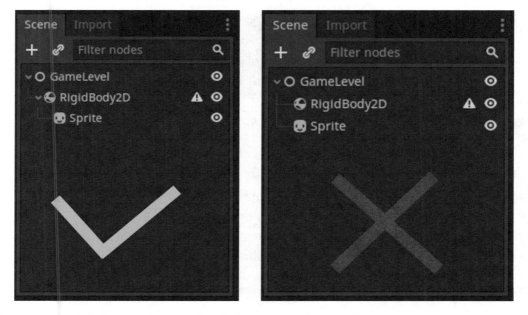

Figure 4-6. *(a) Correct hierarchy, (b) incorrect hierarchy*

Note   To create a child node, you have to keep the intended parent node selected before adding the new node. You'll notice that by default if you don't select any node and just go ahead and add another one, the created node becomes the child of the root node. You can also drag a node on top of its intended parent node, if you want to make the first node a child of the second node.

We still can't see anything on the editor! Why so? This is because every sprite needs an image file as its texture to be able to see it. Select the Sprite node with a single click, and take a look at the inspector on the right side. As shown in Figure 4-7, the Texture field shows "[empty]." We need to add an image to this field. This image will determine how our RigidBody2D will look.

Figure 4-7. *The Texture field of the Sprite node in the Inspector dock is empty*

But where do we get this image from? We can either use the default PNG image that Godot provides or import one into our FileSystem dock. If you want to use your own image, drag and drop it into this dock from anywhere on your computer. For now, let's use the default image, called icon.png. Drag and drop this image from the FileSystem dock onto the Sprite node's Texture field in the Inspector dock. When you do that, you'll see the image pop up on your workspace, as shown in Figure 4-8.

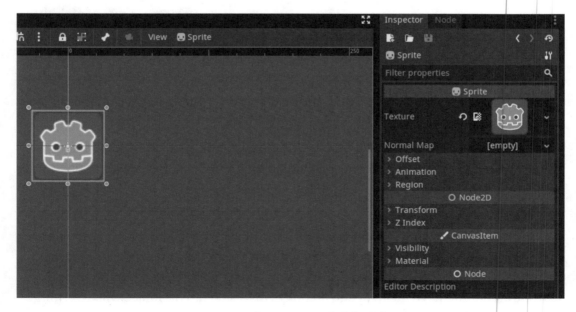

Figure 4-8. *Assigning an image to the Texture field of the Sprite node*

But hold on. Don't move around the sprite yet! If you do that, the RigidBody2D node will stay in its current position (at the origin), while the sprite will move. We don't want that! We want the sprite image to be the display image of the RigidBody2D. To lock them together so that they can move around as one unit, select RigidBody2D, and then click on the ▣ icon next to the lock icon on the 2D toolbar, as shown in Figure 4-9.

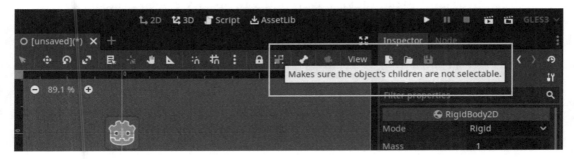

Figure 4-9. *Making sure the parent node's children are not selectable so that they move together as one unit*

As you can see, this icon lets us bundle up the parent-child nodes as one unit by making sure that we cannot separately move around the child nodes. Once we do that, the ▣ icon appears next to the RigidBody2D node in the Scene dock.

But wait, there is another issue we need to solve first: the scary-looking icon ⚠ next to RigidBody2D. When we hover over or click this icon, we get a "Node configuration warning" message, shown in Figure 4-10. This simply means that we have not yet assigned any shape to our rigid body, so it cannot collide or interact with any other objects we might add to the scene. Let's see how to do that next.

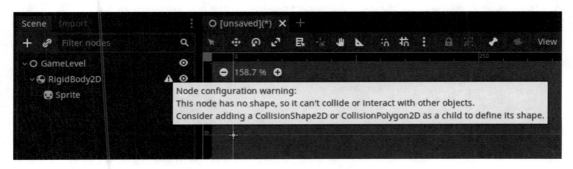

Figure 4-10. *"Node configuration warning" message*

Adding a Collision Shape

When we add a collision body to our scene, we need to tell Godot what kind of shape it has. You can think of this shape as being a force field around the body and will determine the way the body will move after colliding with another body or object.

Let's assign a shape to our RigidBody2D node. To do so, we need to create another node, called CollisionShape2D, as a child of RigidBody2D. Just like we did before, select the RigidBody2D node in the Scene dock by single-clicking it, and then click the ![+] button to create a CollisionShape2D as its child. Either search for *CollisionShape2D* in the search box of the Create New Node window, or navigate to it under Matches by expanding the tree structure as follows:

Node ➤ CanvasItem ➤ Node2D ➤ CollisionShape2D

This is shown in Figure 4-11.

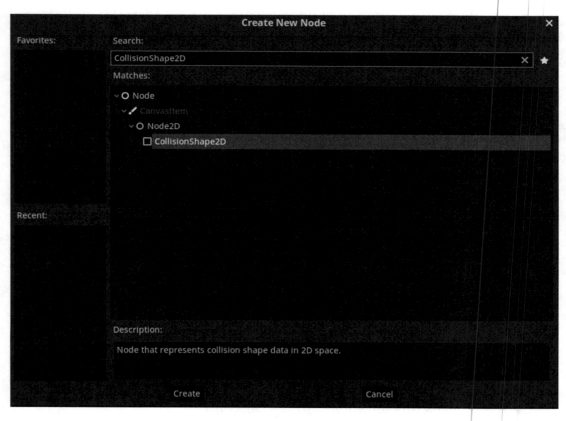

Figure 4-11. *Path to CollisionShape2D node in the Create New Node window*

Your node hierarchy should look like Figure 4-12 (a) and *not* like Figure 4-12 (b).

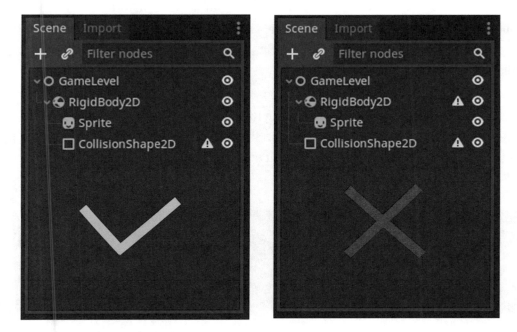

Figure 4-12. *(a) Correct hierarchy, (b) incorrect hierarchy*

Also, Figure 4-13 (a) and (b) are both correct.

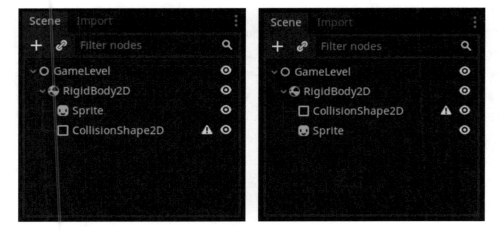

Figure 4-13. *(a) Sprite comes before CollisionShape2D, (b) sprite comes after CollisionShape2D*

Note   The order of the children nodes do not matter here. If your CollisionShape2D node comes before the Sprite node instead, it's correct too. The only important thing is that the CollisonShape2D and Sprite nodes should both be children of RigidBody2D.

You'll notice that the 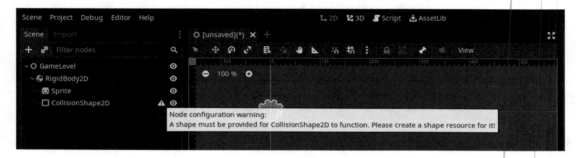 icon next to the RigidBody2D node disappeared, but now another one appeared next to CollisionShape2D! You can see this in Figure 4-14. This time, the warning message tells us that we need to assign a shape to CollisionShape2D. Let's solve this.

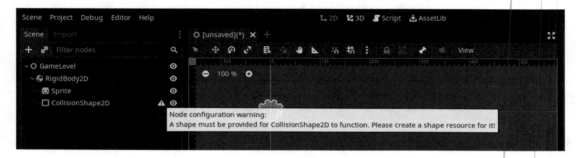

Figure 4-14.   *"Node configuration warning" message prompting you to assign a shape to CollisionShape2D*

In the Scene dock, select the CollisionShape2D node, and then head over to the inspector window. We can assign a shape to this node using the drop-down menu under the Shape field. As shown in Figure 4-15, we can choose from several shapes, such as a capsule, circle, rectangle, etc. Let's select the RectangleShape2D. This creates a rectangular collision area for our rigid body. When we do that, the error message that we encountered earlier is gone.

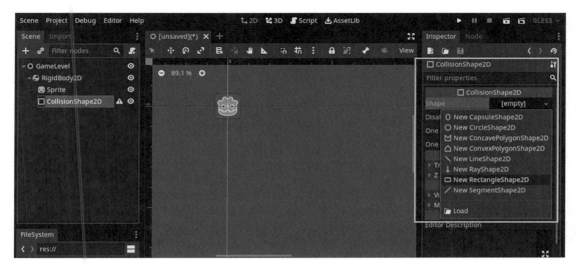

Figure 4-15. *Adding a rectangle shape to CollisionShape2D*

As shown in Figure 4-16 (a), a blue-colored rectangle with small orange dots on its edges appears on top of the sprite in the editor space. If we hide the Sprite node by clicking the toggle visibility icon ⦿ next to it in the Scene dock, we can see this rectangle clearly, as shown in Figure 4-16 (b). This is the body's collision area, which will collide with other physics bodies. But it's too small to see.

Figure 4-16. *(a) The RectangleShape2D appears on top of the sprite, (b) visibility of the Sprite node can be toggled to see the blue RectangleShape2D*

Zoom in the editor either by clicking the Zoom icon on its top-left corner or by using the scroll button on your mouse (if it has the scroll wheel) with your cursor on the editor window. You can move around the editor by moving your mouse around while holding down the right-click button in the editor space. Now, unhide the Sprite node by clicking the ⌄ icon. Next, click and drag the orange dots so that the blue rectangle, that is, the collision shape, is almost equal to the size of the sprite. You should see either Figure 4-17 (a) or 4-17 (b), depending on your node hierarchy.

Figure 4-17. *(a) RectangleShape2D behind the Sprite node,*
(b) RectangleShape2D in front of the Sprite node

Note   If in your scene hierarchy, your CollisionShape2D comes first before the sprite, as shown in Figure 4-13 (b), the rectangle collision shape won't be visible since it will be behind the sprite. It doesn't matter, as long as you can see the orange dots. You can change the order of the nodes in the Scene dock. If your hierarchy looks like Figure 4-13 (b), you can click and drag the CollisionShape2D node and release it on top of the parent node, RigidBody2D (or release it just below the Sprite, on top of a blue line that appears). Now, your hierarchy will look like Figure 4-13 (a), and you will see Figure 4-17 (b) in your editor.

Playing Your First Scene

Now, we haven't saved our scene yet. To do so, navigate to Scene ➤ Save Scene As from the toolbar at the top-left corner of the interface (Ctrl+Shift+S). In the window that pops up, give the scene a name, in this format: SceneName.tscn. By default, the scene is named after the name of our root node. Since we renamed our root node GameLevel, the scene name of GameLevel.tscn is suggested when we try to save the scene, as shown in Figure 4-18. This saved scene appears on the FileSystem dock and is saved as a resource there.

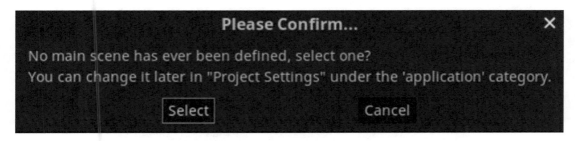

Figure 4-18. *Saving the scene*

We have created our first rigid body! Let's play the scene to see it in action. To do so, click the Play Scene button (keyboard shortcut F6) in the playtest buttons toolbar at the top-right corner of the interface. If you play the project using the ▶ button (keyboard shortcut F5), a window pops up telling us that "No main scene has been defined" and asks us to select one, as shown in Figure 4-19. We saw this in the previous chapter. Click Select, then choose the scene we just created, i.e., GameLevel.tscn, and then click Open.

Figure 4-19. *Prompt to set the main scene*

Once we do that, our scene starts playing in a separate debug window, as shown in Figure 4-20. Notice how the rigid body briefly appears in the top-left corner and then falls down quickly and goes off the screen! This is because our rigid body, being a physics body, follows the rules of in-game gravity. The body will keep falling forever if we don't put another object in the scene to stop it.

Figure 4-20. *The rigid body falls down in the left corner of the game scene*

In the editor, let's drag our rigid body from the top-left corner (the origin) to the center of our game scene so that it appears in the middle, and not the left corner, when we play the scene. The visible area of our game is indicated by the faint purple, pink, and green lines that form a rectangle in the editor. Now when we play the scene, our rigid body falls down from the middle portion of the screen, as shown in Figure 4-21.

Figure 4-21. *The rigid body falls down near the middle of the game scene*

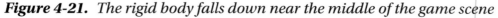

Note   Make sure that the RigidBody2D's children, that is, the Sprite and CollisionShape2D nodes, are set to not selectable before moving around the rigid body in the editor! Remember, you can do this by selecting the parent node (RigidBody2D) and clicking the icon next to the lock button on the 2D toolbar.

Properties of RigidBody2D

Select the RigidBody2D node in the Scene dock, and take a look at the Inspector dock. This node has a bunch of different physics properties that we can play around with, as shown in Figure 4-22.

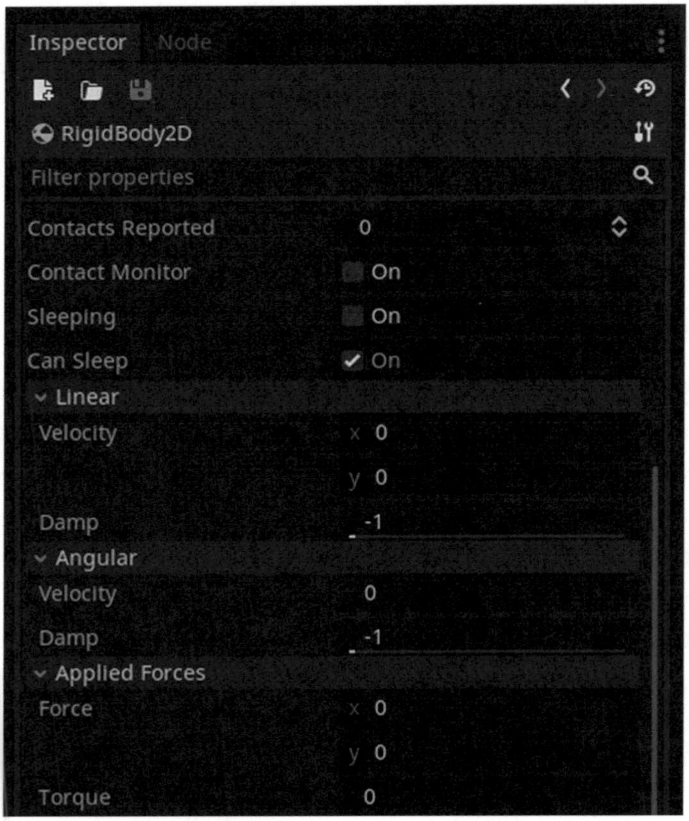

Figure 4-22. *Physics properties of RigidBody2D*

By applying forces to a rigid body such as gravity and by changing its properties, you directly affect the physics simulation that controls the behavior of the body. For example, you can change the mass, weight, and mode of the body.

The mode can be set to rigid, static, character, or kinematic. Different modes change how 2D physics affects the object. For example, if you set the mode as rigid, the body falls under the influence of gravity and can collide with other bodies or objects in the scene. Setting it as static, however, will cause it to remain fixed on the screen. Let's look at more properties that we can change and the effect they will have on our rigid body.

- *Gravity scale*: Increasing the gravity will cause the body in the scene to fall faster, while decreasing it will cause the body to fall slower.

- *Linear velocity*: Increasing the velocity in the x-direction will cause it to move to the right as it falls, while increasing the velocity in the y-direction will cause the body to fall down faster.

- *Angular velocity*: Applying an angular velocity to a rigid body will cause the body to rotate as it falls.

- *Applied force*: An external force can be applied to the body in the x or y direction.

Duplicating a Node

If we want to have a number of similar objects in our scene, it is time-consuming to create each of them, one by one. In such cases, it's more convenient to create multiple copies of a node and change the properties for each individual node. If we want to replicate a node along with all of its children, select the node under the Scene dock, and then use the keyboard shortcut Ctrl+D. Another way is to right-click the node we want to replicate and then select the Duplicate option.

Now, let's use this method to add a second rigid body to our game scene and see how it interacts with the first one. Select RigidBody2D in the Scene dock, and use the keyboard shortcut Ctrl+D. This creates a copy of this node, called RigidBody2D2, as shown in Figure 4-23 (b). This node has exactly the same children, as well as properties, as the original node, RigidBody2D. But the new node gets pasted on top of the first node, as shown in Figure 4-23 (a), so you need to move it around to see it.

Figure 4-23. *(a) The duplicated node RigidBody2D2 pasted on top of RigidBody2D, (b) moving the RigidBody2D2 node next to RigidBody2D node*

After doing that, play the scene by clicking the ▣ button. This time, you'll notice that both the rigid bodies fall at the same time, at the same speed. This is because both of these are identical, as they are duplicates of each other. If you select one of the rigid bodies, say RigidBody2D2, and increase its gravity scale in the Inspector dock, you'll notice that it falls faster than the other one. See Figure 4-24. The same goes for any of its other properties; changing them for one of the rigid bodies will cause both of the rigid bodies to behave differently.

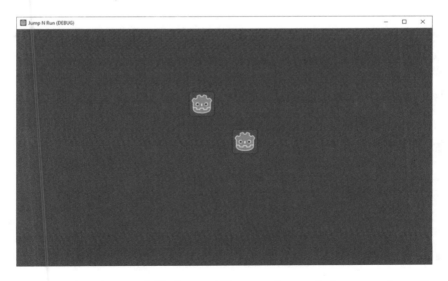

Figure 4-24. *RigidBody2D2 falls faster if its gravity scale is more than that of RigidBody2D*

TRY IT!

Your First Game Scene

1. Create three rigid bodies in your game scene, and assign each of them child nodes: CollisionShape2D and Sprite.

2. Change the properties such as gravity, angular velocity, etc., for each of them.

3. Play the game scene to see them in action!

Creating a Static Body

We've learned how to create a rigid body whose behavior is influenced by game physics. Now, let's add another type of physics body in our scene, one that doesn't fall due to in-game gravity: a static body. As it is independent of the other objects in our scene, that is, the two rigid bodies, we will create a static body as a child of our root node, GameLevel.

First, select the root node, GameLevel, in the Scene dock, and click the Add Child Node ➕ button and add a StaticBody2D node by either searching for it in the search box or navigating to it under the following tree path:

Node ➤ CanvasItem ➤ Node2D ➤ CollisionObject2D ➤ PhysicsBody2D ➤ StaticBody2D

Figure 4-25 shows this path. Click the Create button, and a new node, StaticBody2D, is created as a child of GameLevel.

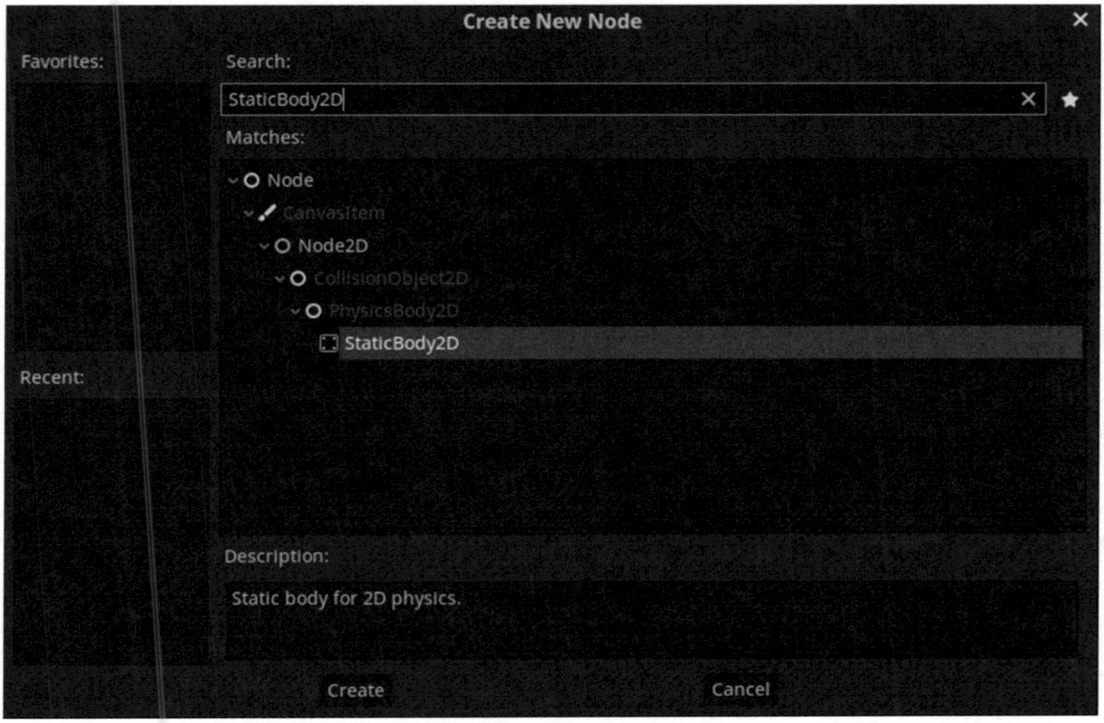

Create New Node   ✕

Favorites: Search:

                  StaticBody2D   ✕   ★

                  Matches:

                  ˅ O Node
                      ˅ ✎ CanvasItem
                          ˅ O Node2D
                              ˅ O CollisionObject2D
                                  ˅ O PhysicsBody2D
                                      ⬚ StaticBody2D

Recent:

                  Description:

                  Static body for 2D physics.

                        Create   Cancel

Figure 4-25. *Path to the StaticBody2D node in the Create New Node window*

Just like every other node, StaticBody2D is created at the origin by default, that is, at the intersection of the green, pink, and red lines in the editor, as shown in Figure 4-26.

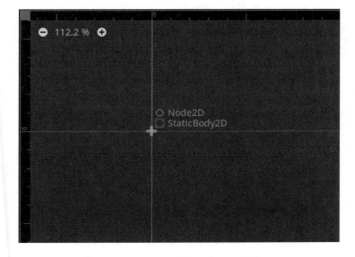

Figure 4-26. *The StaticBody2D is created at the origin*

Make sure that the static body's children are nonselectable; that is, group its children with it by clicking the ▦ icon. This will ensure that when you move the static body around in the editor, its children will move along with it.

The next few steps are the same as the ones for rigid bodies that we implemented before.

1. A ⚠ icon appears next to StaticBody2D, warning us that our static body has no shape assigned to it, so it cannot interact with other scene objects. Fix it by adding a CollisionShape2D as its child.

2. Another warning pops us, prompting us to choose a shape for our static body. Select the CollisionShape2D, and select New RectangleShape2D from the Shape drop-down menu in the Inspector dock.

3. Add a sprite as a child of the static body, and drag and drop an image, e.g., icon.png, found in the FileSystem dock, to the Texture field of the Sprite node in the Inspector dock.

4. Select the CollisionShape2D node that is the child of StaticBody2D, and resize it to fit the sprite.

Just a refresher, the CollisionShape2D node can be found under the path:
Node ➤ CanvasItem ➤ Node2D ➤ CollisionShape2D
And, the Sprite node can be found under this path:
Node ➤ CanvasItem ➤ Node2D ➤ Sprite
We now have two rigid bodies and one static body in our scene, as shown in Figure 4-27.

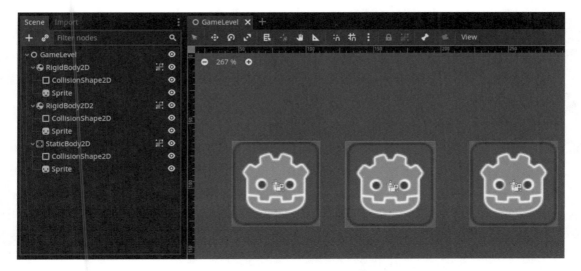

Figure 4-27. *Two rigid bodies and one static body in the game scene*

Unlike a rigid body, the static body isn't affected by gravity; hence, it doesn't fall down when you play the scene. Let's see this in action.

1. First, let's position StaticBody2D under the two rigid bodies in the editor.

2. Next, resize the static body by selecting the CollisionShape2D node of the StaticBody2D in the Scene dock, and making it bigger than both the rigid bodies' lengths by dragging the orange dots, as shown in Figure 4-28.

3. Then, make the sprite of the static body bigger by selecting its node in the Scene dock and then dragging the orange dots that show up in the editor, as shown in Figure 2-29.

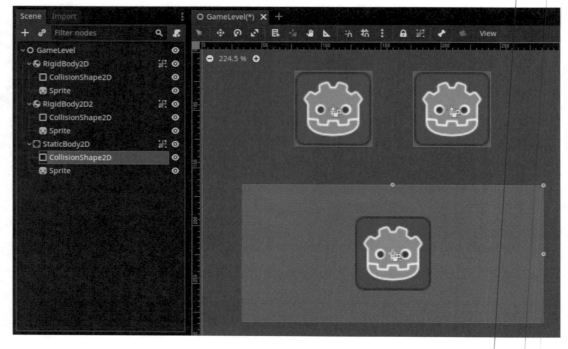

Figure 4-28. *Resizing the collision shape of the static body*

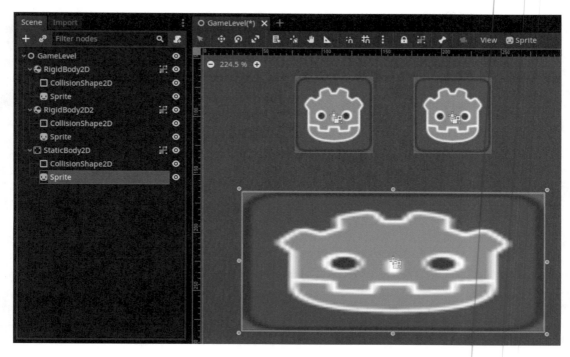

Figure 4-29. *Resizing the sprite of the StaticBody2D*

With the static body positioned under both of the rigid bodies, play the scene by clicking the  button. Notice how the static body breaks the fall of the rigid bodies! When the two rigid bodies come into contact with the static body, they stay on its surface and stop falling further. We can see this in Figure 4-30.

Figure 4-30. *When the two rigid bodies come into contact with the static body, they stop falling*

TRY IT!

A Game Scene with Rigid and Static Bodies

1. Create a game scene with two rigid bodies and four static bodies.

2. Position the static bodies in a row below the two rigid bodies.

3. Play the game scene to see them in action!

Key Takeaways

In this chapter, we learned about Godot's node-scene architecture and how to create and add new nodes to a game scene. We also learned about different collision bodies in Godot and how they are affected by in-game physics. We created two rigid bodies and one static body in a game scene and saw how changing different properties such as gravity affects their behavior when they interact with each other.

PART III

Designing the Game

CHAPTER 5

Adding Game Graphics

In this chapter, you'll learn how to obtain as well as import game assets according to the theme of our game. We'll create a simple game scene with a ground and sky, as well as create our main character. We'll also place our character in this game scene and write a simple script to control it using custom keyboard input.

What Are Game Assets?

Game assets form the basic essence of your game. They include the following:

- Game art for your characters, enemies, coins, and background

- Fonts, buttons, and images for designing the game GUI

- Music and sound effects

- Scripts for making your game work

There are two ways to get the game assets you need. You can make them yourself, or you can easily get them from certain websites. The first option might be time-consuming, based on your skills and your ability to use the tools required to make them. In fact, many people use software such as Blender and Autodesk Maya to make 2D as well as 3D game art and even sell these creations for profit.

But as a first-time game developer, you might want to stick to the second option for now and use the premade assets available online. We'll be following this approach in our book. Now, let's take a look at some popular websites that offer game assets.

© Maithili Dhule 2022
M. Dhule, *Beginning Game Development with Godot*, https://doi.org/10.1007/978-1-4842-7455-2_5

OpenGameArt.org

This website offers a huge number of 2D and 3D art, tilesets, textures, music, and sound effects. All are absolutely free to use, even in commercial projects. You just need to give credit to the creators of these files according to the specified license. See Figure 5-1.

Figure 5-1. *OpenGameArt.org*

Itch.io

This website also provides thousands of free, as well as paid, 2D and 3D art files, music, sound effects, and environment designs for all kinds of game genres. Each file has its own license and terms of use. See Figure 5-2.

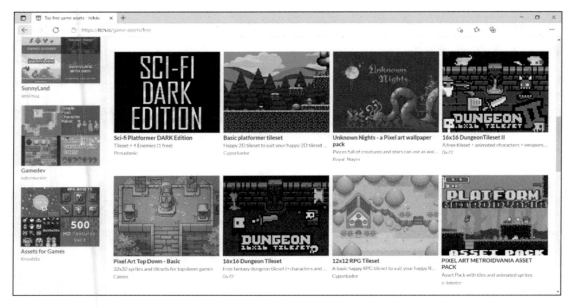

Figure 5-2. *Itch.io*

Gameart2D

The character sprites, tilesets, and game GUI on this website are cute, cartoon-styled creations. Most of the artwork is paid, but there are quite a number of freebies as well. See Figure 5-3.

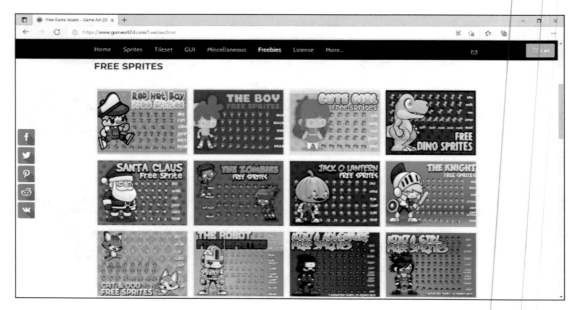

Figure 5-3. *Gameart2D*

Kenney.nl

This website provides a large number of hand-crafted 2D and 3D asset packs, music and background sounds, and UI components. Most of them are free or available at a nominal price. See Figure 5-4.

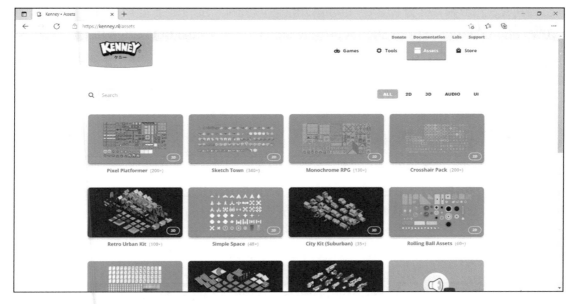

Figure 5-4. *Kenny.nl*

Choosing the Right Assets

When choosing the graphics for your game, you need to first think about its type and theme. The game art for a hyper-realistic first-person shooter will be quite different from the one used for making a 2D, pixel-based platformer!

We'll be focusing on creating a 2D platformer game in this book. Here are some ideas for the type of characters and environment props you can include, according to the theme:

- *Sci-fi*: Aliens, astronauts, spaceships, minerals, planets
- *Fantasy*: Kings and queens, knights, dragons, mythical creatures, dungeons, castles
- *Jungle/forest*: Trees, squirrels, tigers, foxes, mushrooms, grass
- *Horror*: Zombies, ghosts, wizards, dark scenery

93

Once we decide the theme, we need to gather various assets, such as sprites for the player, enemies, and collectibles, as well as tilesets and background images for designing the game world.

Note   An image of a game object such as a character or collectible is called a *Sprite*. A Sprite Sheet is a large image that contains a bunch of sprites arranged in rows and columns. Sprite sheets usually consist of a series of images that can be used for animating a game object, e.g., player actions such as running, jumping, or climbing.

Importing Game Art

The process of importing game art into our Godot project is surprisingly easy. Just drag and drop your images from the computer onto the Godot FileSystem dock, as shown in Figure 5-5. The imported game art may look blurry due to filtering by the engine. To prevent this, select the image files in the FileSystem dock, and, in the Import dock (next to the Scene dock), unselect the Filter property, and then click Reimport.

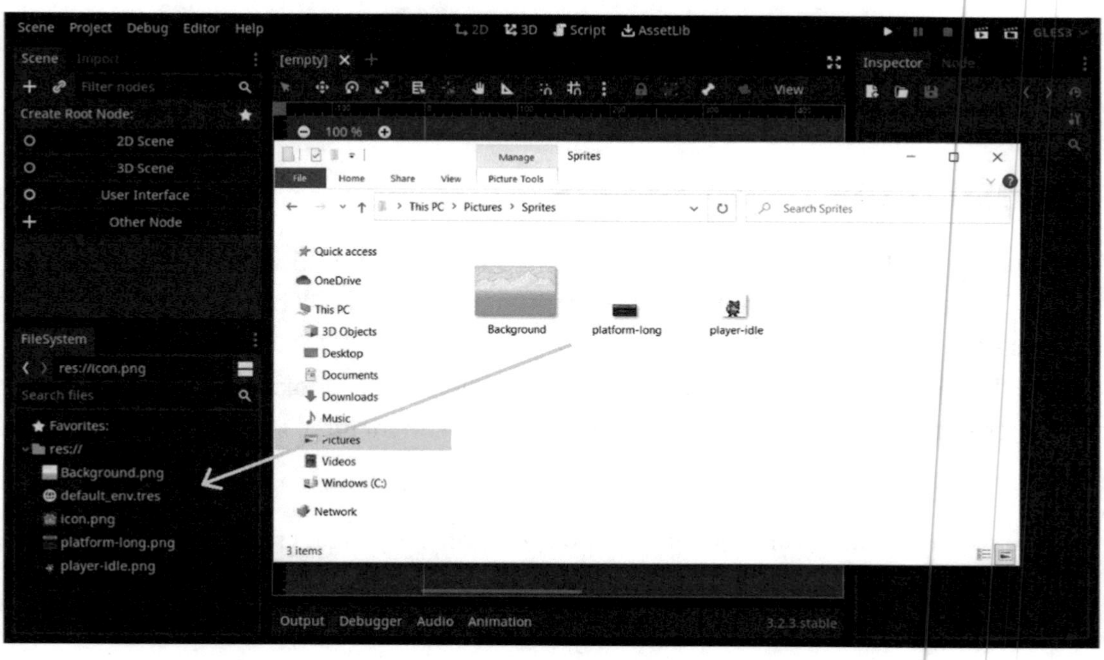

Figure 5-5.   Importing images into Godot

TRY IT!

Importing Game Assets

1. Decide the theme for your game, and think about the type of characters and props you want to include.

2. Find and download some game art that suits the theme.

3. Import them into your Godot project.

Creating the Main Game Scene

At this point, with our assets ready, we can start developing our game. First, we'll create the main game scene. We'll use the image of a platform for creating a ground for the player to move on. Next, we'll create our character that can be controlled with the arrow keys on our keyboard. Finally, we'll place our character in the main game scene with the simple environment that we created! But before all that, let's take a look at how we can create reusable game objects.

Creating Game Objects as Scenes

Each basic component that is placed in our game, such as a character, an enemy, or a collectible, is known as a game object. After creating one for the first time, you might want to use it in different parts of your game. For example, every level of your game might have multiple copies of a certain type of coin. You'll also want your character to be present in every level.

To make game objects such as these reusable, we can create the object (or objects) as its own scene. Then, we can create an instance of that object whenever we want to use it in a particular scene. This means that whenever we want to change some aspects related to that object, we just have to modify it once, and it automatically gets updated in all the scenes in which it is used. For example, we have to create our player in one game scene and hence only once. When we design a game level in another scene, we can just create an instance of our player in this second scene, and our player will pop up in it. If we change a player's sprite in the scene in which it was created, it will change throughout the entire game. Now, let's take a look at a hands-on example. We'll first create the main game scene. In this scene, we'll create static bodies for representing the ground. We'll add the background image for the sky at a later stage.

Designing the Main Game Scene

Follow these steps:

1. Create a new Godot project, giving it the name of your game, such as **Jump N Run**. Then, click on the ⏎2D 2D button at the top of the interface to open and start working in the 2D workspace.

2. Under the Scene dock, click the 2D Scene button to create the root node called Node2D.

3. Next, select the Node2D node in the Scene dock, and click the Add Child Node button (keyboard shortcut: Control ➕ A) to add another node called StaticBody2D as its child, as shown in Figure 5-6. As shown in the previous chapter, we can either search for a particular node by typing it in the Search box or navigate to it by expanding the node hierarchy under Matches.

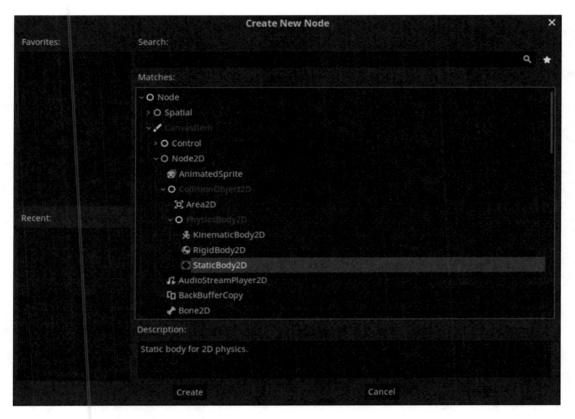

Figure 5-6. *Creating a StaticBody2D node*

4. Once you click the Create button, StaticBody2D will be created as a child of the root node, Node2D. Just as we saw in the previous chapter, a warning icon appears next to StaticBody2D, prompting us to add a collision shape for our static body. This is shown in Figure 5-7.

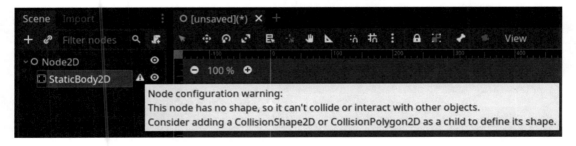

Figure 5-7. *Node configuration warning*

5. Select the StaticBody2D node in the Scene dock, click the ➕ Add
    Child Node button, and then search for or navigate to
    CollisionShape2D. Click the Create button, and this node will be
    assigned to be the child of StaticBody2D, as shown in Figure 5-8.

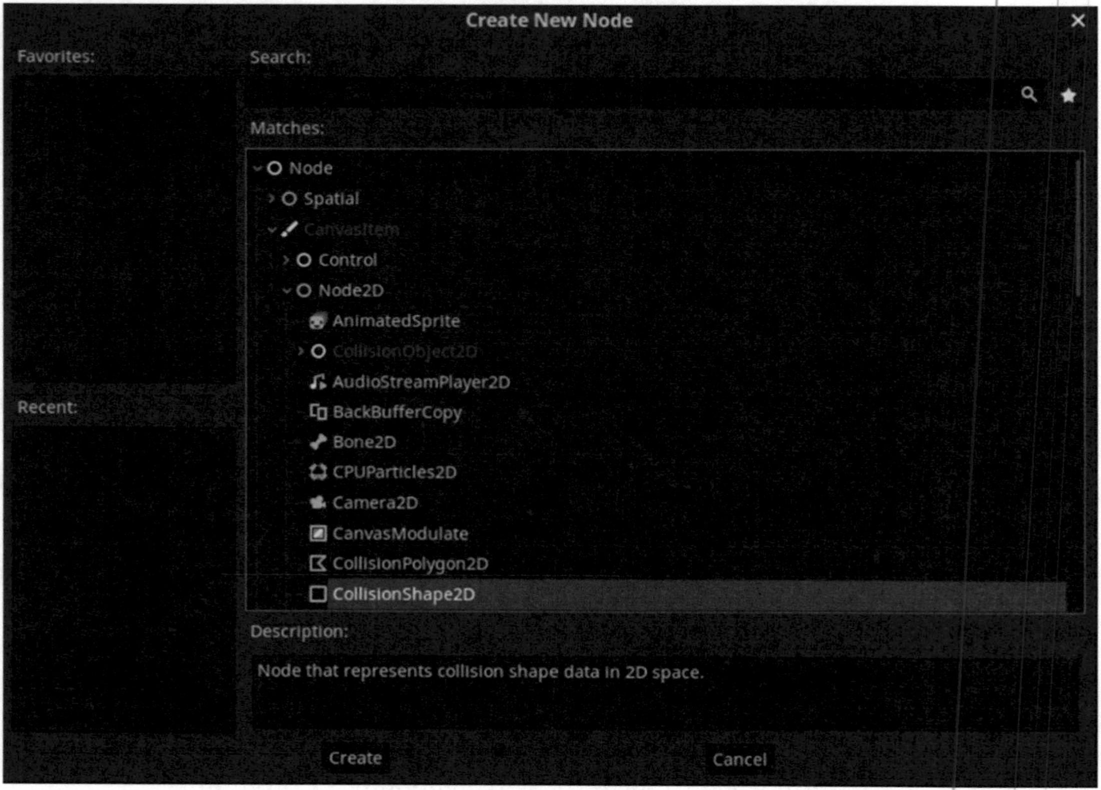

Figure 5-8. *Creating a CollisionShape2D node*

6. We need to assign a collision shape to the CollisionShape2D
    node, as prompted by the warning sign next to it. But first, let's
    add a Sprite node as a child of StaticBody2D. To do so, select
    StaticBody2D under the Scene dock; then navigate to the sprite, as
    shown in Figure 5-9, and click the Create button.

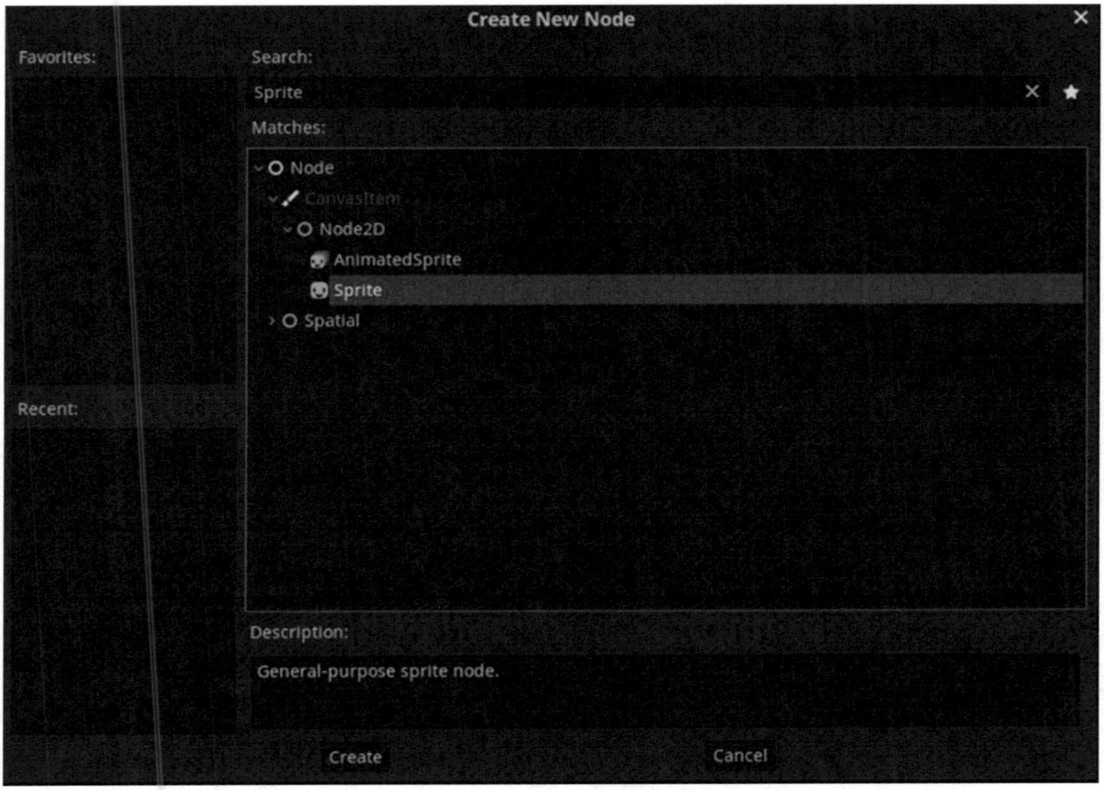

Figure 5-9. *Creating a Sprite node*

7. We need to assign an image as a texture for our Sprite node. Since we want our StaticBody2D to be the platform in this game scene, let's assign an image of a platform as the texture of this node. Just as we saw previously in this chapter, to import an image into your project, just drag and drop the image into the FileSystem dock from your computer. If you haven't already done so, import the image of a platform into your project, as shown in Figure 5-10.

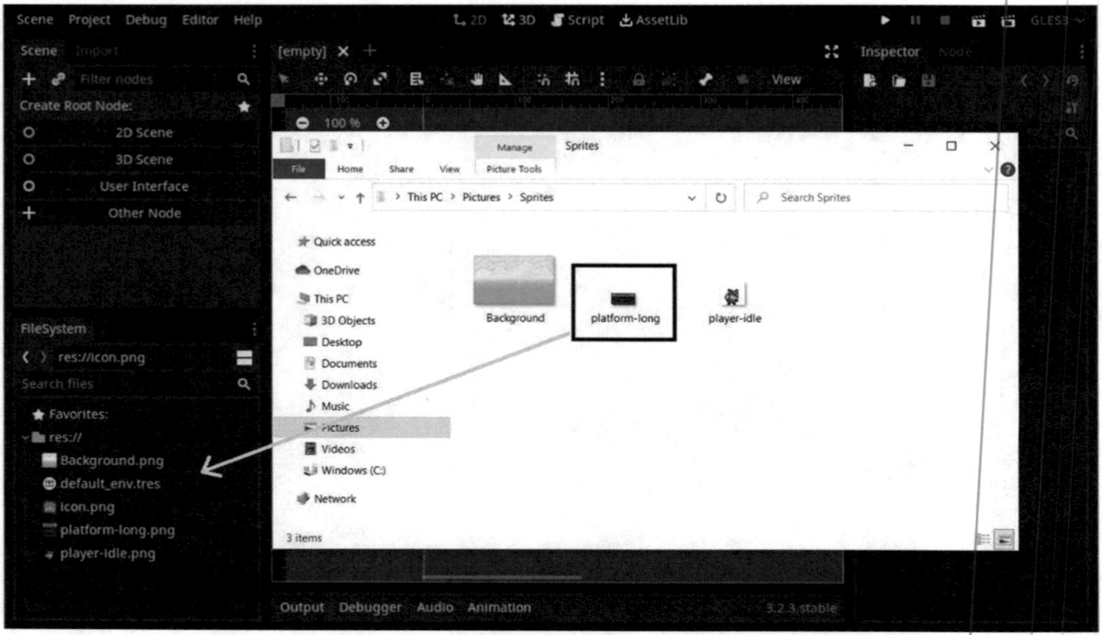

Figure 5-10. *Drag and drop the image of a platform into the FileSystem dock*

Select the Sprite node in the Scene dock, and then drag and drop
the image of the platform (platform-long.png in this case) from
the FileSystem dock onto the Texture field of the Sprite node
(under the Inspector dock), as shown in Figure 5-11.

Figure 5-11. *Assigning an image to the Texture field of the sprite*

8. Now that we have our platform, let's assign a collision shape to it. Select the CollisionShape2D node under the Scene dock, and then head over to the inspector. Under the Shape drop-down menu, select New RectangleShape2D to add a rectangular collision shape, as shown in Figure 5-12. Now, you'll notice that the warning sign next to CollsionShape2D disappears.

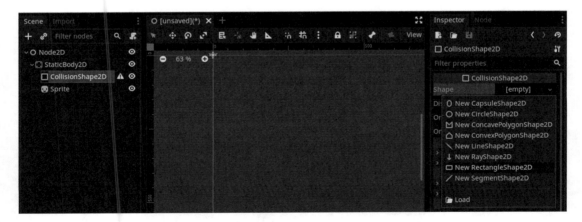

Figure 5-12. *Adding a RectangleShape2D*

9. Now, zoom in on the platform by scrolling on your mouse or using the zoom in ⊕ button on the workspace. Drag the orange dots to adjust the collision shape to fit the size and shape of the platform, as shown in Figure 5-13.

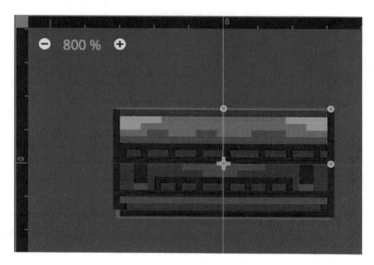

Figure 5-13. *Adjusting the size of the collision shape*

10. Let's group the StaticBody2D node with its children, i.e., the CollisionShape2D and Sprite nodes so that they move together as one unit. Under the Scene dock, select StaticBody2D, and then Click on the bind ⊞ button next to the lock icon on the 2D toolbar near the top of the workspace. Once we do that, the icon will appear next to StaticBody2D, and we can freely move the static body around in the workspace. This is shown in Figure 5-14.

Figure 5-14. *Group the StaticBody2D, CollisionShape2D, and Sprite nodes together*

11. Zoom out and adjust the workspace until you can see the rectangle formed by the faint pink, green, and purple lines, shown in Figure 5-15. The space enclosed by this rectangle is what is visible to us when we play the game scene. Let's call this the *game screen area*. Since the static body represents the ground in our game, click and drag it toward the bottom of the game screen area in the workspace, as shown in Figure 5-15.

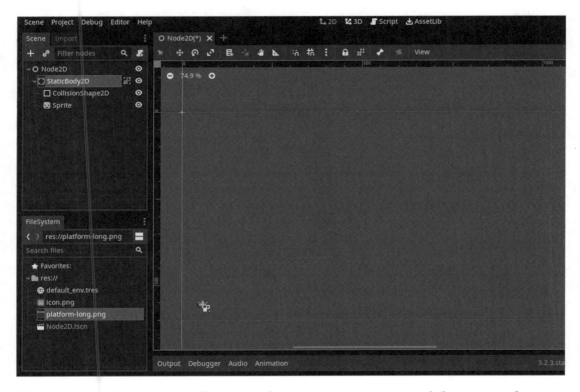

Figure 5-15. *Zoom out until you see the game screen area and then move the platform to the bottom of it*

12. As you can see in Figure 5-15, the platform is tiny compared to the game scene area! Let's make it bigger by changing its scale. Select the StaticBody2D node in the Scene dock; then, under the Transform field in the Inspector, change its x and y scale values in the Inspector. As shown in Figure 5-16, we've set the x scale to 5 and the y scale to 4. Increasing the x scale makes the static body longer, while increasing the y scale makes it taller. Do note that non-uniform scaling can lead to stretched game art!

Figure 5-16. *Making the static body larger by increasing its x and y scale*

13. Make sure to adjust the position of the platform to be within the boundary of the game screen area. If any part of the platform goes out of the boundary, that part will get cut off and won't be visible when we play the game scene. See Figure 5-17.

Figure 5-17. *(a) The portion of the platform on the left of the green line gets cut off, (b) The platform doesn't get cut off*

14. Now, let's create a long line of platforms for our character to walk on. Select StaticBody2D in the Scene dock and press Ctrl+D on your keyboard to duplicate the node. Alternatively, you can right-click StaticBody2D and select the "duplicate" option. Once you do that, an identical node called StaticBody2D2 is created under the Scene dock. But the static body of this node gets placed on top of our first static body in the workspace, as shown in Figure 5-18.

Figure 5-18. *The duplicated static body gets placed on top of the first static body*

Note   A better practice for creating multiple copies of an object would be to create a separate scene for the object and then to create multiple instances of that object in our main game scene. We'll take a look at creating instances of scenes in the next section.

---

15.   Click it, and then drag it away from the first static body by holding down your left mouse button and moving your mouse. Place it next to the first static body, as shown in Figure 5-19, for creating a longer platform. You can choose to enable Smart Snap (Shift+S) by clicking the ![icon] icon and Grid Snap (Shift+G) by clicking the ![icon] icon on the 2D toolbar to make it easier for you to place the platforms. You can configure snapping by clicking the Snapping options ![icon] icon on the toolbar.

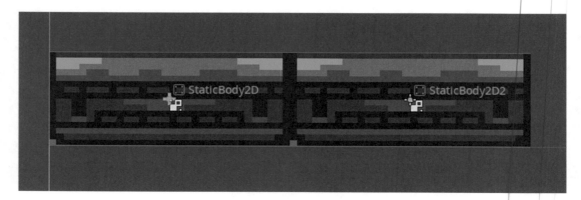

Figure 5-19. *The second static body is moved and placed next to the first static body to create a longer platform*

16.   We can repeat the previous step a number of times to create a line of platforms that forms the ground for our character to move on, as shown in Figure 5-20.

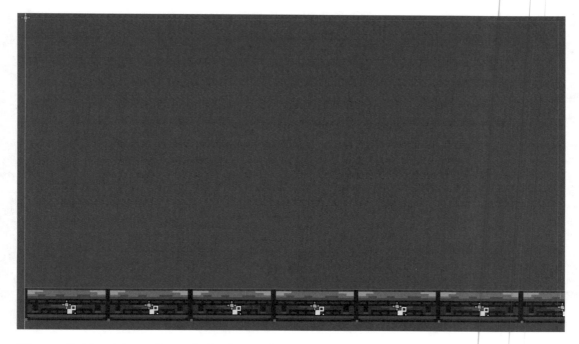

Figure 5-20. *A long line of platforms forming the ground of the game*

17. We've created the first scene of our game! Let's rename the scene
     Game Level by double-clicking the root node, Node2D in the
     Scene dock, and then typing in the new name. Save the scene
     by clicking Scene ➤ Save Scene As at the top-left corner of the
     interface (keyboard shortcut: Ctrl+Shift+S). By default, Godot
     names the scene Game Level.tscn, since this is the current name
     of our root node. Replace this with GameLevel.tscn, as shown in
     Figure 5-21. Then click Save.

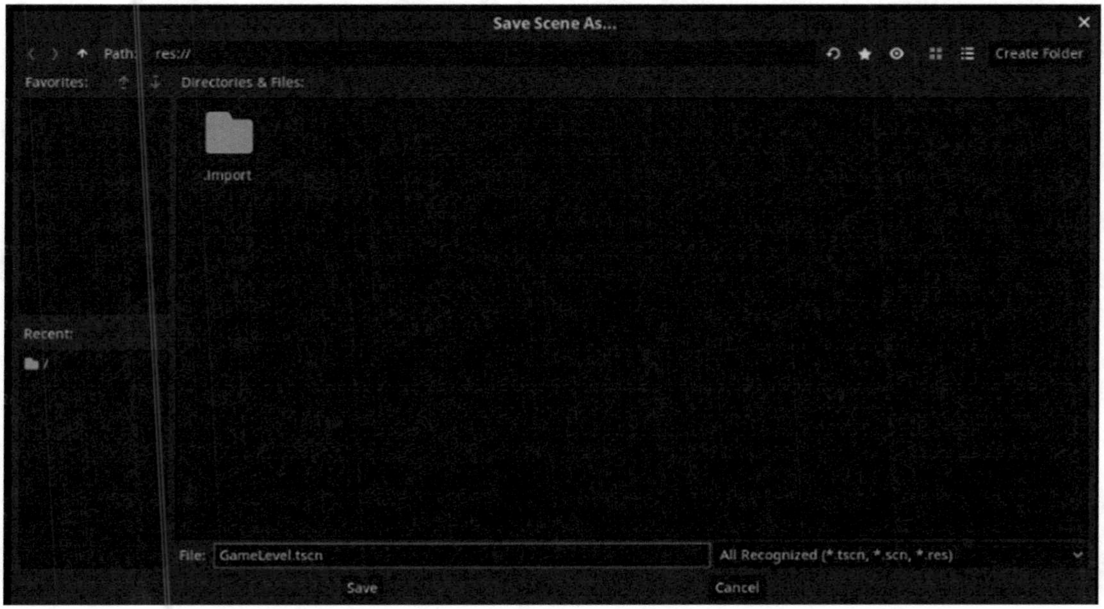

Figure 5-21. *Save the scene as GameLevel.tscn*

18. Play the scene by clicking the Play Scene 🎬 button (keyboard
     shortcut: F6) on the Playtest tab on the top-right corner of the
     interface. You'll see the debug window pop up, as shown in
     Figure 5-22.

Figure 5-22. *Play the game scene*

Creating the Player

Follow these steps:

1. Create another scene by clicking the ➕ button next to our first scene, GameLevel, as shown in Figure 5-23.

Figure 5-23. *Creating a new game scene*

2. Now, we'll create a game object for our character. Since we'll be creating this object as a scene, we don't need to add a root node. Instead, in the empty Scene dock of this new scene, click the ➕ Add Child Node button

and add a node called KinematicBody2D by searching for it in the window that pops up. This is shown in Figure 5-24.

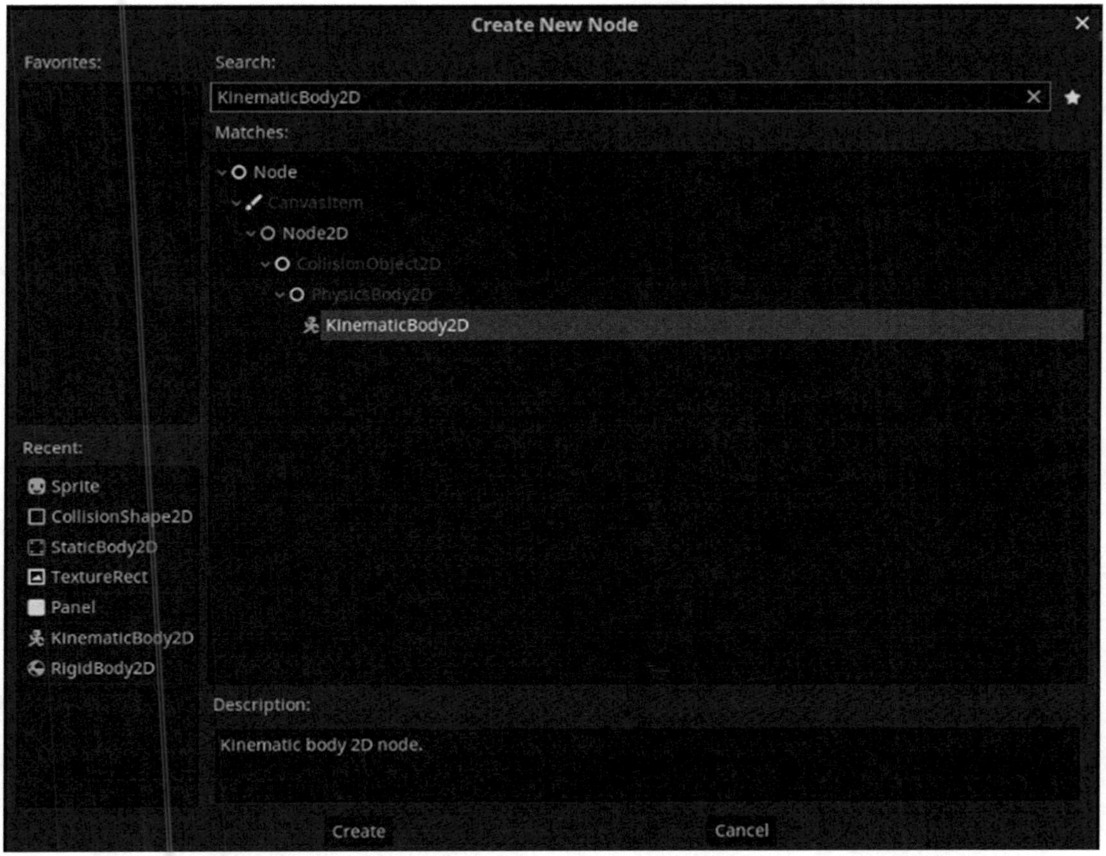

Figure 5-24. *Creating a KinematicBody2D node*

3. Just like in the case of any physics body, we also need to add CollisionShape2D and Sprite nodes as its children. We can do that by selecting KinematicBody2D in the Scene dock, clicking the ➕ Add Child Node button, and then searching for and creating the respective child nodes.

4. Import the sprite (image) for the player from your computer by dragging and dropping it into the FileSystem dock from the file on your computer. Re-import the image by selecting it in the FileSystem dock, then unselecting the Filter property (untick it) in the Import dock (Next to Scene dock), and clicking on the Reimport button.

5. Select the Sprite node in the Scene dock, and then drag and drop the image of the Player from the FileSystem dock into the Texture field of the Sprite node (in the Inspector dock).

6. Zoom in on the Player on the workspace by scrolling with your mouse or using the zoom in ⊕ button on the workspace.

7. We need to assign a collision shape to our player. Select the CollsionShape2D node in the Scene dock, and then head over to its shape field in the Inspector dock. This time, let's select a capsule shape. Adjust the capsule shape to fit the sprite's shape and size by dragging the orange dots on the workspace. You can adjust the x and y positions under the Transform field in the inspector for moving the capsule shape up/down or left/right, as shown in Figure 5-25.

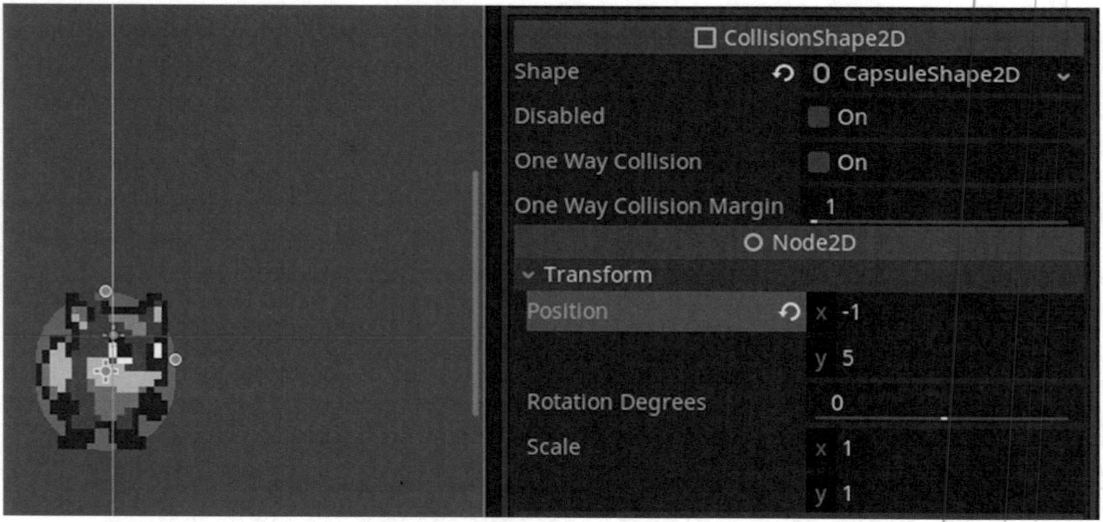

Figure 5-25. Adjusting the size and shape of the CapsuleShape2D

8. Select KinematicBody2D in the Scene dock; then click the 🔳 button to bind it with its child nodes, i.e., CollisionShape2D and Sprite. Now, you can freely move the player around in the workspace in the current scene.

110

9. Save the scene by clicking Scene ➤ Save Scene As at the top-left corner of the interface (keyboard shortcut: Ctrl+Shift+S). Rename the scene to `Player.tscn`.

10. Move the player on the workspace so that it is within the boundaries of the game screen area (rectangle formed by the green, pink, and purple lines on the workspace).

11. But the player is too small compared to the game screen area! Let's increase its size by selecting the Sprite node in the Scene dock and then changing its x and y scale on the Inspector dock. Let's make the x and y value equal to, say, 4. Do the same for the CollisionShape2D, and make the x and y values equal to, say, 3. You can also change the x and y scale of the KinematicBody instead, as shown in Figure 5-26.

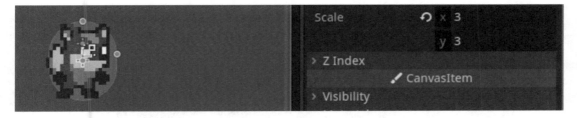

Figure 5-26. *The player's size is increased by changing the x and y scale of its KinematicBody2D*

12. Now when you play the scene by pressing Play Scene button (keyboard shortcut F6), you can see that the player's size is bigger. Make sure to save the scene.

TRY IT!

Creating Your First Game Character

1. Create a game character with the sprite (image) of your choice.

2. Increase the size of the character to five times its original size.

Linking the Player to the Main Scene

Follow these steps:

1. Go to the Game Level scene (the first scene that we created), and then select the root node, Game Level.

2. Next, click the 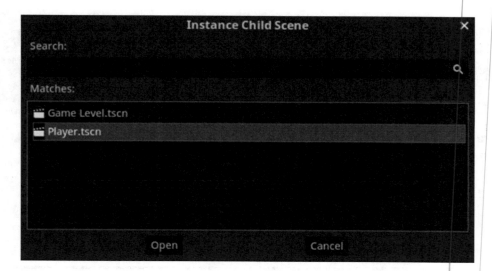 icon (next to the Add Child node icon) on the Scene dock for creating an instance of our player scene in the Game Level scene.

3. You can now select the scene to be instanced. Select the Player.tscn scene, and click Open, as shown in Figure 5-27. Our player game object appears in this scene. Next, move the player toward the bottom of the workspace so that it's standing on the platform.

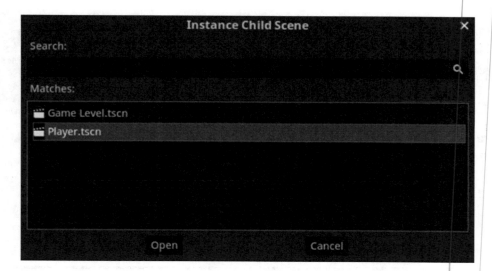

Figure 5-27. *Select Player.tscn to create an instance of it in GameLevel.tscn*

4. Click the play scene button to see the player standing on the ground! We can see this in Figure 5-28.

112

Figure 5-28. *Our player now appears in the Game Level scene*

Moving the Player Using Keyboard Input

We finally have a scene with our player in it! But when you play the game scene, it doesn't move no matter what keyboard key you press. We need to write a simple script for controlling our player. Let's take a look at how to do this.

1. Go to the scene in which you created the player (in our case, Player.tscn). Select KinematicBody2D (the node that represents our player) in the Scene dock; then click the ▣ icon to attach a script to it. This is shown in Figure 5-29.

Figure 5-29. *Attaching a new script to KinematicBody2D*

2. The Attach Node Script window pops up, as shown in Figure 5-30.
    We can select different properties of the script such as its name, the
    language (we'll be using GDScript), the node that it is attached to, and the
    path it's saved under. By default, the script is named after the scene name.
    As shown in Figure 5-30, since our scene name is Player, the default script
    name shows up as Player.gd, under the path res://Player.gd.

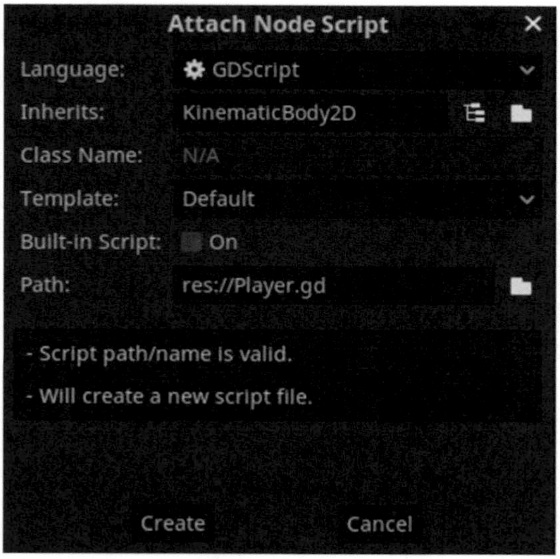

Figure 5-30. *Attaching a node script*

3. Once you click Create, Godot's scripting IDE opens up. As shown in Figure 5-31, the script has a default function called _ready(), and a few lines of comments (starting with #). You can go ahead and delete all the lines in this script, as we'll replace them with our own lines of code.

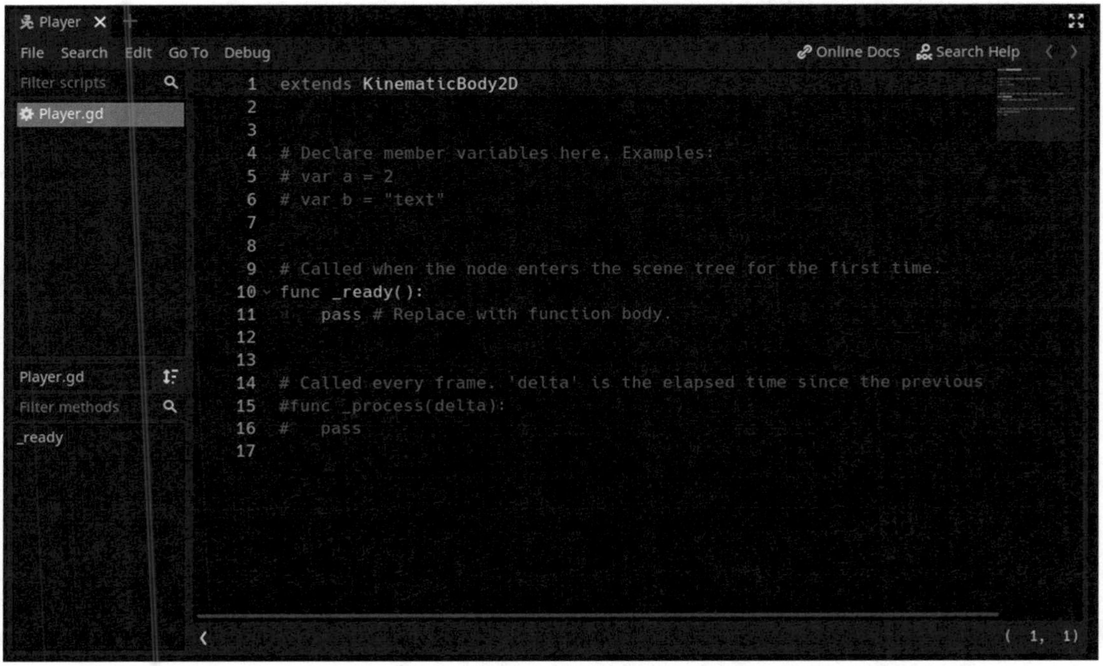

Figure 5-31. *The Godot scripting IDE*

Note   The script, Player.gd, is saved under res:// in the FileSystem dock.

4. Type in the following code in the Scripting space:

```
extends KinematicBody2D

var velocity = Vector2(0,0)

func _physics_process(delta):
        if Input.is_action_pressed("left_arrow"):
                velocity.x = -200
```

```
if Input.is_action_pressed("right_arrow"):
    velocity.x = 200

move_and_slide(velocity)

velocity.x = lerp(velocity.x,0,0.1)
```

- We declare a variable called `velocity` and use the data type called `Vector2 (x,y)` to define the initial velocity of our kinematic body (player) in the x and y directions. `Vector2 (0,0)` implies that the x, as well as y velocities, are both 0.

- The function `_physics_process (delta)` checks if either the left or right keyboard key is pressed and increases the velocity in the left or right direction, respectively.

- If the left arrow key is pressed, the kinematic body moves left (its horizontal velocity is set to -200). Similarly, if the right arrow key is pressed, the body moves right (its horizontal velocity is set to 200). NOTE: You can replace -200 and 200 with other values for changing the velocity by different amounts.

- `move_and_slide()` is a Godot function that moves a body along a specific vector. Since we're passing the parameter `velocity` to it, and `velocity` is defined as a two-dimensional vector, `move_and_slide()` moves the kinematic body in the x and y directions.

- `lerp()` is another Godot function that we use for smoothly bringing the player to a stop when you let go of the arrow keys. If we don't include this last line in the code, the player will keep moving in one direction! The player velocity in the x-direction (`velocity.x`) transitions to 0 from either -200 or 200 (depending on which key was pressed) by 0.1 or 10 percent, 60 times per second. Using `lerp()` causes an exponential falloff of the velocity, with the velocity being dependent on the fixed physics frame rate.

Make sure to use proper indentation while writing the script, as shown in Figure 5-32.

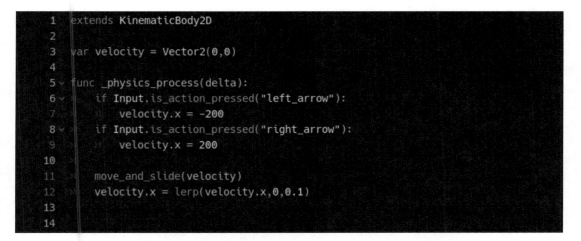

```
1    extends KinematicBody2D
2
3    var velocity = Vector2(0,0)
4
5    func _physics_process(delta):
6        if Input.is_action_pressed("left_arrow"):
7            velocity.x = -200
8        if Input.is_action_pressed("right_arrow"):
9            velocity.x = 200
10
11       move_and_slide(velocity)
12       velocity.x = lerp(velocity.x,0,0.1)
13
14
```

Figure 5-32. *The script for moving the character using the arrow keys*

Assigning Keyboard Input

Before playing the scene to see the script working, we need to tell Godot that `left_arrow` and `right_arrow` represent the left and right keyboard keys. We do this by defining this in the input map.

1. On the Project tab in the top-left corner of the interface, click Project Settings, and then open the Input Map tab on the window that pops up. This is shown in Figures 5-33 and 5-34.

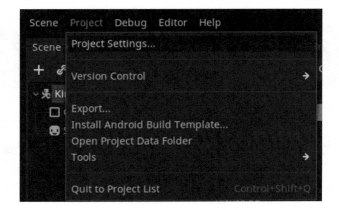

Figure 5-33. *Opening the Project Settings*

Figure 5-34. *The Input Map tab in the Project Settings window*

2. In the Action field, type in **left_arrow**, and then click the Add button, as shown in Figure 5-35.

Figure 5-35. *Adding a new action called left_arrow*

3. Our newly added action, left_arrow, gets added to the bottom of the list of actions. Click the ➕ button next to it and select the option that says Key, as shown in Figure 5-36. We use the Key option for assigning a keyboard key.

Figure 5-36. *Select the Key option for assigning a keyboard key*

Note   You can also assign other options such as Joy Button, Joy Axis, or Mouse Button, in case you're using other input devices such as a handheld controller or mouse.

---

4. Next, you'll be prompted to press the corresponding arrow key on your keyboard, as shown in Figure 5-37. Press the left keyboard arrow key, and click OK.

Figure 5-37. *(a) Prompt to press a keyboard key, (b) confirming that the left arrow key was pressed*

5. You can repeat this for assigning multiple buttons for our `left_arrow` action. For example, we can also add the A keyboard key for moving left.

6. In this way, the left arrow key and A key on the keyboard are assigned to `left_arrow`, as shown in Figure 5-38.

Figure 5-38. *The left arrow key and the A key are assigned to the left_arrow action name*

7. To assign the right arrow key on the keyboard to the `right_arrow` action, repeat steps 2 to 6. In the Action field at the top of the Input Map tab, type in **right_arrow** and click Add. Once it appears at the bottom of the list of actions, click the ➕ button next to right_arrow, and then select the Key button. Once prompted, press the right arrow key on your keyboard to confirm assigning this key to right_arrow. Let's repeat this for assigning the D key on the keyboard to right_arrow as well. We should then see the assignment, as shown in Figure 5-39.

Figure 5-39. *The right arrow key and the D key are assigned to the right_arrow action name*

8. Click Close to exit the Project Settings. Now, save the scene (Ctrl+S), and then press the play button ▶ (F5) to play the game project. Since we haven't yet defined the main scene for our game, a dialog window will pop up asking us to select one. In this window, click the Select button, and choose GameLevel.tscn in the Pick a Main Scene window prompt. Then, click the Open button to set it as the main scene of the project.

9. Now, once the main game scene starts playing, you can press the left arrow or A keyboard key to move the player left, and press the right arrow or D keyboard key to move it to the right. Figure 5-40 shows the player moving toward the right after we press either the right arrow key or the D keyboard key.

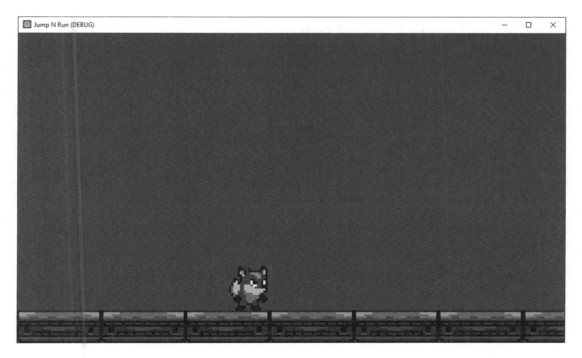

Figure 5-40. *The player moves toward the right after pressing the right arrow key or the D keyboard key*

Note   You can also click the ▣ Play Scene (F6) button for playing a scene, but this will only play the current scene you're in.

TRY IT!

Writing a Script for Moving the Player

1. Write a script for moving the player left or right on the game screen with corresponding key presses on the keyboard.

2. Add different keyboard key assignments to the input map for doing this.

3. Change the value of `velocity.x` by different values, and then play the scene to see how it affects the player.

Adding a Background Image

To add a background image to your main game scene (GameLevel.tscn), follow these steps:

1. Go to the main game scene (GameLevel.tscn).

2. Import the image that you want to use as the background into your project by dragging and dropping it into the FileSystem dock. Reimport it by selecting it in the FileSystem dock, then unselecting the Filter property in the Import dock, and clicking Reimport.

3. Select the root node, that is, Game Level, and click the ➕ button to add a child node. Search for *TextureRect* (or navigate to it at this path: Node ➤ CanvasItem ➤ Control ➤ TextureRect), and click the Create button.

4. Select TextureRect in the Scene dock, and then drag and drop the image of the background from the FileSystem dock onto the Texture field of TextureRect in the Inspector dock, as shown in Figure 5-41.

Figure 5-41. *Drag and drop the background image onto the Texture field of TextureRect*

5. As shown in Figure 5-41, select the Expand option. This will make sure that the background image scales properly when we try to expand it.

6. Drag the orange dots on the edges of the background image on the workspace to increase its size until it fills the entire game screen area, as shown in Figure 5-42. In cases where you want to ensure uniform scaling, you can hold down the Shift key while expanding the image.

Figure 5-42. *Expanding the background image to fill the game screen area*

7. But now, the background image is covering all the static bodies in our scene! Let's send it to the back by selecting TextureRect in the Scene dock and selecting the Show Behind Parent option under Visibility in the Inspector dock. This is shown in Figure 5-43.

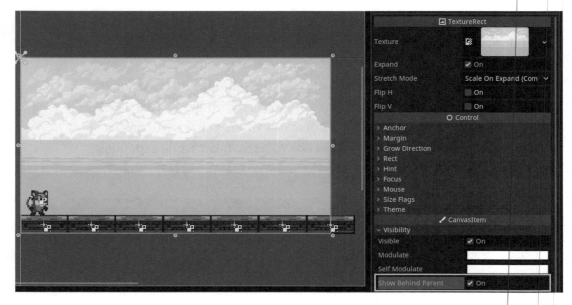

Figure 5-43. *Selecting the Show Behind Parent option in the Inspector, for the TextureRect node*

8. Play the game scene by pressing the playtest ▣ Play Scene (F6) button! You'll see that the game scene now has the newly added background, as shown in Figure 5-44.

Figure 5-44. *The final game scene with the newly added background*

Key Takeaways

In this chapter, we learned about game assets and how to choose the right ones for our game based on the theme. We were introduced to a few online sources that we could use for obtaining our game assets and learned how to import game art into our Godot project. We created a scene with simple environmental props such as the ground and sky and also created our game character. We learned how to create an instance of our player in another scene. Using this knowledge, we wrote a simple script to make a playable scene in which the player moved on the ground when certain keyboard keys were pressed.

CHAPTER 6

Game Animations

In this chapter, we'll learn how to create player animations for performing different actions such as running, jumping, and staying idle. We will use the game assets obtained in the previous chapter for creating animated image frames. We will also learn how to write a player script for making the animations work when certain keyboard keys are pressed.

Giving Life to the Player

In the previous chapter, we created our first character using the game assets that we downloaded. We also made it move left and right by pressing various keyboard keys. Now, let's learn how to create various player actions that are involved in making a platformer, such as running, jumping, or staying idle.

Importing Images for Animation

First, let's import all the images we need for animating our main character, the player. We saw how to do this in the previous chapter—a simple drag and drop from the computer system into the FileSystem dock, as shown in Figure 6-1.

© Maithili Dhule 2022
M. Dhule, *Beginning Game Development with Godot*, https://doi.org/10.1007/978-1-4842-7455-2_6

Figure 6-1. *Drag and drop the player animation sprites into the project*

As shown in Figure 6-1, we have downloaded the sprites for different player actions such as climbing, crouching, getting hurt, being idle, and jumping. Each folder consists of a set of images that, when played one after another animation, would result in that action. For example, as shown in Figure 6-2, the run sprite folder has six different images that can be used to create the running animation. Make sure to name the images according to the order in which they should be played during the animation, for example, player-run-1, player-run-2, player-run-3, etc. You can download the asset pack that provides the images shown in Figure 6-1 here: https://ansimuz.itch.io/sunny-land-pixel-game-art. This pack, called SunnyLand, has been designed by Ansimuz.

Figure 6-2. *Individual images for the running animation*

Now, let's organize the images in our FileSystem into different folders. To create a new folder, right-click `res://`, and then select the New Folder option, as shown in Figure 6-3 (a). Give this folder a suitable name, e.g., `player_animation`, and then click the OK button. This is shown in Figure 6-3 (b).

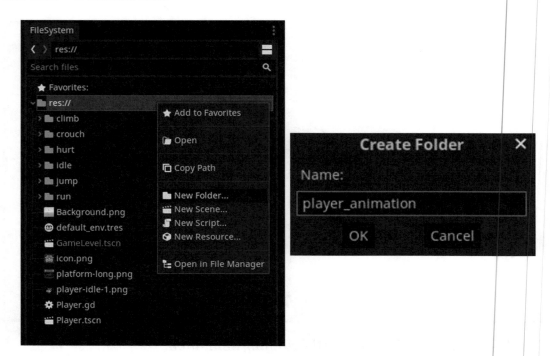

Figure 6-3. *(a) Creating a new folder, (b) naming the new folder*

Next, select all the animation image folders in the FileSystem dock and right-click and select the Move To option, as shown in Figure 6-4 (a). In the Choose a Directory window that pops up, choose the folder we want to move all the image folders to, e.g., the `player_animation` folder, as shown in Figure 6-4 (b), and then click the Move button.

Figure 6-4. *(a) Selecting the image folders to be moved, (b) selecting the player animation folder*

We can see the updated hierarchy in Figure 6-5.

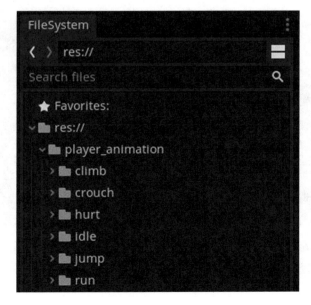

Figure 6-5. *New hierarchy after moving the image folders*

Now, sometimes when you import images into Godot, especially Pixel Art, they might appear blurry in the 2D workspace, if they are being filtered by the engine. Let's make sure that all of our imported images are crisp and clear.

1. First, select all the images in the FileSystem dock, as shown in Figure 6-6 (a), by holding down the Ctrl button on your keyboard and clicking the images one by one.

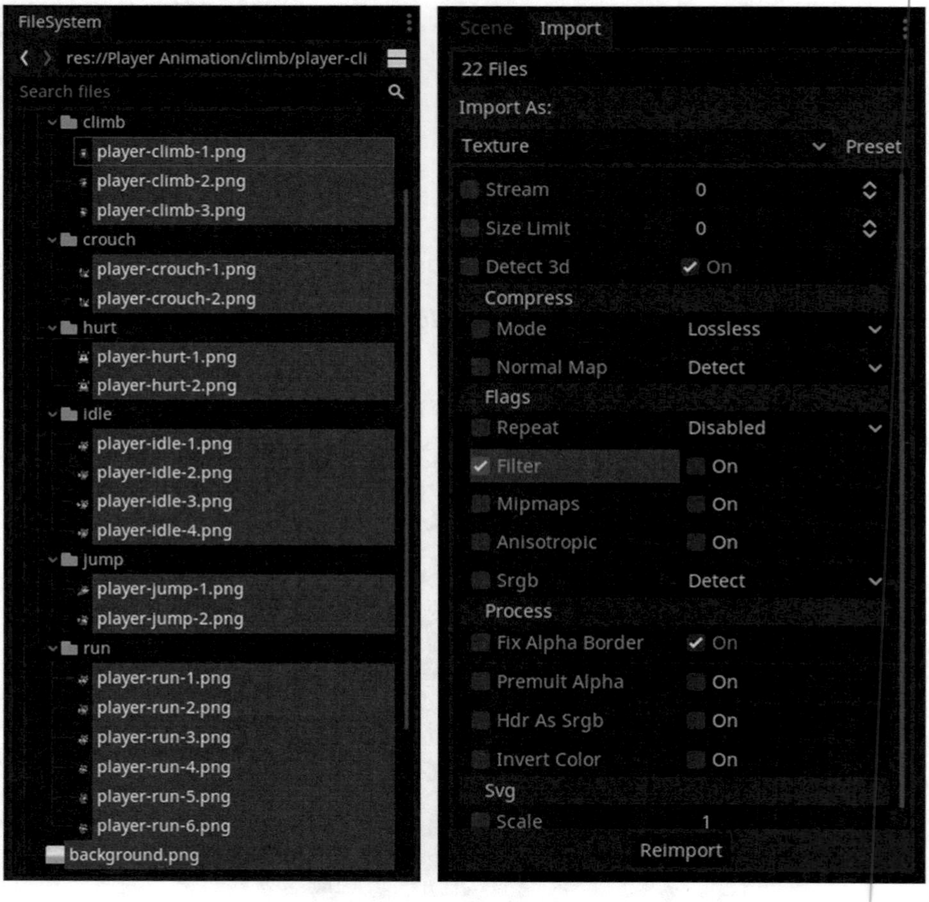

Figure 6-6. *(a) Select all the images in the FileSystem dock, (b) uncheck the Filter option on the Import tab in the Scene dock*

2. Then, head over to the Import tab under the Scene dock, and make
    sure that the Filter field is unchecked, as shown in Figure 6-6 (b). If
    it is selected, then uncheck it and click the Reimport button. This
    will sharpen all the images that we import into our Godot project.

We can now start creating our player animations!

Animating the Player

Follow these steps:

1. First, open the player scene (`Player.tscn`) that we created
    in our previous chapter. The Scene dock should have three
    nodes—the KinematicBody2D (parent node) and its child nodes,
    CollisionShape2D, and the Sprite node.

2. Now, for animating our kinematic body, i.e., our player, we need to
    replace this Sprite node with an AnimatedSprite node. To do this,
    we can right-click the Sprite node in the Scene dock and select
    the Change Type option, as shown in Figure 6-7, then search and
    choose the AnimatedSprite node. Another option is to delete the
    original Sprite node and create a new node called AnimatedSprite.

Figure 6-7. *Changing the type of the Sprite node*

3. Let's go ahead and delete the existing Sprite node by right-clicking it in the Scene dock and selecting the Delete Node option.

4. Now, our Scene dock will only have KinematicBody2D as the parent node, and CollisionShape2D as its only child. Select KinematicBody2D, and click the ➕ button to create another child node.

5. In the Create New Node window, search for *AnimatedSprite*, then select the AnimatedSprite node and click the Create button, as shown in Figure 6-8. You can also navigate to this node using this path:

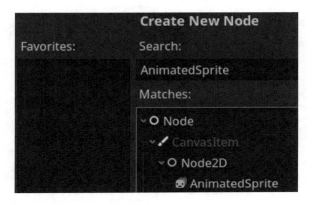

Figure 6-8. *Creating an AnimatedSprite node*

Node ➤ CanvasItem ➤ Node2D ➤ AnimatedSprite

6. You need to assign the frames that make up the animation to the Frames property of the new AnimatedSprite node. As shown in Figure 6-9, when we select the AnimatedSprite node in the Scene dock, the Frames field in its Inspector dock shows "[empty]."

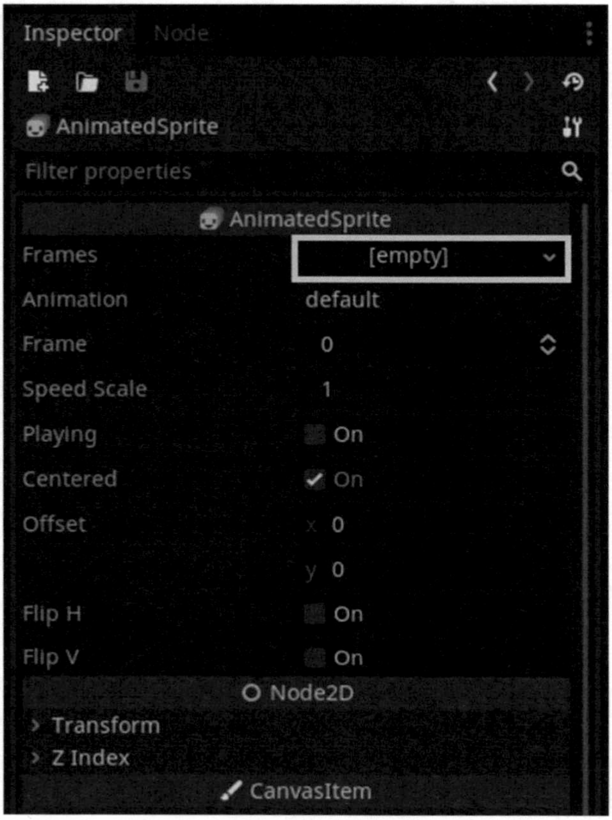

Figure 6-9. *We need to assign images to the Frames field of the AnimatedSprite*

7. Click the small arrow on the Frames field in the Inspector dock to open the drop-down menu, and select the New SpriteFrames option, as shown in Figure 6-10.

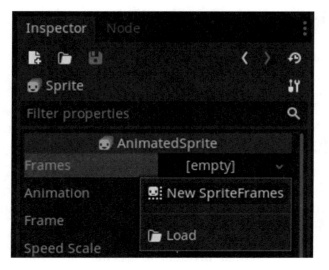

Figure 6-10. *Select the New SpriteFrames option*

8. Once you do that,  SpriteFrames appears in the Frames field. Click it to open the SpriteFrames editor, as shown in Figure 6-11.

Figure 6-11. *The SpriteFrames editor*

Creating Animations with Individual Images

For each player action to be animated, we have to add its name to the Animations list, and we have to add the corresponding images to the area under Animation Frames. Let's do this for different player actions.

Idle Animation

Follow these steps:

1. In the SpriteFrames editor shown in Figure 6-11, click default and replace it with the word *idle*.

2. Next, drag and drop the individual images that represent the idle action from the FileSystem dock, onto the Animation Frames area, as shown in Figure 6-12.

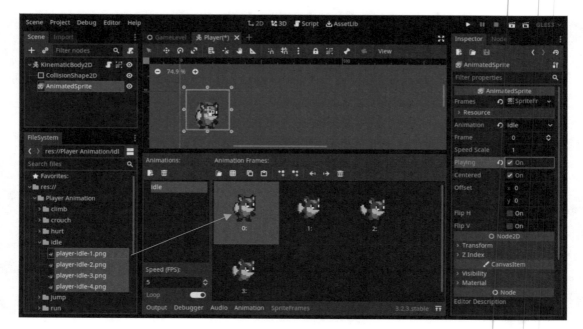

Figure 6-12. *Creating the idle animation*

3. If you want to see the animation play, select the Playing option
    in the inspector window. When you do this, the frames are
    continuously cycled in the order in which they appear in the
    Animation Frames area, forming an animated image in the
    workspace area.

Now, for this animation to work, we need to add the following line of code to our
player script:

```
$AnimatedSprite.play("idle")
```

Open the player script (Player.gd) we created in the previous chapter, and add this
line of code in the _physics_process(delta) function. Add it within an else statement,
right after the two if statements that check whether either the left or right keyboard key
is pressed, as shown here:

```
func _physics_process(_delta):
    if Input.is_action_pressed("left_arrow"):
        velocity.x = -200
    if Input.is_action_pressed("right_arrow"):
        velocity.x = 200
    else:
        $AnimatedSprite.play("idle")
```

Now, change the second if to an elif, as shown here:

```
func _physics_process(_delta):
    if Input.is_action_pressed("left_arrow"):
        velocity.x = -200
    elif Input.is_action_pressed("right_arrow"):
        velocity.x = 200
    else:
        $AnimatedSprite.play("idle")
```

This ensures that the idle animation is played only when none of the keyboard keys
assigned to the "left arrow" or "right arrow" is pressed. Here, play() is a Godot function
that plays the animation specified within the brackets. Since we want to play the idle
action animation, we specify idle within the brackets.

The code inside the Player.gd script should look similar to the following snippet:

```
extends KinematicBody2D

var velocity = Vector2(0,0)

func _physics_process(_delta):
    if Input.is_action_pressed("left_arrow"):
        velocity.x = -200
    elif Input.is_action_pressed("right_arrow"):
        velocity.x = 200
    else:
        $AnimatedSprite.play("idle")
    move_and_slide(velocity)
    velocity.x = lerp(velocity.x,0,0.1)
```

Note   The player velocity in the x direction (left/right) is velocity.x, while the player velocity in the y direction (up/down) is velocity.y. You can assign different values to these variables to change the player's speed in the corresponding direction. Take note that negative values indicate the left or up directions, while positive values indicate the right or down directions.

Make sure to follow proper indentation when writing the code, as shown in Figure 6-13.

```
 1   extends KinematicBody2D
 2
 3   var velocity = Vector2(0,0)
 4
 5 ⌄ func _physics_process(_delta):
 6 ⌄     if Input.is_action_pressed("left_arrow"):
 7           velocity.x = -200
 8 ⌄     elif Input.is_action_pressed("right_arrow"):
 9           velocity.x = 200
10 ⌄     else:
11           $AnimatedSprite.play("idle")
12       move_and_slide(velocity)
13       velocity.x = lerp(velocity.x,0,0.1)
14
```

Figure 6-13. *The script for the idle animation*

Next, save your script using Ctrl+S or navigating to the Save button using the toolbar on the top left of the engine. Then click the ▶ Play button (F5) to play the project (the ▶ Play Scene button (F6) plays the current scene). The debug window opens, and we see the idle animation playing, as shown in Figure 6-14. But this animation continues to play even when we press the left or right keyboard arrow keys (along with the A and D keys if you've set them in the input map)! Let's change that by creating a run animation.

Figure 6-14. *The idle player animation plays in the debug window*

Run Animation

Follow these steps:

1. Open the player scene, Player.tscn, and click the AnimatedSprite node in the Scene dock. Since this is an animated sprite, the SpriteFrames editor should then open up at the bottom panel of the interface.

2. In the SpriteFrames editor, click the  New Animation icon (next to the trash can icon) to create a new animation, and replace the default name, New Anim, with `run`. This is shown in Figure 6-15.

Figure 6-15. *Creating a new animation in the SpriteFrames editor*

3. Just as we did for the idle animation, drag and drop the player run images from the FileSystem dock, into the Animation Frames area, as shown in Figure 6-16.

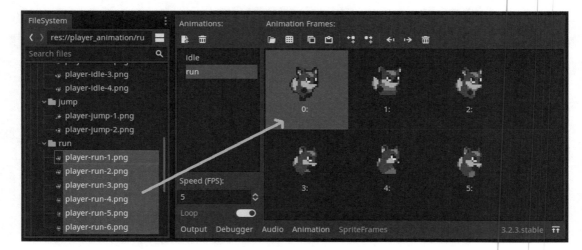

Figure 6-16. *Drag and drop the player run images into the Animation Frames editor*

4. If you click the box next to the Playing field in the Inspector dock for the AnimatedSprite, you'll see the player in the workspace "running," that is, playing all the image frames in order.

5. Now, open the player script Player.gd, and add $AnimatedSprite.play("run") in the player script, as shown here:

```
extends KinematicBody2D

var velocity = Vector2(0,0)

func _physics_process(_delta):
    if Input.is_action_pressed("left_arrow"):
        velocity.x = -200
        $AnimatedSprite.play("run")
    elif Input.is_action_pressed("right_arrow"):
        velocity.x = 200
        $AnimatedSprite.play("run")
    else:
        $AnimatedSprite.play("idle")
    move_and_slide(velocity)
    velocity.x = lerp(velocity.x,0,0.1)
```

Make sure to use proper indentation when writing the code, as shown in Figure 6-17.

6. Save the script, and then play the project using the ▶ Play button (F5). Once the debug window opens, you can see that the run animation plays when you press the left or right arrow keys (and A or D keys if you've set them in the input map), and the idle animation plays when you don't press any key.

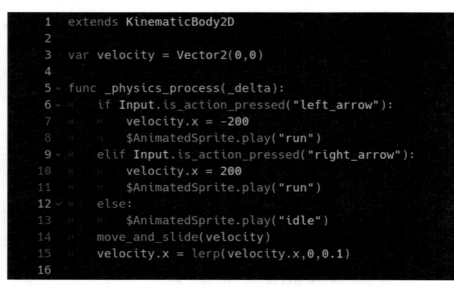

```
 1    extends KinematicBody2D
 2
 3    var velocity = Vector2(0,0)
 4
 5    func _physics_process(_delta):
 6        if Input.is_action_pressed("left_arrow"):
 7            velocity.x = -200
 8            $AnimatedSprite.play("run")
 9        elif Input.is_action_pressed("right_arrow"):
10            velocity.x = 200
11            $AnimatedSprite.play("run")
12        else:
13            $AnimatedSprite.play("idle")
14        move_and_slide(velocity)
15        velocity.x = lerp(velocity.x,0,0.1)
16
```

Figure 6-17. *Script for player run animation*

But one issue still exists—when you press the left arrow, the player seems to run backward, instead of turning around and running in the left direction! We can fix this by modifying the code as follows:

```
extends KinematicBody2D

var velocity = Vector2(0,0)

func _physics_process(_delta):
    if Input.is_action_pressed("left_arrow"):
        velocity.x = -200
        $AnimatedSprite.play("run")
        $AnimatedSprite.flip_h = true
    elif Input.is_action_pressed("right_arrow"):
        velocity.x = 200
        $AnimatedSprite.play("run")
        $AnimatedSprite.flip_h = false
    else:
        $AnimatedSprite.play("idle")
    move_and_slide(velocity)
    velocity.x = lerp(velocity.x,0,0.1)
```

Here, flip_h is a property of an animated sprite that flips the texture, i.e., image assigned to it, horizontally. Setting it true creates a mirror image of the player's animated sprite, while setting it false keeps the original image. We set the property to true when the player runs left, as shown in Figure 6-18 (a), and set it to false when the player runs right, as shown in Figure 6-18 (b).

Figure 6-18. *(a) Player running left, (b) player running right*

Make sure that your properly indented code looks like Figure 6-19.

```
1   extends KinematicBody2D
2
3   var velocity = Vector2(0,0)
4
5 v func _physics_process(_delta):
6 v      if Input.is_action_pressed("left_arrow"):
7           velocity.x = -200
8           $AnimatedSprite.play("run")
9           $AnimatedSprite.flip_h = true
10 v     elif Input.is_action_pressed("right_arrow"):
11          velocity.x = 200
12          $AnimatedSprite.play("run")
13          $AnimatedSprite.flip_h = false
14 v     else:
15          $AnimatedSprite.play("idle")
16      move_and_slide(velocity)
17      velocity.x = lerp(velocity.x,0,0.1)
18
```

Figure 6-19. *Player script with flip_h property added*

Jump Animation

Follow these steps:

1. Open the player scene, `Player.tscn`, and click the AnimatedSprite node in the Scene dock.

2. In the SpriteFrames editor, click the ![icon] button to create a new animation, and replace the default name, New Anim, with **jump**. This is shown in Figure 6-20.

![Animations editor showing idle, jump, run animations with jump selected]

Figure 6-20.   *Creating a new animation for Jump*

3. Next, drag and drop the images for the jump animation from the FileSystem dock into the Animation Frames area, as shown in Figure 6-21.

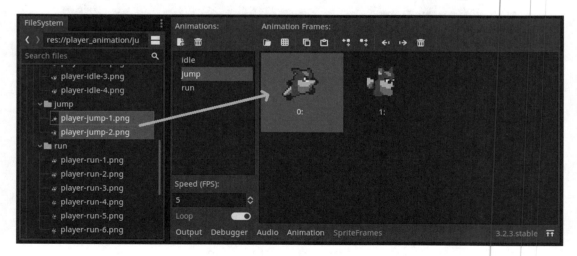

Figure 6-21.   *Dragging and dropping the Jump Animation images into the SpriteFrames editor*

In the previous chapter, we set the project input map to detect the left arrow, right arrow, and the A and D keyboard keys for controlling our player. We need to set a keyboard key for the player's jump action in the same way.

1. Open Project Settings by clicking the Project button in the menu at the top-left corner of the interface and selecting the Project Settings option.

2. Open the Input Map tab, and type in **jump** in the Action field, as shown in Figure 6-22, and click the Add button.

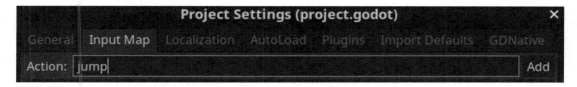

Figure 6-22. *Adding the Jump action in the input map*

3. The "jump" action gets added to the bottom of the list of actions, as shown in Figure 6-23. Next, click the ➕ button next to jump, and select the Key option, shown in Figure 6-24, for assigning the corresponding keyboard keys to it.

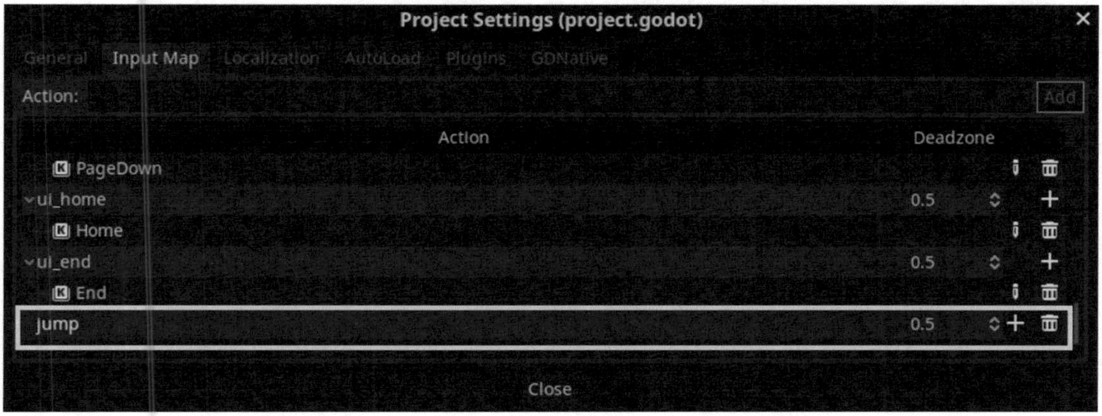

Figure 6-23. *The jump action is added to the list in the Input Map*

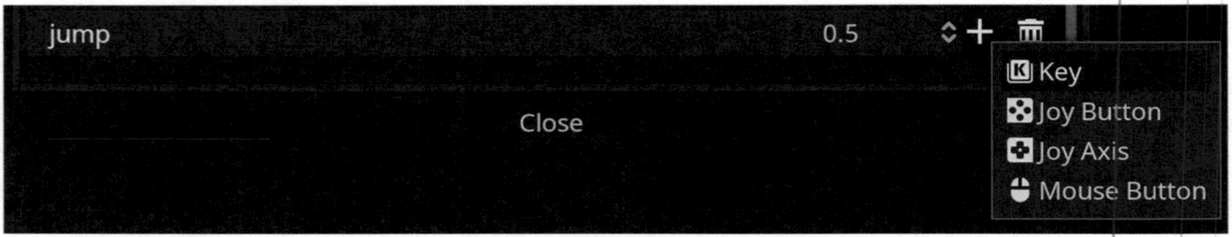

Figure 6-24. *Select the Key option for assigning a keyboard key to the jump action*

4. A window will pop up, prompting you to press the keyboard
    key you want to assign to jump. Press the spacebar key on your
    keyboard to assign it to jump, and click the OK button to confirm
    the key press.

5. Just as we did in the previous chapter, we can assign multiple
    keys to any action. For example, we can assign the up arrow key,
    as well as the W key on the keyboard for jumping, by clicking the
    Key option and entering the corresponding key. This is shown in
    Figure 6-25.

Figure 6-25. *Assigning the spacebar, Up arrow, and W keyboard keys to the
Jump action*

6. Close the Project Settings.

7. Open the player script (`Player.gd`), and modify it as follows:

```
extends KinematicBody2D

var velocity = Vector2(0,0)
var gravity = 2000
func _physics_process(_delta):
    if Input.is_action_just_pressed("jump")and is_on_floor():
        velocity.y= -1000
        $AnimatedSprite.play("jump")
```

```
    if Input.is_action_pressed("left_arrow"):
        velocity.x = -300
        $AnimatedSprite.play("run")
        $AnimatedSprite.flip_h = true
    elif Input.is_action_pressed("right_arrow"):
        velocity.x = 300
        $AnimatedSprite.play("run")
        $AnimatedSprite.flip_h = false
    else:
        $AnimatedSprite.play("idle")
    if not is_on_floor():
        $AnimatedSprite.play("jump")

    velocity.y = velocity.y + gravity * (_delta)
    move_and_slide(velocity, Vector2.UP)
    velocity.x = lerp(velocity.x,0,0.1)
```

- is_action_just_pressed() is a Godot function that returns true only at that instant (or frame) when the keyboard key is pressed. We use this, since we want to just press and release a keyboard key to cause the player to jump, and we don't want to hold down the keyboard key for this purpose.

- When any of the keyboard keys assigned to the jump action is pressed, and when the player is on the floor (platform), the velocity of the player is set to -1000, in the negative y direction (upward). We can choose any value to assign to our y velocity. The height the player jumps to will depend on this value. For example, setting velocity.y to -2000 will make the player jump higher than if we set it to velocity.y to -1000.

- is_on_floor() is a Godot function that detects whether the physics body, i.e., the player, is on the floor. We add this to the first if statement to make sure that the Jump action works only when the player is on the platform, and not when the player is in the air.

- `move_and_slide()` can take many arguments, out of which the first one is the linear velocity, and the second one is the up direction vector. We use `Vector2.UP`, where UP is a constant that represents `Vector2(0, -1)` (where x=0, y=-1), and we include this in the `move_and_slide()` function to enable the player to move in the –y direction. This up direction parameter allows us to determine what counts as a wall and what counts as a floor, enabling the `is_on_floor()` check to work properly. In a similar way, DOWN represents `Vector2(0,1)`, LEFT represents `Vector2(-1,0)`, and RIGHT represents `Vector2(1,0)`.

- We declare a variable called `gravity`, and assign it a value, e.g., 2000. This will be the downward force acting on our player. The line `velocity.y = velocity.y + gravity *(_delta)` cumulatively adds the gravity to the y velocity. In this case, we've set the y velocity to be negative (causing the body to move upward). When we add gravity to it, it pulls the body down toward the ground, over time. Multiplying the gravity value with `_delta` ensures that the game's behavior stays consistent even if the FPS changes.

- We add an if statement (`if not is_on_floor()`) to cover the case in which the player is midair, either during a fall or during a jump. If the player is not on the floor, i.e., the platform, we assume that it's airborne. In this case, we play the `jump` animation frames that we created previously. Since this condition is independent of the other if-else conditions, we use an `if` statement, instead of an `elif`.

- `velocity.x` can be changed to 300 (right direction) and -300 (left direction) to make the player move faster (compared to if the values of velocity.x are equal to 200 and -200 in the right and left directions respectively). You can change these values to change the player's horizontal velocity.

Note   In Godot, negative values of x and y indicate the left and up direction respectively, while positive values of x and y indicate the right and down directions, respectively.

Figure 6-26 shows the final script for the player jump, run, and idle actions.

```
1    extends KinematicBody2D
2
3    var velocity = Vector2(0,0)
4    var gravity = 2000
5  ˅ func _physics_process(_delta):
6  ˅ ⧽    if Input.is_action_just_pressed("jump")and is_on_floor():
7    ⧽    ⧽    velocity.y= -1000
8    ⧽    ⧽    $AnimatedSprite.play("jump")
9  ˅ ⧽    if Input.is_action_pressed("left_arrow"):
10   ⧽    ⧽    velocity.x = -300
11   ⧽    ⧽    $AnimatedSprite.play("run")
12   ⧽    ⧽    $AnimatedSprite.flip_h = true
13 ˅ ⧽    elif Input.is_action_pressed("right_arrow"):
14   ⧽    ⧽    velocity.x = 300
15   ⧽    ⧽    $AnimatedSprite.play("run")
16   ⧽    ⧽    $AnimatedSprite.flip_h = false
17 ˅ ⧽    else:
18   ⧽    ⧽    $AnimatedSprite.play("idle")
19 ˅ ⧽    if not is_on_floor():
20   ⧽    ⧽    $AnimatedSprite.play("jump")
21   ⧽    velocity.y = velocity.y + gravity * (_delta)
22   ⧽    move_and_slide(velocity, Vector2.UP)
23   ⧽    velocity.x = lerp(velocity.x,0,0.1)
```

Figure 6-26. *Final script for run, jump, and idle actions*

TRY IT!

Creating Player Animations

1. Create animations for jumping, running, and idle actions, and assign player sprites to them in the SpriteFrames editor.

2. Write and run the script shown in Figure 6-26, for different values of `gravity`, `velocity.x`, and `velocity.y`.

Other Player Actions

In the previous part of this chapter, we created player animations for jumping, running, and staying idle. We can do the same for other actions as well, such climbing or crouching, or when the player gets hurt. Just as we did before, we have to create a new animation in the SpriteFrames editor and drag and drop the corresponding images into it. As shown in Figure 6-27, animation actions called climb, crouch, and hurt have been created. In the figure, the image frames for the player climb action have been copied from the FileSystem dock into the Animation Frames editor, through drag and drop. The same can be done for the rest of the actions. If you're using individual images to animate the Player, instead of using a Sprite Sheet, you can skip the next few sections in this chapter.

Figure 6-27. *Creating the climbing animation*

Creating Animations Using a Sprite Sheet

Sometimes, we might have a Sprite Sheet that contains all the image frames on it, instead of individual player images. Figure 6-28 shows an example of a Sprite Sheet. This Sprite Sheet can be found in the same asset pack that we used previously, designed by Ansimuz (https://ansimuz.itch.io/sunny-land-pixel-game-art).

Figure 6-28. *A Sprite Sheet with running sprites*

We can break, i.e., *splice*, the Sprite Sheet into its individual image frames using an online Sprite Sheet splicer and then use the procedure discussed in the previous sections for animation. Another option is to use Godot's built-in animation player for animating it.

For simpler animations, we can use the SpriteFrames editor for an AnimatedSprite. In the SpriteFrames panel under Animation Frames, you can click the 🎞 Add Frames from a Sprite Sheet icon to add frames from a Sprite Sheet. Then, select the Sprite Sheet you want to use in the Open a File window, and click the Open button. In the Select Frames window, set the Horizontal and Vertical frames (equal to 6 and 1 respectively in the example shown in Figure 6-29). Then, click the individual frames (a blue box appears around each selected frame), and finally click the Add Frames button. The number of frames that you select will appear on this button, e.g., Add 6 Frame(s) as seen in Figure 6-29.

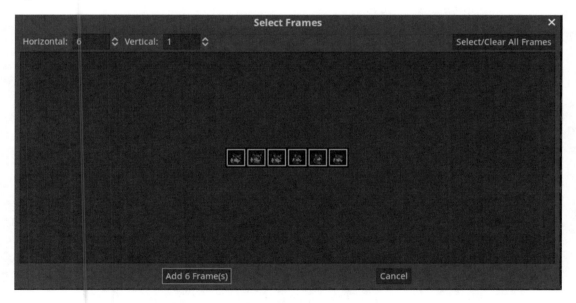

Figure 6-29. *Selecting the frames in the Sprite Sheet*

Introduction to Godot's Animation Player

We can use the Scene dock that we created in the previous chapter, with the KinematicBody2D being the parent node, along with two child nodes: CollisionShape2D and the Sprite node.

Note   For animating the player using Godot's Animation Player, make sure that you have a Sprite node, not an AnimatedSprite node in your Scene dock as a child of KinematicBody2D.

1. Add a node called AnimationPlayer as a child of KinematicBody2D. We can do this by selecting the KinematicBody2D node in the Scene dock, clicking the Add Child Node button, searching for the AnimationPlayer node in the Create New Node window, and then clicking the Create button.

2. Next, select the Sprite node in the Scene dock, and assign the Sprite Sheet you want to animate as its texture by dragging and dropping the Sprite Sheet from the FileSystem dock onto the Texture field in the Inspector dock, as shown in Figure 6-30.

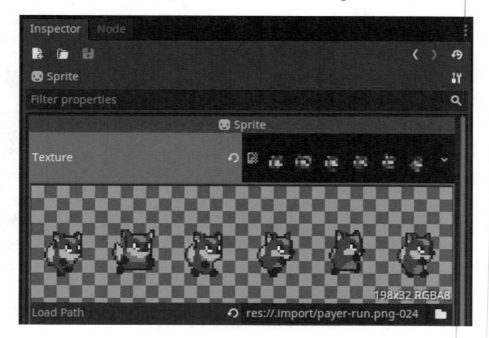

Figure 6-30. *Assigning a spritesheet as a texture of a sprite*

The Sprite Sheet appears on the workspace as a single image, and we need to tell Godot how to split it into individual images.

3. Expand the Animation tab in the Inspector dock of the Sprite node, as shown in Figure 6-31. Here, the Vframes determines the number of rows, and the Hframes determines the number of columns in the Sprite Sheet for splitting it into individual images.

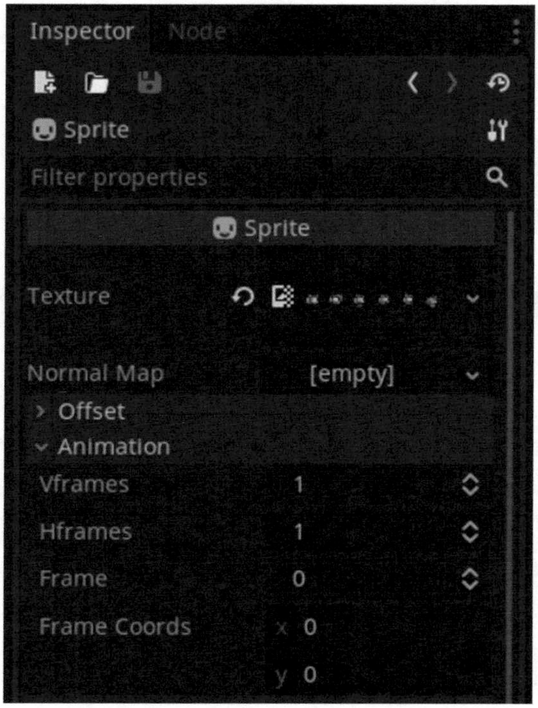

Figure 6-31. *Expanding the Animation tab in the Inspector dock of the Sprite node*

4. As we are animating the Sprite Sheet given in Figure 6-28 and it has one row and six columns, set the Vframes to 1, and set the Hframes to 6.

5. Godot now successfully splits up the Sprite Sheet into six individual images and places them on top of each other on the workspace. As shown in Figure 6-32, one of the frames (Frame 0, in this case) is displayed in the workspace. We can toggle the frame number by clicking the small arrows next to the Frame field on the Animation tab.

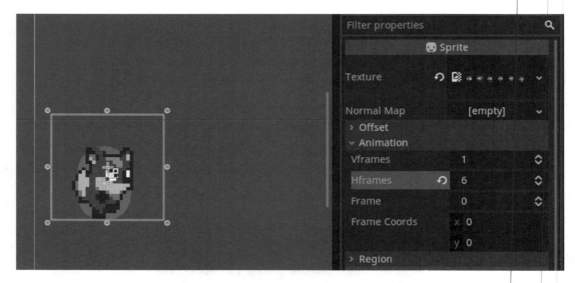

Figure 6-32. *The workspace displays one of the six frames at a time*

Note   If the images in the workspace are blurry, select the Sprite Sheet in the FileSystem dock and head over to the import dock next to the Scene dock. Untick the Filter field, and click Reimport to get clearer image frames.

---

6.   Click the AnimationPlayer in the Scene dock, and the Animation panel opens up at the bottom of the Godot interface, as shown in Figure 6-33. Click the Animation button, and select the [+ New] option.

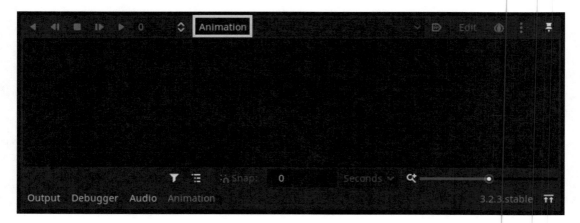

Figure 6-33. *The Animation panel*

7. Give the animation a name, such as **run**, and then click the OK button.

8. Set the animation interval to 0.6 (next to the clock icon ), and slide the pointer next to the magnifying glass to zoom into the interval, as shown in Figure 6-34.

Figure 6-34. *Set the animation interval to 0.6*

9. Select the Sprite node in the Scene dock, and then head over to the Inspector dock. Click the key icon next to the Frame field on the Animation tab to add the first image frame (Frame 0) to the Animation track. Make sure that Frame is set to 0.

10. In the window that pops up asking to confirm creation of a new track, click the Create button. This adds the first frame to the animation track.

11. Once the blue pointer in the Animation panel moves to 0.1, toggle to frame 1 in the Animation tab in the Inspector dock, and click the key icon again to add this next frame.

12. Repeat the previous step until all six image frames have been added to the track, as shown in Figure 6-35.

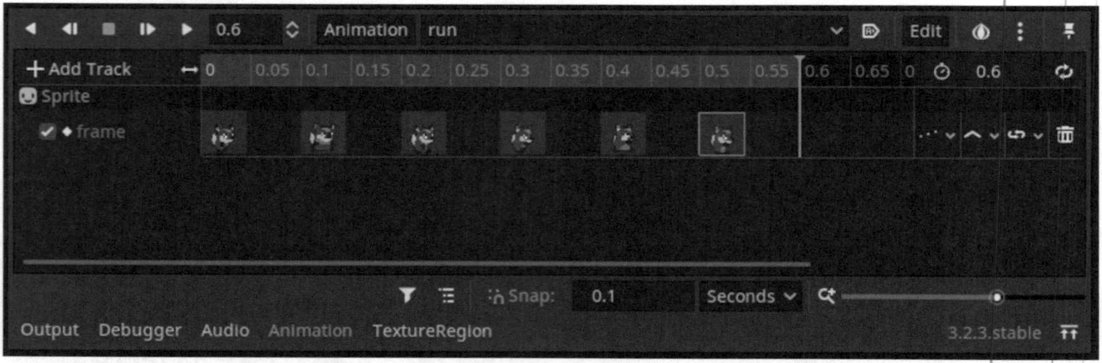

Figure 6-35. *Adding all the image frames to the animation track*

13.   Click the ⟳ button for playing the animation in a loop, and then
       click the Play button on the Animation Panel ▶. Once you do that,
       you can see the running animation playing in the workspace. Save
       the project (Ctrl+S).

14.   Now that we have our animation, we have to modify our player
       script (Player.gd) to play it using the animation player. Enter the
       following code in the scripting space:

```
extends KinematicBody2D

onready var _animation_player = $AnimationPlayer
onready var _sprite = $Sprite

var velocity = Vector2(0,0)

func _physics_process(_delta):
    if Input.is_action_pressed("left_arrow"):
        velocity.x = -200
        _animation_player.play("run")
        $Sprite.flip_h = true
    elif Input.is_action_pressed("right_arrow"):
        velocity.x = 200
        _animation_player.play("run")
        $Sprite.flip_h = false
    else:
        _animation_player.stop()
```

```
move_and_slide(velocity)
velocity.x = lerp(velocity.x,0,0.1)
```

- When using the animation player for player animation, we need to declare

```
onready var _animation_player = $AnimationPlayer
onready var _sprite = $Sprite
```

- To play an animation, use _animation_player.play(), and specify the name of the animation created in the animation panel within the brackets.

- To stop playing an animation, use _animation_player.stop().

Your properly indented code should look like Figure 6-36.

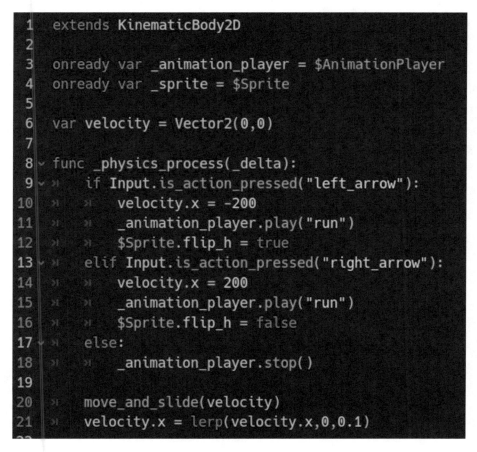

```
1   extends KinematicBody2D
2
3   onready var _animation_player = $AnimationPlayer
4   onready var _sprite = $Sprite
5
6   var velocity = Vector2(0,0)
7
8   func _physics_process(_delta):
9       if Input.is_action_pressed("left_arrow"):
10          velocity.x = -200
11          _animation_player.play("run")
12          $Sprite.flip_h = true
13      elif Input.is_action_pressed("right_arrow"):
14          velocity.x = 200
15          _animation_player.play("run")
16          $Sprite.flip_h = false
17      else:
18          _animation_player.stop()
19
20      move_and_slide(velocity)
21      velocity.x = lerp(velocity.x,0,0.1)
```

Figure 6-36. *Script for player run animation using AnimationPlayer*

Click the play button to play the project, and the running animation plays when you press the keyboard keys to move the Player to the left or right!

TRY IT!

Using Godot's Animation Player

1. Use a player action Sprite Sheet (e.g., run, jump, walk, etc.) and animate the actions using the animation player.

2. Modify the script for making the animations work.

3. Run the project to see the player animation.

Key Takeaways

In this chapter, we learned the basics of animating a player using individual image frames. We created animations for different player actions such as running, jumping, and staying idle, and we modified our player script to make them work. We also learned how to split a player action Sprite Sheet into individual images and explored how to use Godot's animation player for player animation.

CHAPTER 7

Building the Game World

In this chapter, we'll learn how to design a game level for a platformer using a game asset pack. We'll learn techniques for splicing a TileMap into its individual image tiles and placing them into our Godot workspace. We'll also see how to configure the game camera to follow the player. Further, we will learn how to create an infinite-scrolling, parallax background for our game.

Now that we've animated our player, let's dive into the exciting part—building the game world. In the previous chapter, we saw how we can use individual image frames of a Sprite Sheet for character animation. For designing a game level, we can use a similar game asset called a TileMap (or TileSet), which is a single image file that contains objects and props that you can use for creating the game environment, including the following:

- Trees

- Ground

- Wall

- Rocks

- Doors

- Buildings

Figure 7-1 (a) and Figure 7-1 (b) show TileMaps of environmental props and platforms. They are part of the game asset pack called Sunny Land (which we used previously), created by an artist called Ansimuz. We will use it for designing the game levels for our platformer. You can download it here: https://ansimuz.itch.io/sunny-land-pixel-game-art.

© Maithili Dhule 2022
M. Dhule, *Beginning Game Development with Godot*, https://doi.org/10.1007/978-1-4842-7455-2_7

Figure 7-1. *(a) A TileMap of environmental objects, (b) a TileMap of platforms and other props*

Since we are now designing the game level from scratch, let's delete the StaticBody2D nodes (the platforms) and the TextureRect node (the background) from our Scene dock. Make sure that you don't delete the root node Game Level or the KinematicBody2D node (the player).

To delete a node, right-click it in the Scene dock, and select the 🗑 Delete Node(s) option, as shown in Figure 7-2 (a). You can also click on the node to be deleted in the Scene dock and press the Delete key on your keyboard.

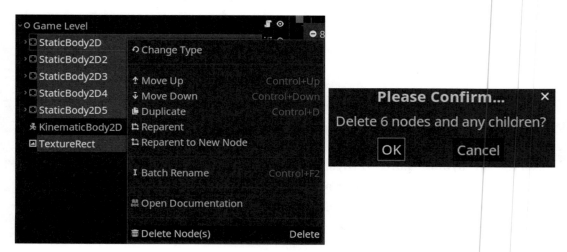

Figure 7-2. *(a) Delete nodes, (b) confirm deletion of the nodes*

Click the OK button once the Please Confirm window pops up, as shown in Figure 7-2 (b). Doing so will remove the StaticBody2D node, along with both of its child nodes, that is, CollisionShape2D and Sprite.

Figure 7-3 (a) and Figure 7-3 (b) show the Scene dock node hierarchy before and after the deletion of the TextureRect node and all the StaticBody2D nodes.

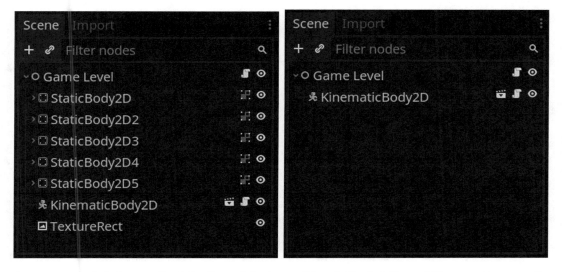

Figure 7-3. *(a) Scene dock before deletion of StaticBody2D and TextureRect nodes, (b) Scene dock with only the root node and KinematicBody2D node*

Note   If you accidently delete a node, you can always get it back by pressing Ctrl+Z on your keyboard.

Importing the TileMaps

Next, let's import the TileMaps into our Godot project, by dragging and dropping them into the FileSystem dock, as shown in Figure 7-4. To make sure that the images are sharp and not blurry, select them in the FileSystem dock, open the Import tab in the Scene dock, and make sure to unselect the Filter field. Then, click the Reimport button. This is shown in Figure 7-5.

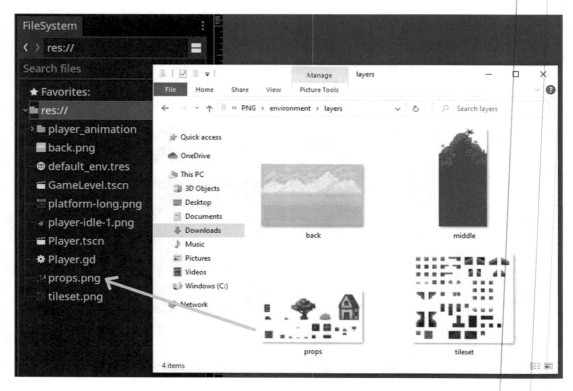

Figure 7-4. *Importing the TileMaps into the project*

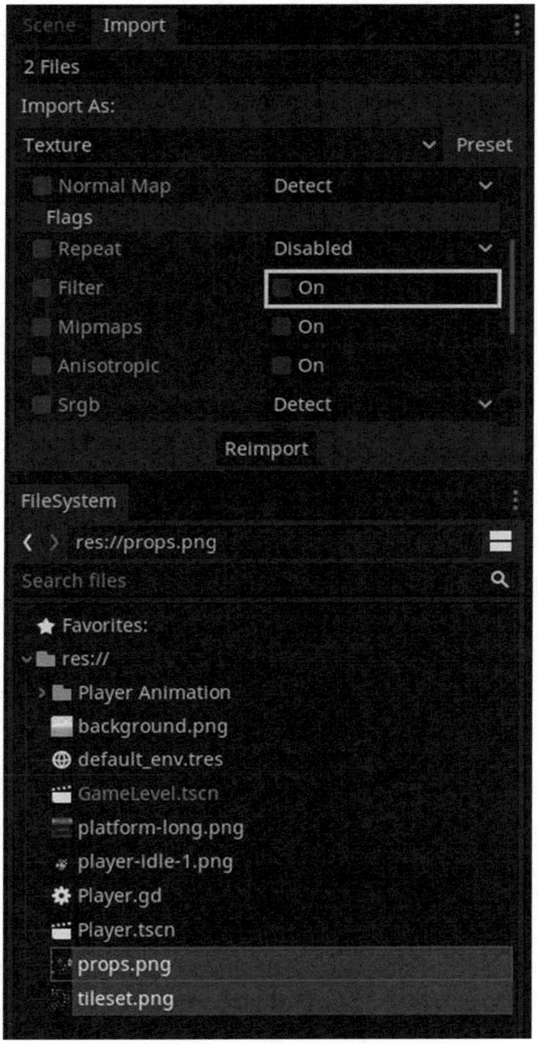

Figure 7-5. *Reimporting the images with Filter unselected*

Creating Individual Tiles

Let's see how to use Godot's TileMap editor to break our TileMap down into its individual images.

1. In the main game scene (GameLevel.tscn), select the root node (Game Level) in the Scene dock, and click the ➕ button to add node TileMap as its child. In the Create New Node window, search for *TileMap*, or navigate to it under the following path:

    Node ➤ CanvasItem ➤ Node2D ➤ TileMap

    Then, click the Create button. This is shown in Figure 7-6.

Figure 7-6. *Creating a TileMap node*

    If you select the TileMap node in the Scene dock, you'll notice an orange-colored grid shows up in your workspace, as shown in Figure 7-7.

Figure 7-7. *The grid for the TileMap shows up in the workspace*

Note   The cells/boxes of the grid shown in Figure 7-7 represent the positions where we will place the image tiles into our game. We will add images from our TileMap to a panel called the Tile palette. We can then pick and choose images from the Tile palette and paint them into our workspace.

---

2. Now, with the TileMap node selected in the Scene dock, head over to the Inspector dock. If you expand the tab called Cell, you'll see a field called Size, which gives us the length and width of each cell of the grid in our workspace. By default, it is 64 × 64, and we can modify it according to the size of the images of our TileMap. Change the x and y fields both to 16, as shown in Figure 7-8 (a).

TileMap

Filter properties

TileMap	
Mode	Square
Tile Set	[empty]
Compatibility Mode	On
Centered Textures	On
Cell Clip Uv	On
˅ Cell	
Size	x 16
	y 16
Quadrant Size	16

Inspector   Node

TileMap

Filter properties

TileMap	
Mode	Square
Tile Set	[empty]
Compatibility Mode	On New TileSet
Centered Textures	On
Cell Clip Uv	On Load
˅ Cell	
Size	x 16
	y 16
Quadrant Size	16
Custom Transform	
x 64	y 0
x 0	y 64
x 0	y 0

Figure 7-8. *(a) Changing the Cell Size to 16x16, (b) creating a new TileSet resource*

3. In the Tile Set field, click the small arrow next to "[empty]," and select New TileSet, as shown in Figure 7-8 (b).

4. Click **TileSet** on the TileSet icon that now appears in the Tile Set property field, and the TileSet editor opens up at the bottom panel of the interface, as shown in Figure 7-9.

Figure 7-9. *TileSet editor*

5. Click the ⊞ button on the bottom-left corner of the TileSet editor, shown in Figure 7-9, and select the TileMaps that we've imported into our project, as shown in Figure 7-10. Click the Open button to open them in the editor. You can also drag and drop the TileMaps from the FileSystem dock onto the dark blue area on the left side of the TileSet editor panel.

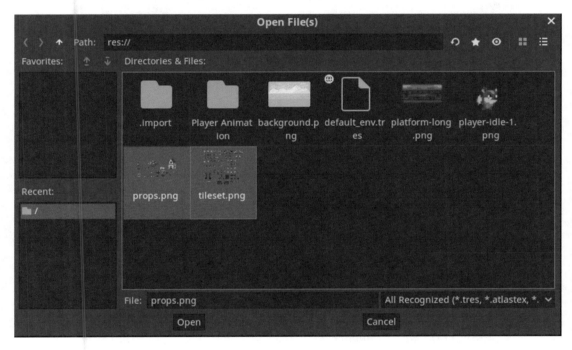

Figure 7-10. Opening the TileMaps

Note   On your keyboard, press the Shift+F12 keys to expand this editor panel to take up the whole workspace. You can also click and drag the panel upward to fill up the workspace.

A preview of the two TileMaps can be seen on the left side of the TileSet editor, as shown in Figure 7-11. To start editing a particular TileMap, select its corresponding preview on the left, and it will open up in the editor on the right.

Figure 7-11. *TileMaps opened in the TileSet editor*

6.   Now, let's create individual tiles from the TileMaps. Click the
      second TileMap (`tileset.png`) in the TileSet editor, as shown in
      Figure 7-12. To zoom into the TileMap, click the Zoom in ⊕
      button at the top-right corner.

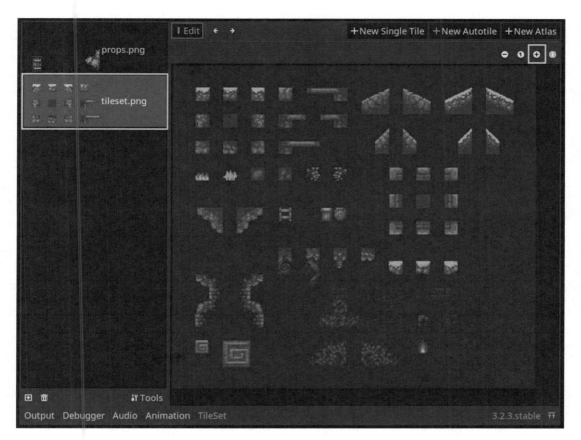

Figure 7-12. *Opening tileset.png by clicking its preview on the left of the editor*

7. Click the New Single Tile button 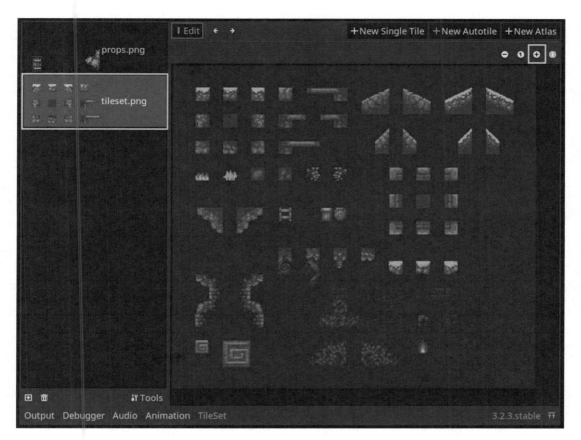 at the top-right corner of the editor. This opens the region mode in the editor toolbar, as shown in Figure 7-13 (a).

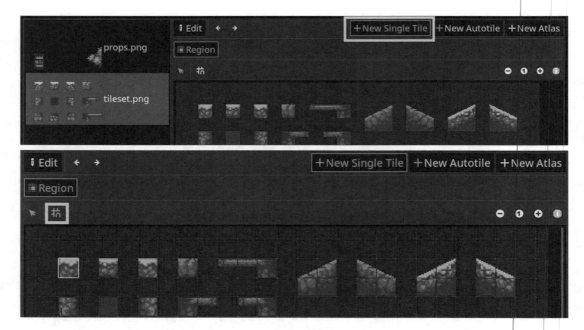

Figure 7-13. *(a) Creating a new tile, (b) toggling the purple grid*

8. Click the grid icon to show the purple grid on the editor space, as shown in Figure 7-13 (b).

9. Now, we can select the tile of the image that we want to add to our Tile palette. First, let's add an image tile that has the same size as the grid cell. Click the image in the top-left corner in the editor, as shown in Figure 7-14. This is one of the images that we will use to create the ground of our game.

    Make sure that the x and y Step size (under the Snap Options property in the Inspector dock) is 16. This is seen in Figure 7-14. Recall that we had set the grid size of our workspace to 16x16 as well, during Step 2.

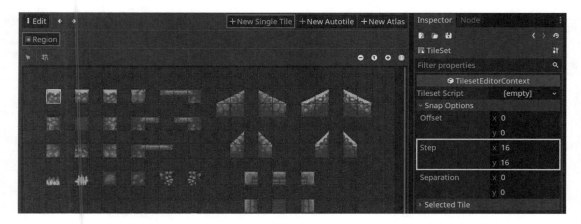

Figure 7-14. *Selecting the first image tile*

10.   Now, click the Collision button   to add a collision shape
to the tile. This opens a toolbar with options to create a new
rectangular or polygon-shaped collision area, as shown in
Figure 7-15.

Figure 7-15. *The Collision Shape toolbar*

11.   Click the square icon ▣ in the toolbar, and then click the image
tile for adding a square/rectangular collision shape to it, as shown
in Figure 7-16. That's it! This tile gets automatically added to the
Tile palette.

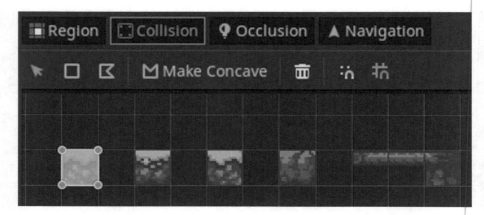

Figure 7-16. *Adding a rectangular collision shape to the image tile*

12. Now, let's add an image tile to the Tile palette that is larger than the purple grid cell size or is irregular in shape. Click the New Single Tile button on the top right of the editor. With the region button (next to the Collision button) selected, click and drag your cursor across the image so that the yellow square completely surrounds the entire image, as shown in Figure 7-17.

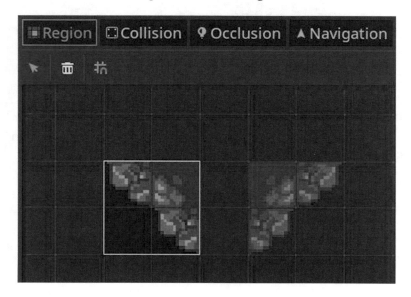

Figure 7-17. *Drawing the square around the tile*

Note   Once you add a tile to the Tile palette, it stays bordered by a yellow square, as shown in Figure 7-17, even while you've selected another tile.

13.   Now, we need to add a collision shape to it, just as we did before. Click the Collision button ⬚Collision to open up the Collision Shape toolbar. This time, since our image is not square-shaped, we will manually draw an exact, triangular collision shape around it. Select the Polygon-shaped icon ◺ on the toolbar, as shown in Figure 7-18.

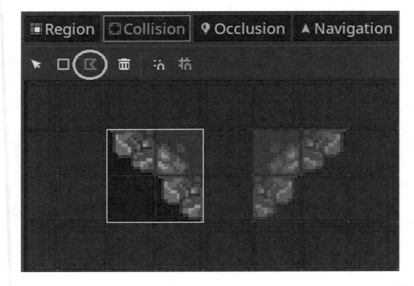

Figure 7-18. *Click the Polygon icon to draw a collision shape manually*

14.   Next, click the ⛏ icon on the toolbar to turn off (disable) the Enable Snap and Show Grid option, as shown in Figure 7-19. This allows us to manually draw an irregular collision shape. If the option is turned on, we can only draw the collision shape using the sides of the purple grid.

Figure 7-19. *Enable Snap and Show Grid option turned off*

Note   When the icon on the toolbar is highlighted in blue, it means that the corresponding option is enabled (on). If it's in white, it implies that the option is disabled (off).

15.   To draw the collision shape, click different points along the outer edges of the image, on the editor. Doing so will create a vertex (orange dot) on the position clicked. Whenever you click a new point, i.e., create a new vertex, the previous one gets connected to the new one, as shown in Figure 7-20 (a) and (b). Do this until the last vertex connects with the first one, as shown in Figure 7-20 (b). The region enclosed by the vertices forms the collision shape of the image.

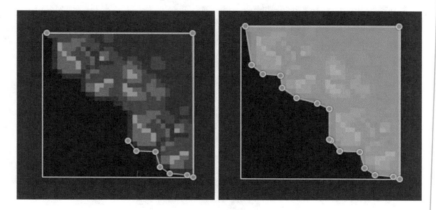

Figure 7-20. *(a) Click the outer edges to create vertices. (b) Once the last vertex is connected to the first one, a collision shape is created*

Note   The first vertex, or orange dot, becomes visible only once you click the spot where you want to create the second one. Also, if you make a mistake when drawing the vertices of the collision shape, you can start all over by clicking the delete polygon icon (trash can icon) on the toolbar.

So far, we have added two of the images from the TileMap to our Tile palette. We can repeat the entire process for the rest of the images in our TileMap that we want to add as well. Every time you want to add another tile to the Tile palette, click the New Single Tile button on the editor, then select the image on the TileMap in the editor, and finally add a collision shape to it. Note that if you want to use the tile for creating a background object such as a tree or a rock (which won't collide with the player), it doesn't need a collision shape.

16. Once you've created all the tiles that you want to use for building the game, click the TileMap node in the Scene dock. You'll notice that the Tile palette pops up on the workspace and has all the tiles that you created! Figure 7-21 shows one such example of a Tile palette.

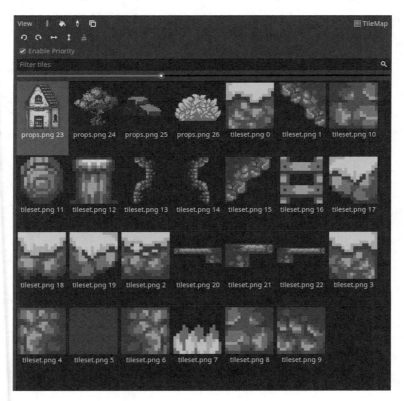

Figure 7-21. *Tile palette*

Now, we can use the tiles in our palette to paint our game world! The process is simple—select the tile from the palette, and then click one of the grids in the workspace to place it there, as shown in Figure 7-22 (a). Once you place a tile in the workspace, hold down your left mouse button, and drag your mouse around to "paint" the workspace.

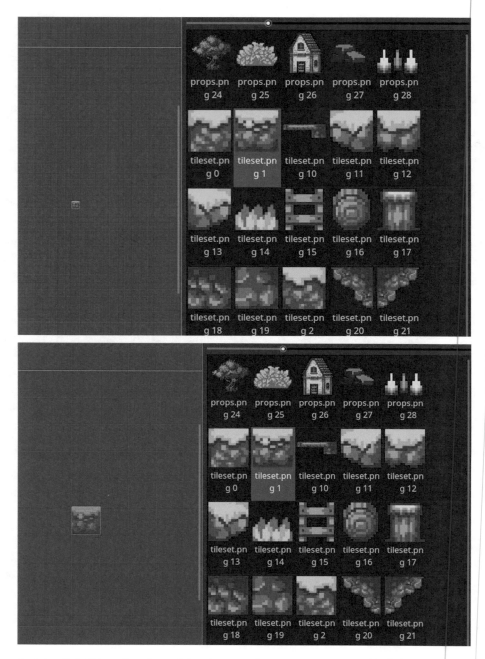

Figure 7-22. *(a) The tile placed in the workspace is too small. (b) The tile is scaled up in proportion to the player*

But the tile is tiny compared to the player! Let's fix this by changing the scale. With the TileMap node selected in the Scene dock, head to the Inspector dock and expand the Transform tab. Then, change the x and y scales to 4, as shown in Figure 7-23. Now, the tile is scaled up, as shown in Figure 7-22 (b).

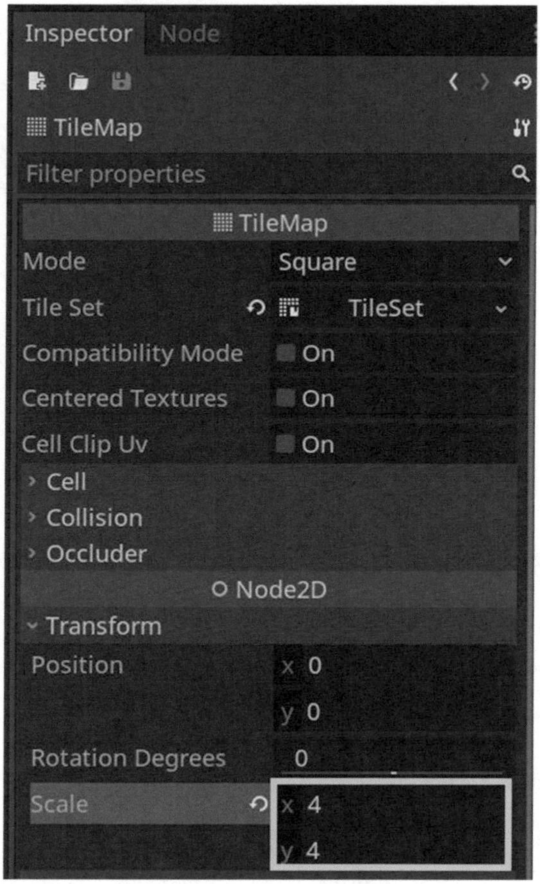

Figure 7-23. *Setting both the x and y scales of the TileMap equal to 4*

Note   To delete a tile, hover over it in the workspace, and right-click it once the blue border appears around it. For deleting a tile that takes up multiple grid cells in the workspace, put your cursor on the top-left corner of the image (with its rectangular outline), and once you right-click the blue cell, the image gets deleted. This is shown in Figure 7-24 (a) and (b).

Figure 7-24. *(a). Deleting a single-cell-sized tile, (b) deleting a large tile*

Now, you can design your game world using all the props and objects from your Tile palette.

TRY IT!

Painting Your First Game Level

1. Download a TileMap that includes the game objects that you want to use in your game level, such as platforms, ledges, trees, houses, bushes, rocks, etc.

2. Create image tiles using the TileMap editor.

3. Get creative and paint the game level!

Note   If in your Scene dock the hierarchy of your nodes looks like Figure 7-25 (a), the player will appear behind the props and objects in your game. Figure 7-26 shows an example of this. On the other hand, if the hierarchy looks like the one shown in Figure 7-25 (b), the player will appear in front of the objects in your game scene, as shown in Figure 7-27. In case your Scene dock looks like Figure 7-25 (a), you can move the player's node to the bottom of the hierarchy by clicking the KinematicBody2D node and dragging and releasing it onto the parent node (Game Level). This results in the hierarchy shown in Figure 7-25 (b).

Figure 7-25. *(a) The KinematicBody2D is the first child node in the hierarchy. (b) The TileMap is the first child node in the hierarchy*

Figure 7-26. *The player appears behind an object in the game scene*

Figure 7-27. *The player appears in front of an object in the game scene*

Camera-Follow

Now, in the game, we want the camera to follow our player as it moves across the game level. To do this, we can implement camera-follow:

1. Select the KinematicBody2D node in the Scene dock, and click the
    ➕ button to add a child node to it. In the Create New window that
    pops up, search for *Camera2D*, and then click the Create button.
    Alternatively, you can also navigate to this node under the path:

    Node ➤ CanvasItem ➤ Node2D ➤ Camera2D

    Once you click the Create button, Camera2D will be created as a
    child of KinematicBody2D, as shown in Figure 7-28.

Figure 7-28. *Camera2D is created as a child node of KinematicBody2D*

When we look at the 2D workspace, a purple-colored rectangle appears around the player. This represents the boundaries of the game's camera, i.e., the area that we see when the game scene is playing. This area moves along with the player, effectively "following" the player around in the game. This is shown in Figure 7-29.

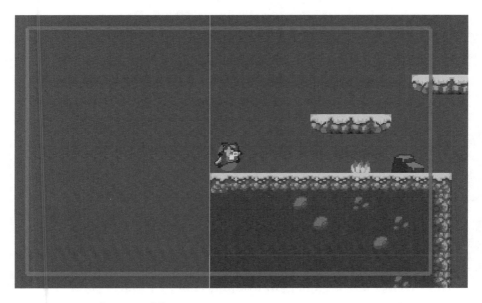

Figure 7-29. *Boundaries of the game camera*

2. Select the Camera2D node in the Scene dock, head over to the Inspector dock, and turn on the Current property, as shown in Figure 7-30. This sets our camera as active for the current game scene (GameLevel.tscn).

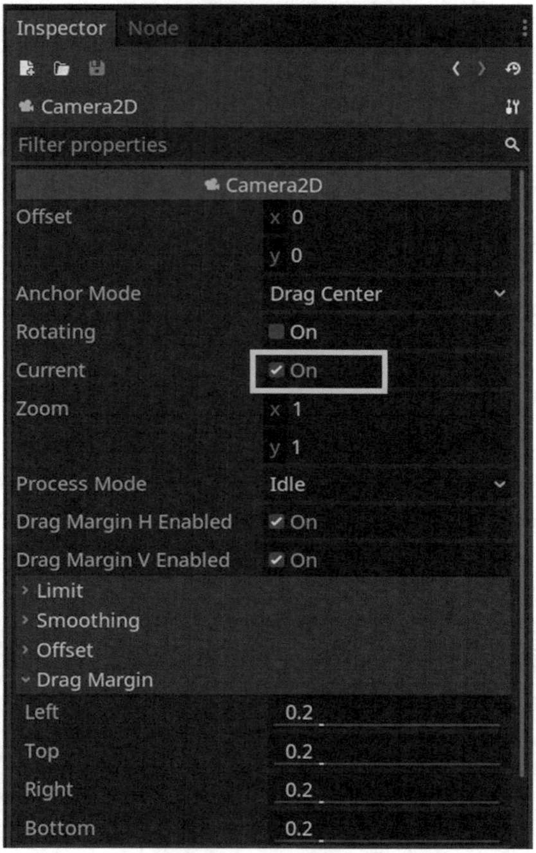

Figure 7-30. *Turn on the current property*

3. Also, turn on the Drag Margin H Enabled and Drag Margin V Enabled fields, as shown in Figure 7-30. This gives the player some grace margin to move around left/right or up/down in the game. This means that the camera moves only when the player gets close to either the left/right or top/bottom edges of the screen, ensuring that the camera doesn't continuously move as the player moves.

If you expand the Drag Margin tab in the inspector, as shown in Figure 7-30, you can see that the default margins are 0.2 on all four sides, that is, 20 percent of the distance between the center of the player to one of the edges of the game screen. Increasing this value will allow the player to move a greater distance toward one of the edges of the camera boundary without the camera moving.

4. Change the Left, Top, Right, and Bottom margins to 0.5 to give the player more room to move without the camera moving.

5. Play the game scene to see the camera following the player when it moves along the game level.

Note   Notice how once you add Camera2D and play the game scene, you will first see the portion of the workspace that has the camera (with the thick purple boundaries), instead of seeing the default game screen area (rectangle formed by the faint purple, pink, and green lines on the workspace).

But as shown in Figure 7-31, the player starts from the middle portion of the game screen. This is because the camera shows the portion of the workspace that is on the left of where our platform actually starts. To fix this, we can change the limits of the camera's leftmost position.

Figure 7-31. *The player starts from the middle of the game screen*

6.   Select the Camera2D node in the Scene dock, and, in the Inspector dock, expand the Limit tab. Change the Left field to 0, as shown in Figure 7-32. By doing this, we are ensuring that when the game scene starts playing, the camera's leftmost limit corresponds to the left side of the game screen area on the workspace (indicated by the green vertical line).

˅ Limit		
Left	0	◇
Top	-10000000	◇
Right	10000000	◇
Bottom	10000000	◇
Smoothed	▣ On	

Figure 7-32. *Set the Left limit of Camera2D to 0*

7. Now, play the game scene. You'll see that now the player starts from the left portion of the game screen, as shown in Figure 7-33.

Figure 7-33. *The player starts from the left part of the game screen*

Creating a Parallax Background

We created our first game level, but our game doesn't have a background! Instead of a simple background that stays in one position throughout the game, we can create what's called a *parallax background*. What makes it so different from a regular one is that it is made up of a number of background layers, each of which moves at a different speed.

So if we have mountains, trees, and clouds in our background, making them move at different speeds gives an amazing 3D effect to our 2D game. For creating a parallax effect, we will be using the background image from the same asset pack that we used for getting the TileMaps. Once you've downloaded an image of a background you'd like to use for your game, follow these steps:

1. Import the background image into your Godot project by dragging and dropping it into the FileSystem dock from your computer. This is shown in Figure 7-34. Next, to ensure that the image is not blurry, be sure to re-import without filtering. Select the image in the FileSystem dock, open the Import tab next to the Scene dock, unselect the Filter property under the Flags tab, and click the Reimport button.

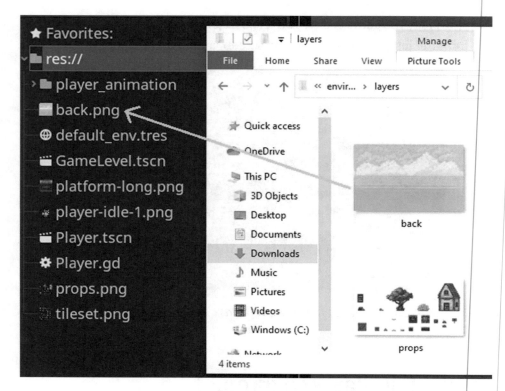

Figure 7-34. *Drag and drop the background image into the FileSystem*

2. Add a new node as a child of Game Level (root node). Select the
    root node (Game Level) in the Scene dock, and then click the ➕
    button to add a child node to it. In the Create New Node window,
    search for *ParallaxBackground* or navigate to it under the
    following path:

    Node ➤ CanvasLayer ➤ ParallaxBackground

    Click the Create button to create ParallaxBackground as a child of
    Game Level.

3. Next, add a ParallaxLayer node as a child of the
    ParallaxBackground node. Select the ParallaxBackground node in
    the Scene dock; then click the ➕ button to add a child node to it.
    In the Create New Node window, search for ParallaxLayer or
    navigate to it under the following path:

Node ➤ CanvasItem ➤ Node2D ➤ ParallaxLayer

Click the Create button to create ParallaxLayer as a child of
ParallaxBackground.

4. Add a Sprite node as a child of ParallaxLayer, in the same way
    that we did the previous two steps. You can navigate to it under
    the following path: Node ➤ CanvasItem ➤ Node2D ➤ Sprite.
    The node hierarchy of the Scene dock should now look like
    Figure 7-35.

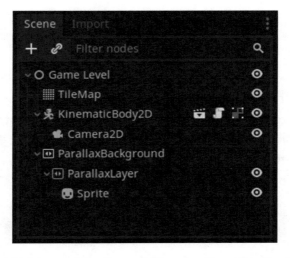

Figure 7-35. *The node hierarchy after adding the ParallaxBackground,*
ParallaxLayer, and Sprite nodes

5. Select the Sprite node in the Scene dock and then assign the
    background image to its Texture property. You can do this by
    dragging and dropping the image from the FileSystem dock into
    the Texture property of the Sprite in the Inspector dock. This is
    shown in Figure 7-36.

Figure 7-36. *Assign the background image to the Texture property of the Sprite node*

6. The sky is too small and is centered at the origin of the workspace! Let's make it larger, and make sure that the top-left corner of the sky image coincides with the origin of the workspace instead. With the Sprite node selected in the Scene dock, expand the Offset property in the Inspector dock, and uncheck the Centered field, as shown in Figure 7-37.

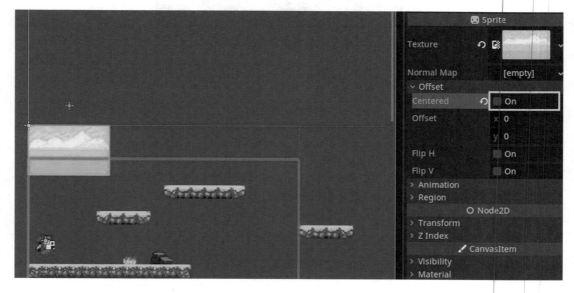

Figure 7-37. *Uncheck the Centered property of the Sprite node*

Now, the left side of the sky image is aligned with the leftmost limit of our game screen, as shown in Figure 7-37.

7. Next, let's make the background larger. Expand the Transform property in the Inspector dock, and change the x and y scales to 8. (This will differ if you use another background image of a different size.) This is shown in Figure 7-38.

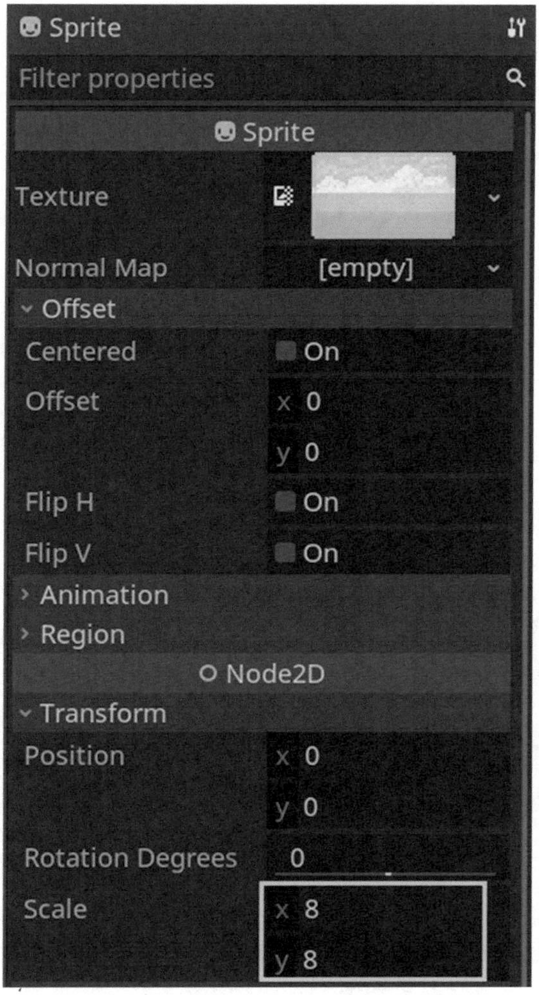

Figure 7-38. *Set the x and y scales of the Sprite node to 8*

We can't make it large enough to fit the entire length of the game; otherwise, the clouds in the image will be huge! Adjust the x and y scale until the proportion of the background image with respect to the game looks okay.

8.   Save the scene (Ctrl+S on your keyboard).

When you play the game scene (with the 🎬 button), you'll notice that the background ends after you reach a certain point in the game, i.e., when you reach the right edge of the image. This is shown in Figure 7-39. To fix this, we can use an important property called Mirroring to our advantage. This property enables you to repeat the background multiple times along the length of your game— potentially forever! Let's see how to set this property in the next step.

Figure 7-39. *The background ends at a certain point in the game*

9.   Select the ParallaxLayer node in the scene dock, and head over to the Inspector dock. Expand the Motion field, and you'll see the Mirroring property, which helps you create an infinitely repeating scrolling background.

10. Now, since we want the background to repeat after it reaches the right edge of the image, we need to set the x value of the Mirroring field equal to the length of the background image. We can measure it in the in our workspace using Ruler Mode. With the Sprite node selected in the Scene dock, click the ruler icon ◣ on the 2D toolbar near the top center of the interface, as shown in Figure 7-40.

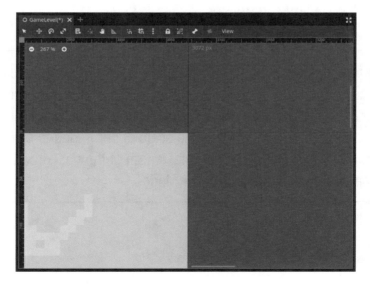

Figure 7-40. *Click the ruler icon on the toolbar to open Ruler Mode*

11. Next, click the vertical ruler on the left of the workspace, and drag your mouse toward the right to generate the vertical ruler. Drag it toward the right until it coincides with the right edge of the background image, and note the pixel measurement that shows up. As shown in Figure 7-41, the length of background image is measured to be 3072 pixels. You can zoom into the image for greater accuracy, before taking the measurement. You can also enable Smart Snap (Shift+S).

Figure 7-41. *The length of the background image is 3072 pixels*

Note   To remove the horizontal ruler marker, click its left endpoint that intersects with the vertical ruler (on the left of the workspace), drag it upward, and release it on the horizontal ruler at the top.

12. Select the ParallaxLayer in the Scene dock, and expand its Motion property in the Inspector dock. Set the x field of the Mirroring property to 3072, as shown in Figure 7-42.

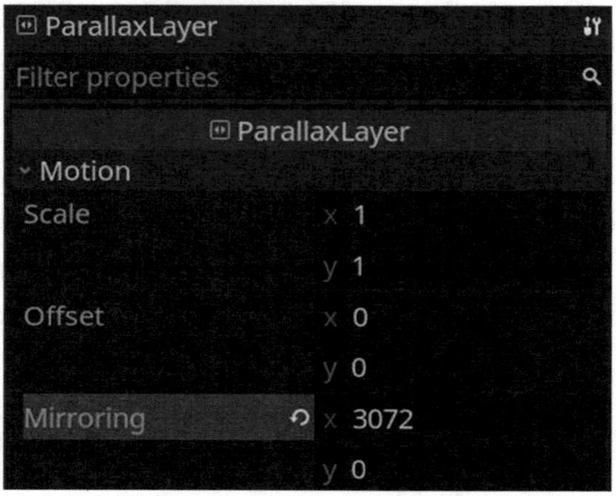

Figure 7-42. Set the x value of the Mirroring property to 3072

Note   A shortcut to calculating the length of the background is to select the Sprite node in the Scene dock, and click the image loaded in the Texture property. The dimensions of the original image can be seen in the lower-right corner, as shown in Figure 7-43. Since we have changed the scale of our image to eight times the original, we get 384 × 8 = 3072 as the total length of the background image—the same value that we measured using Ruler Mode.

Figure 7-43. *Dimensions of the original background image*

13. Play the game scene, and you'll see that the background repeats every 3072 pixels, giving the illusion that it is repeating endlessly!

But one issue still persists—the top of the background might get cut off if your player reaches a certain height during the game, as shown in Figure 7-44. We can fix this issue by changing the limits of our game camera to only show the game area that's within the boundaries of the background. But first, we need to measure the distance of the top and bottom sides of the background image from the origin of the workspace. We can do this in a similar way as we did for measuring the length of our background.

Figure 7-44. *The top portion of the background image is cut off*

14.   Select the Sprite node (child of ParallaxLayer) in the Scene dock, and click the ruler icon ▲ on the 2D toolbar to enable Ruler Mode. For generating the horizontal ruler marker, click and hold your left mouse button down anywhere on the horizontal ruler on the top of the workspace, and drag your mouse downward. This is shown in Figure 7-45.

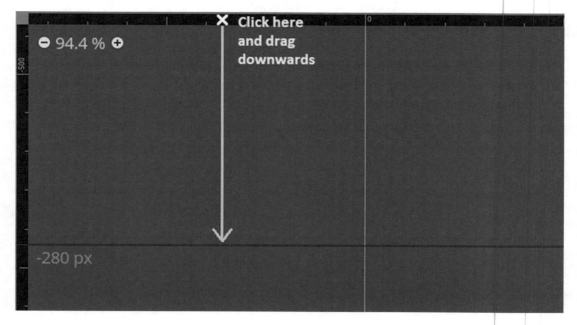

Figure 7-45. *Click the horizontal ruler at the top of the interface, and drag downward to get the horizontal ruler marker*

15.   Move the dark pink horizontal marker downward until it coincides with the top of the background in the workspace. As shown in Figure 7-46, the upper limit of the background is present at 0 pixels above the origin (that is, it is along the line passing through origin). You can zoom into the background image by pressing the zoom ⊕ button on the workspace.

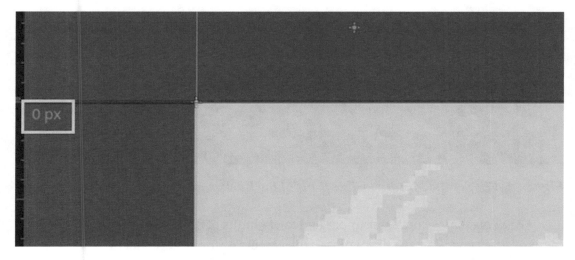

Figure 7-46. *The top of the background image is at 0 pixels from the origin*

16.   The bottom limit of the background can be measured in a similar way, by dragging the horizontal ruler marker from the ruler at the top of the workspace until it coincides with the bottom side of the background image. You can also choose to cut off some portion of the background, as shown in Figure 7-47. As we don't want to see the entire blue portion of the background, let's keep the distance as 1661 pixels below the origin.

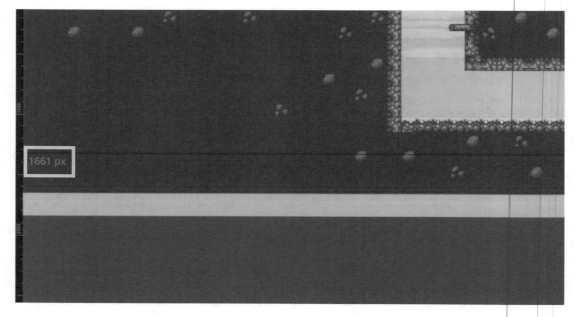

Figure 4-47. *Set the bottom visible limit of the background image to be 1661 pixels*

17. Now that we have our upper and lower limits of the background, we can adjust the properties of the camera accordingly. Select the Camera2D node in the Scene dock, and then expand its Limit property in the Inspector dock.

18. Based on these measurements that we took in the previous steps, set the Top limit to 0, and set the Bottom limit to 1661 (these might differ according to the size and scale of your background image). This is shown in Figure 7-48.

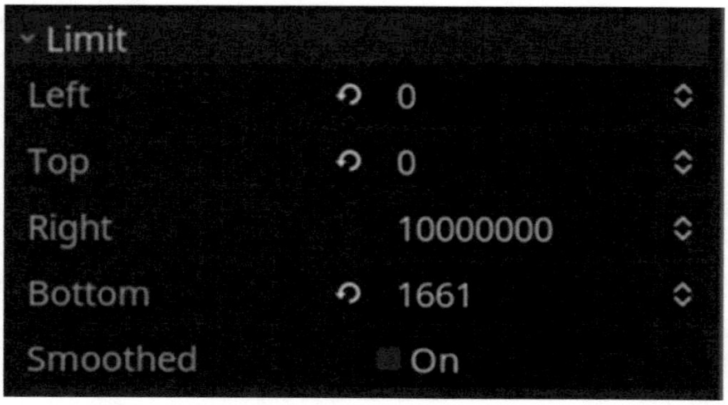

Figure 7-48. *Adjust the top and bottom limits of the Camera2D's Limit property*

19.   Next, let's apply the parallax effect—where the sky appears to be moving slower than the trees, ground, and other props, giving the game a depth effect. Select the ParallaxBackground node in the Scene dock, and expand its Scroll property in the Inspector dock. Set Base Scale to 0.5 for both x and y, as shown in Figure 7-49.

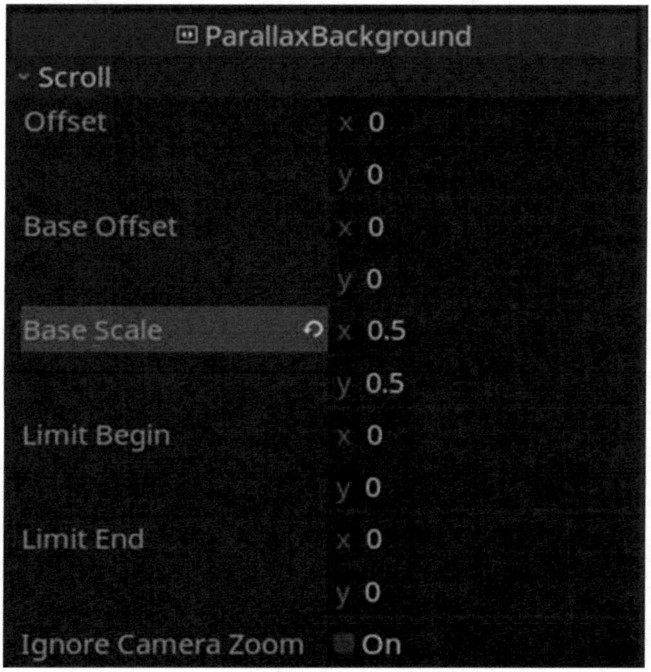

Figure 7-49. *Setting both the x and y values of Base Scale of the ParallaxBackground to 0.5*

Note   The original Base Scale of x=1 and y=1 implies that the background moves at the same rate as the foreground, which makes it seem like it is not moving at all! When you set x=0.5 and y=0.5, the background moves 50 percent slower than the foreground, which makes it seem like the clouds in the sky are far away and hence are moving slower.

20.   Play the game scene to see the parallax effect being applied!

TRY IT!

Creating a Parallax Background

1. Create a parallax background by following the steps in the chapter.

2. Play the game scene for different values of the Base Scale property.

Design Ideas

Take a look at some design ideas shown in Figures 7-50 through 7-53!

Figure 7-50. *Design idea 1*

Figure 7-51. *Design idea 2*

Figure 7-52. *Design idea 3*

Figure 7-53. *Design idea 4*

Key Takeaways

After creating animations for our player in the previous chapter, we learned the basics of designing a game level in this chapter. We used a TileMap to paint the images of props and objects such as platforms, trees, bushes, rocks, and houses in our game. Moreover, we saw how to splice the TileMap into its individual images and assign a collision shape for each of them. In addition, we also learned the concept of implementing camera-follow, as well as how to create parallax backgrounds for our game.

CHAPTER 8

Counting Wins and Losses

📷 In this chapter, we'll learn how to add animated coins and enemies to our game. We'll learn how to create instances of the various objects in the main game scene and use them to keep track of the player score and lives. We'll dive into important concepts such as signals, RayCast2D, collision masks and layers, and changing scenes.

Introducing a reward system in your game can make it more interesting and exciting to play. The challenge of leveling up by collecting coins and dodging or defeating enemies along the way motivates the player to keep playing the game!

Let's see how to add animated coins that the player can collect and enemies that the player has to avoid!

Adding Coins to the Game

Follow these steps:

1. First, let's import the images of the coins by dragging and dropping them onto the FileSystem dock, as shown in Figure 8-1. We'll be using the Gold, Red, and Silver coins from the Collectibles & Buttons Asset Pack created by Mihika Dhule. You can download it here: `https://mihikad.itch.io/collectibles-buttons`.

© Maithili Dhule 2022

M. Dhule, *Beginning Game Development with Godot*, https://doi.org/10.1007/978-1-4842-7455-2_8

Figure 8-1. *Importing the Coin Sprite Sheets into the project*

2. To keep things organized, let's create a separate folder to store
    the coin Sprite Sheets. Right-click `res://` in the FileSystem dock
    and select the New Folder option. In the Create Folder pop-
    up window, type in a suitable name, such as **Coin Animation**,
    and then click the OK button. Select all the coin images in the
    FileSystem dock, as shown in Figure 8-2, and drag and drop them
    into the coin_animation folder, as shown in Figure 8-3.

Figure 8-2. *Select all the coin images in the FileSystem dock*

3. Now, you can see the three image files, `pixel_coins_gold.png`,
    `pixel_coins_red.png`, and `pixel_coins_silver.png`, within the
    coin_animation folder by expanding it, as shown in Figure 8-3. To
    make sure that the images don't appear blurry in the editor, select
    all of them in the FileSystem dock, then unselect the Filter option
    in the Import dock, and click Reimport.

Figure 8-3. *Drag and drop the coin images into the coin_animation folder*

4. Next, create a new scene for one of the coins by clicking the ⊞ button on top of the 2D workspace toolbar, as shown in Figure 8-4.

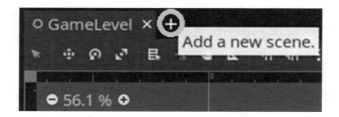

Figure 8-4. *Creating a new scene for the coin*

5. In the new, empty scene that opens up in the 2D workspace, click the new node ⊞ button in the Scene dock, and search for the Area2D node in the Create New Node window, as shown in Figure 8-5. You can also navigate to it under this path:

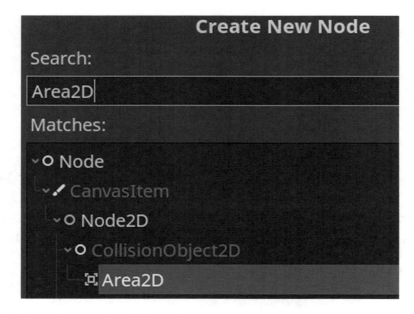

Figure 8-5. *Creating an Area2D node*

Node ➤ CanvasItem ➤ Node2D ➤ CollisionObject2D ➤ Area2D

Click the Create button to create Area2D as the root node of this scene.

6. Next, add a CollisionShape2D node and a Sprite node as the child nodes of Area2D. Do this by selecting Area2D in the Scene dock, clicking the new node button ⊞ in the Scene dock, and searching for the respective child node in the Create New Node window. This is shown in Figure 8-6 (a) and (b).

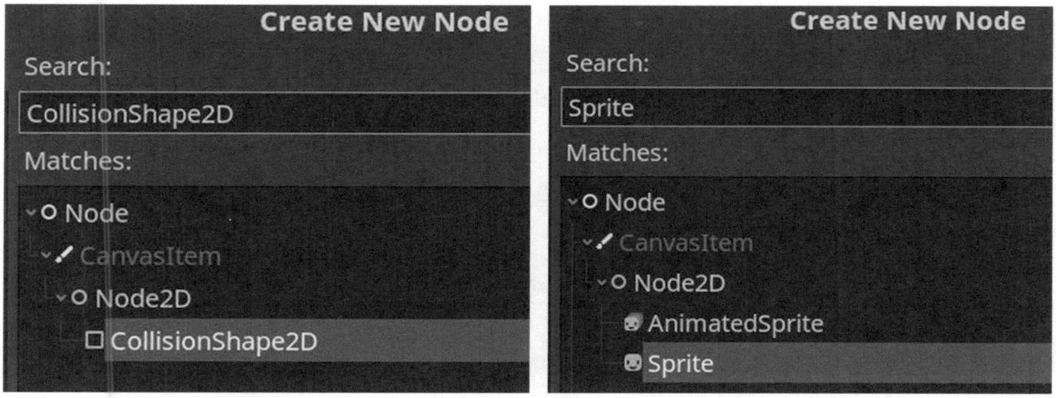

Figure 8-6. *(a) Creating a CollisionShape2D node, (b) creating a Sprite node*

7. Now, there is a warning sign next to the CollisionShape2D in the Scene dock. When we hover our mouse over it, we see that it's a node configuration warning that indicates that we need to assign a shape to this node. To do this, select the CollisionShape2D node in the Scene dock, and then head over to the Inspector dock. Click the drop-down menu next to the Shape field, and select New CapsuleShape2D, as shown in Figure 8-7.

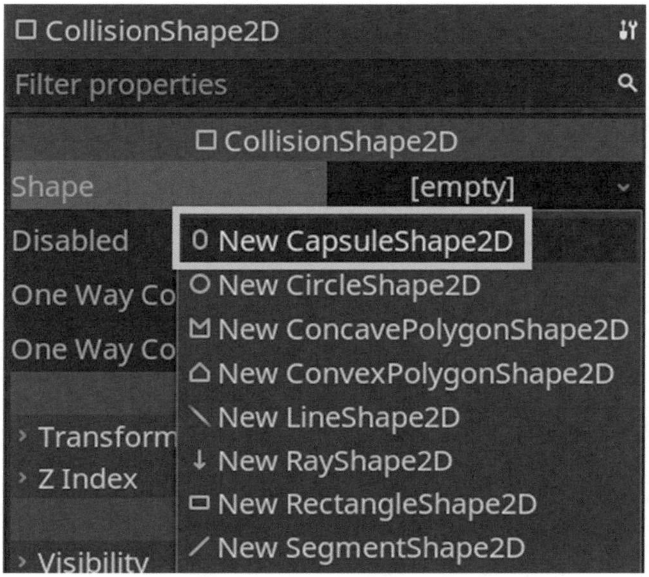

Figure 8-7. *Assigning a capsule shape to the CollisionShape2D*

8. When you zoom into the origin on the workspace, you'll see that the capsule-shaped collision shape is created there. Your node hierarchy in the Scene dock should look like the one shown in Figure 8-8.

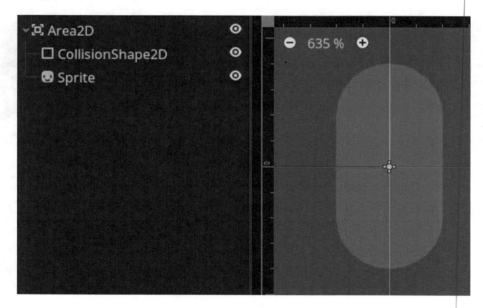

Figure 8-8. *Node scene hierarchy with the Capsule shape assigned to CollisionShape2D*

9. Next, select the Sprite node in the Scene dock and then drag and drop one of the coin Sprite Sheet images into its Texture property in the Inspector dock, as shown in Figure 8-9. Select the CollisionShape2D in the Scene dock, and adjust its size with the help of the orange vertices so that it fits the size of the coin as closely as possible.

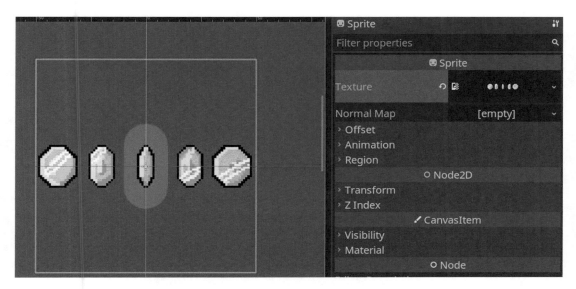

Figure 8-9. *Assigning the coin Sprite Sheet to the Texture property of the Sprite node*

Now, we need to break the coin Sprite Sheet into its individual coin images and use them for creating a rotating coin animation. We can easily do this using Godot's animation player, in the same way that we animated our player Sprite Sheet in Chapter 6. Let's take a look at how to do it for our gold coin.

Animating the Coin

Follow these steps:

1. Select the Area2D node in the Scene dock and click the ➕ button to add a child node to it. In the Create New Node window, search for *AnimationPlayer* or navigate to it under this path: Node ➤ AnimationPlayer. This is shown in Figure 8-10.

Figure 8-10. *Creating an AnimationPlayer node as a child of Area2D*

On clicking the Create button, the node-scene hierarchy in the Scene dock should look like the one shown in Figure 8-11.

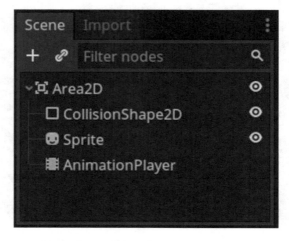

Figure 8-11. *Area2D node with its three child nodes—CollisionShape2D, Sprite, and AnimationPlayer*

2.   Select the AnimationPlayer node in the Scene dock, and the Animation panel should open up at the bottom of the interface, as shown in Figure 8-12.

Figure 8-12. *The Animation panel*

For Godot to break our coin Sprite Sheet down into its individual image frames, we need to tell it how many rows and columns there are in it. As shown in Figure 8-13, we can break down the Sprite Sheet into a single row and five columns of images.

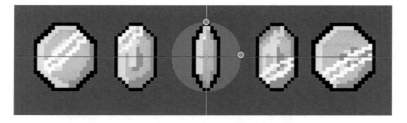

Figure 8-13. *The coin Sprite Sheet has one row and five columns of images*

3. Select the Sprite node in the Scene dock, and then expand the
    Animation tab under the Inspector dock. The Vframes property
    specifies the number of rows in the Sprite Sheet, while the Hframes
    specifies the number of columns. Both of the properties have
    a value of 1 by default. Let's go ahead and change the Hframes
    property to 5. Once you do that, you should see a single coin image
    frame on the Godot workspace, as shown in Figure 8-14.

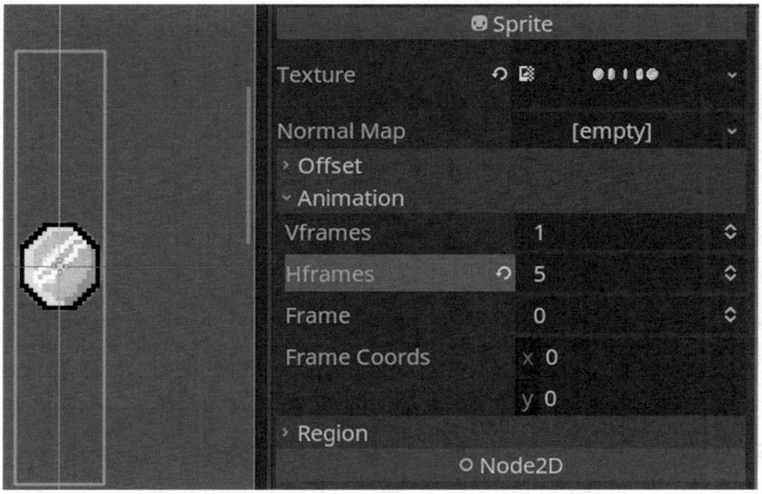

Figure 8-14. *The coin Sprite Sheet is broken down into five separate image frames*

In this way, our Sprite Sheet is broken down into five different
image frames. The value next to the Frame field in the Inspector
dock indicates the frame number being displayed in the workspace.
As shown in Figure 8-14, frame 0 is currently being shown in the
workspace. We can click the small up and down arrows next to this
field to change the current image frame number.

211

4. Select the Sprite node in the Scene dock, click the Animation
    button on the Animation panel, as shown in Figure 8-15, and
    select the  option.

Figure 8-15. Click the Animation button and select the New Option

5. A Create New Animation window pops up prompting you to name
    your new animation. Let's name it **Rotate_Coin** and then click the
    OK button. Note that you can rename the animation by clicking
    on the Animation button and selecting the Rename option. Now,
    your animation player should look like Figure 8-16, with a blue
    marker that you can slide over the different time intervals.

Figure 8-16. Animation player with time intervals

As shown in Figure 8-16, the Snap option is turned on with the
snap time being 0.1 seconds, implying that when you slide the blue
marker, it will move by exactly 0.1 second every time.

6. Also, a value of 1 next to the ⏱ stopwatch (Animation Length)
    icon indicates that the entire animation will last for 1 second.
    Change it to 0.5, and press Enter on your keyboard. This will make
    the total animation duration equal to 0.5 seconds, with each of the
    five image frames being displayed for 0.1 seconds. Your Animation
    panel should look like the one shown in Figure 8-17.

Figure 8-17. *The animation interval is set to 0.5 second*

7. Make sure that the Sprite node is selected in the Scene dock, and the blue marker on the animation player is at the beginning of the timeline (as shown in Figure 8-17). Then, click the key icon next to the Frame field, for image frame 0 in the Inspector dock. A window pops ups, asking you to confirm whether you want to insert the key on the timeline. Click the Create button, and you'll see that frame 0, that is, the first coin image in the Sprite Sheet, appears on the timeline, as shown in Figure 8-18.

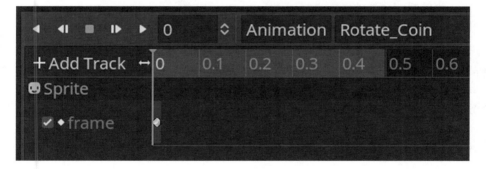

Figure 8-18. *Frame 0 appears on the animation timeline*

8. Now, click the 0.1-second mark on the timeline in the animation player for the blue marker to move to that position, as shown in Figure 8-19.

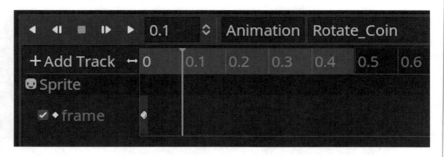

Figure 8-19. *Clicking the 0.1s mark on the animation timeline moves the blue marker to that position*

9.   Next, toggle the Frame property in the Inspector dock, change it to 1, and click the key icon . This adds image frame 1 to the animation timeline, as shown in Figure 8-20.

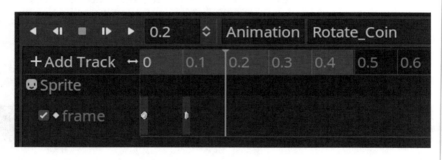

Figure 8-20. *Image frame 1 is added to the animation timeline*

10.   This time, the blue pointer automatically moves ahead by 0.1 seconds, that is, at the 0.2-second position on the timeline, once you add image frame number 1 to it. If not, you can click the timeline at the 0.2-second position to place the blue marker there. The Frame property should also automatically increase by one in the Inspector dock, each time.

11.   In this way, we can add the rest of the image frames onto the animation track, which should look like the one shown in Figure 8-21 after adding all the image frames.

Figure 8-21. *All the image frames are added to the animation track*

12. To play the animation in a loop, click the  icon on the animation timeline, and then click the Play (F5) button. Once you do that, the animation player continuously cycles through all the image frames in a loop.

Note   To change the speed of the animation, we can modify the total animation duration and the Snap position and then add the image frames at different timing positions.

---

13. We now have the animation for rotating the gold coin! Go ahead and save the scene (Ctrl+S on the keyboard or Scene ➤ Save Scene As). Let's name the scene Gold_coin.tscn, as shown in Figure 8-22, and then click the Save button.

File:	Gold_coin.tscn		All Recognized (*.tscn, *.scn, *.res) ⌄
	Save		Cancel

Figure 8-22. *Save the scene as Gold_coin.tscn*

TRY IT!

Creating a Collectible

1. Import images or Sprite Sheets of collectibles such as coins, gems, keys, etc., into the Godot project.

2. Animate the collectibles using the animation player.

3. Play around with different speeds of rotation.

Creating a Coin in the Game Level

Now that we have our gold coin, let's put it in the game. We can do this by creating an instance of our coin scene, Gold_coin.tscn, in our main scene, GameLevel.tscn. Let's see how to do that:

1. Open the main game scene (GameLevel.tscn) by double-clicking it in the FileSystem dock.

2. Next, click the 🔗 icon (next to the Add Child node icon) on the Scene dock, as shown in Figure 8-23, and then select Gold_coin. tscn, as shown in Figure 8-24. This creates an instance of our gold coin, and its corresponding node, called Area2D, appears in the Scene dock as a child of the root node (Game Level).

Figure 8-23. *Creating an instance as a scene as a node*

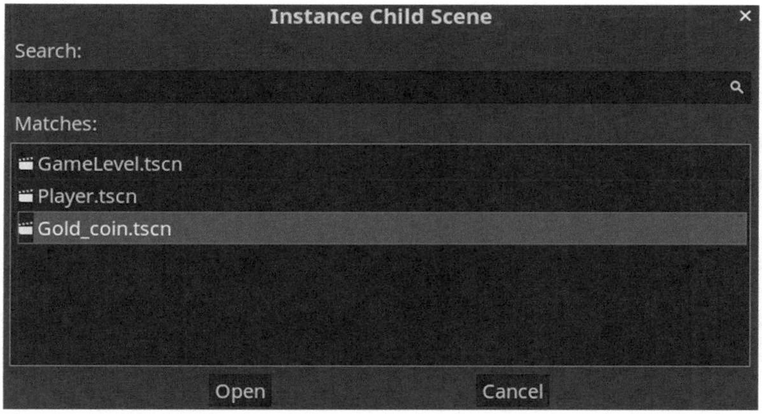

Figure 8-24. *Selecting Gold_coin.tscn*

3. Let's rename the node Area2D to **Gold coin**. But instead of
    changing the name locally in the main game scene, do it in
    Gold_coin.tscn, as shown in Figure 8-25. This will ensure that
    every time you create another instance of the coin in your main
    game scene, it will be named Gold coin, and not Area2D. Open
    Gold_coin.tscn, and then double-click Area2D in the Scene dock.
    Type in the new name, **Gold coin**.

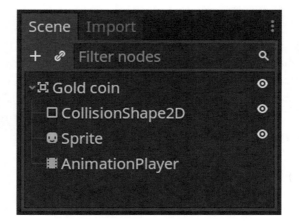

Figure 8-25. *Rename the Area2D node to Gold coin*

4. If you go back to GameLevel.tscn and zoom into the origin on the workspace, you'll notice that the "Gold coin" node has been created there. But it's too small! Let's change its size in the original scene in which it was created. Open Gold_coin.tscn and select the root node, Gold coin, and then expand the Transform tab on the Inspector dock. Change to x and y Scale properties to, say, 3 (to scale up the coin). Save the scene.

5. Next, go back to GameLevel.tscn. You'll notice that the size of the coin gets scaled up this time. In the workspace, drag the coin and place it near the platform, as shown in Figure 8-26.

Figure 8-26. *Creating a gold coin in the game level*

Note   When you are changing the properties of an object, make the changes in the scene in which they are created so that the change is reflected in all created instances of the object.

Collecting Coins

Follow these steps:

1. Open the scene Gold_coin.tscn, and then select the root node (Gold coin) in the Scene dock. Next, click the ⬛ icon to attach a script to it.

2. A window called Attach Node Script pops up, as shown in Figure 8-27 (a). As shown, the default name of the script is Gold_coin.gd. This can be changed if we want to give the script a different name. Let's leave it as it is. We can also change the Template property by expanding its drop-down menu. Go ahead and select the No Comments option, as shown in Figure 8-27 (b). Click the Create button.

Figure 8-27. *(a) Creating a new script for the "Gold coin" node, (b) setting the No Comments option*

This will give us a default script without any comments. Now, let's type in the code for playing the coin rotation animation using the animation player. In the func _ready(), replace the "pass" with the following line of code:

```
$AnimationPlayer.play("Rotate_Coin")
```

3. Save the script (Ctrl+S on the keyboard).

Collecting the Coin Using Signals

Now, if you play the game using the ▶ Play (F5) button, you'll see the coin rotating in the game, but your player can't yet collect the coin; it just passes behind it. Since our coin is represented by a node of the type Area2D, we can modify our script such that every time our player passes through the Area2D(the coin), the coin is "collected," and the score increases by 1. We can use the concept of signals for this purpose.

In Godot, every node is associated with a number of signals that can be emitted each time something happens to that particular node. Let's understand this with the help of an example. In the Gold_coin.tscn scene, select the "Gold coin" node in the Scene dock, and then open the Node dock next to the Inspector dock. As shown in Figure 8-28, this displays all the signals that can be emitted for "Gold coin."

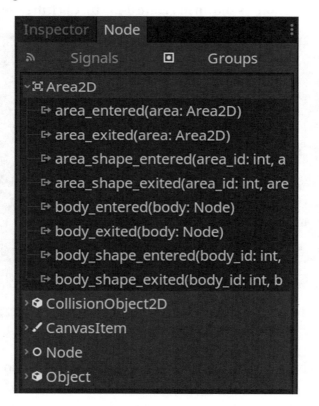

Figure 8-28. *Signals that can be emitted for "Gold coin"*

For example, the area_entered signal is emitted when another area enters, that is, comes into contact with the "Gold coin" node. Another signal, area_exited, is emitted when another area exits, that is, stops being in contact with "Gold coin." Since a coin is collected once the player comes in contact with it, we'll be using the body_entered signal for collision detection. This signal is emitted when a physics body enters the "Gold coin" node. Let's see how to use this signal for coin collection.

1. With the "Gold coin" node selected in the Scene dock, double-click the body_entered signal, as shown in Figure 8-29. Make sure to do this in Gold_coin.tscn and not the main game scene (GameLevel.tscn).

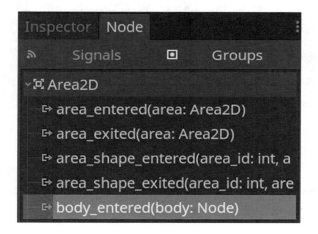

Figure 8-29. *The body_entered signal*

2. Once you do that, the Connect a Signal to a Method window pops up. Select the "Gold coin" node and click the Connect button, as shown in Figure 8-30. This will create a function called _on_Gold_coin_body_entered in the script of Gold coin.

Figure 8-30. *Connect the body_entered signal to "Gold coin"*

3. Once you click the Connect button, the script Gold_coin.gd will
    open, and you'll see two functions called _ready() and _on_Gold_
    coin_body_entered(body) in it, as shown here:

```
extends Area2D
```

```
func _ready():
    $AnimationPlayer.play("Rotate_Coin")
```

```
func _on_Gold_Coin_body_entered(body):
    pass
```

Now, let's create another function for counting the collected coins.
Open the script of the KinematicBody2D called Player.gd from
the FileSystem dock.

4. Declare a variable called score at the top of the script, and intialize it to 0, as follows:

```
var score = 0
```

5. Next, create a function called score_count(), as follows:

```
func score_count():
    score = score + 1
```

Your script should look like the one shown here:

```
extends KinematicBody2D

var velocity = Vector2(0,0)
var gravity = 2000
var score = 0
func _physics_process(_delta):
    if Input.is_action_just_pressed("jump") and is_on_floor():
        velocity.y= -1000
        $AnimatedSprite.play("jump")
    if Input.is_action_pressed("left_arrow"):
        velocity.x = -300
        $AnimatedSprite.play("run")
        $AnimatedSprite.flip_h = true
    elif Input.is_action_pressed("right_arrow"):
        velocity.x = 300
        $AnimatedSprite.play("run")
        $AnimatedSprite.flip_h = false
    else:
        $AnimatedSprite.play("idle")
    if not is_on_floor():
        $AnimatedSprite.play("jump")

    velocity.y  = velocity.y + gravity *(_delta)
    move_and_slide(velocity, Vector2.UP)
    velocity.x = lerp(velocity.x,0,0.1)

func score_count():
    score = score + 1
```

The score_count() function continually increments the score by 1 each time a new coin is collected. We can call this function in our script for "Gold coin," as follows:

6. Open Gold_coin.gd from the FileSystem dock or by clicking the ■ icon next to the "Gold coin" node in the Scene dock, in Gold_coin.tscn.

7. In func _on_Gold_coin_body_entered(body), replace the pass keyword with these lines:

```
body.score_count()
queue_free()
```

Your code should now look like this:

```
extends Area2D

func _ready():
    $AnimationPlayer.play("Rotate_Coin")

func _on_Gold_coin_body_entered(body):
    body.score_count()
    queue_free()
```

- body.score_count(): This line of code calls the score_count() function of the body that enters the "Gold coin" node. In our case, the body is the player, and the score_count() function that we added to Player.gd previously will get called every time the player enters or comes into contact with the coin, and the number of coins will then increase by one.

- queue_free(): This is a built-in function to delete an object. We use this function to delete the coin as soon as it is collected.

8. Now, let's go back to our main game scene, GameLevel.tscn. To insert another coin object in the game, we can just duplicate our "Gold coin" node in the Scene dock, by selecting it and pressing Ctrl+D on the keyboard (or right-clicking the node and selecting the Duplicate option). This copies and pastes the new coin on top of the original one in the workspace. Click it, and drag it to place it

somewhere else in the game. We can do it as many times as we want to create a new coin in the game. As shown in Figure 8-31, three coins have been created and placed in the game.

Figure 8-31. *Creating and placing coins in the game*

Creating More Collectibles

We can also create different kinds of collectibles such as different coloured coins, gems, cherries, keys, etc. We can repeat the process that we followed for the "Gold coin" node and create new scenes for different collectibles.

1. Create two different scenes for the animated Red and Silver coins, and name them Red_coin.tscn and Silver_coin.tscn, respectively. The procedure remains the same as that of creating the Gold_coin.tscn, with the only difference being in the textures assigned to the sprites.

We can now create instances of the Red and Silver coins in the main game scene, GameLevel.tscn.

2. Now, open the main game scene, GameLevel.tscn, and, with the Game Level node (root node) selected, click the 🔗 icon in the Scene dock. Select Red_coin.tscn in the Instance Child Scene window that pops up, as shown in Figure 8-32.

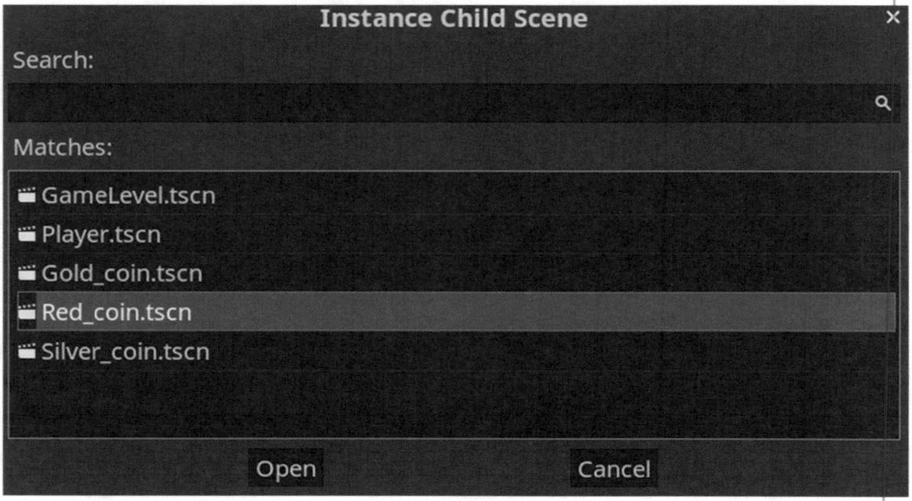

Figure 8-32. *Creating an instance of Red_coin.tscn*

3. Click the Open button to create an instance of the red coin in GameLevel.tscn, as a child node of Game Level. The red coin now appears at the origin at the workspace and can be moved and placed anywhere in the game.

4. For creating an instance of a Silver coin, click the 🔗 icon again, and select Silver_coin.tscn this time. Now, we have instances of the Red coin, as well as an instance of a Silver coin in the Scene dock. This is shown in Figure 8-33.

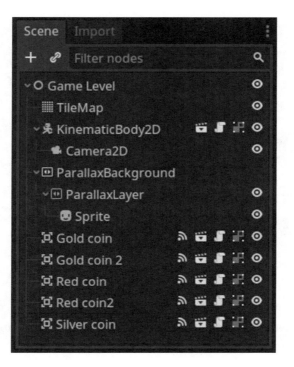

Figure 8-33. *Scene dock after creating instances of different coins*

5. Create copies of the red and silver coin (Ctrl+D on the keyboard).
    Drag and place the different coins at various points in your game
    level in the workspace, as shown in Figure 8-34.

Figure 8-34. *Placing different coins in the game level*

6.   Now, when we play the main game scene by clicking the ▶ Play
      button (F5), our player can collect each coin, which disappears as
      soon as it is collected.

TRY IT!

Placing Collectibles in the Game

1.   Create instances of collectibles such as coins in the main game scene.

2.   Place different collectibles throughout the game level.

3.   Write a script for increasing the score by 10 every time a collectible is collected.

Adjusting the Rewards

Now, according to our current scripts, the score count increases by one any time any of
the coins is collected. Instead, if we want to increase the score by a different value for
each different collectible, we can make slight modifications to our scripts as follows:

1. Open the player script, Player.gd, by double-clicking it in the FileSystem dock.

2. Replace the score_count() function with the following three functions:

```
func score_count_gold():
    score = score + 1
```

```
func score_count_red():
    score = score + 5
```

```
func score_count_silver():
    score = score + 10
```

3. Now, we need to change the scripts for each of the Gold, Silver, and Red coins.

4. Now, open the script of the Gold coin, Gold_coin.gd. In the function _on_Gold_coin_body_entered(body), replace body. score_count() with body.score_count_gold(). Your script should look like this:

```
extends Area2D
```

```
func _ready():
    $AnimationPlayer.play("Rotate_Coin")
```

```
func _on_Gold_coin_body_entered(body):
    body.score_count_gold()
    queue_free()
```

5. In the script of the Red coin, Red_coin.gd, in the function _on_ Red_coin_body_entered(body), replace body.score_count() with body.score_count_red(). Your script should look like this:

```
extends Area2D

func _ready():
    $AnimationPlayer.play("Rotate_Coin")

func _on_Red_coin_body_entered(body):
    body.score_count_red()
    queue_free()
```

6. Lastly, in the script of the Silver coin, `Silver_coin.gd`, in the function `_on_Silver_coin_body_entered(body)`, replace the `body.score_count()` with `body.score_count_silver()`. Your script should look like this:

```
extends Area2D

func _ready():
    $AnimationPlayer.play("Rotate_Coin")

func _on_Silver_coin_body_entered(body):
    body.score_count_silver()
    queue_free()
```

7. With this, the score will increase by 1 for every Gold coin collected, by 5 for every Red coin collected, and by 10 for every Silver coin collected. We can change these values according to the rules of our game.

Adding Enemies

No game is complete without an enemy that the player can defeat! Let's see how to add an enemy to our game.

1. Import the images of the enemy into the FileSystem dock by dragging and dropping them from a file on your computer.

We'll be using the Opossum enemy included in the asset pack called Sunny Land, created by an artist called Ansimuz, as shown in Figure 8-35. This is the same game art pack that we used for our player sprites and TileMaps. You can download it here: https://ansimuz.itch.io/sunny-land-pixel-game-art.

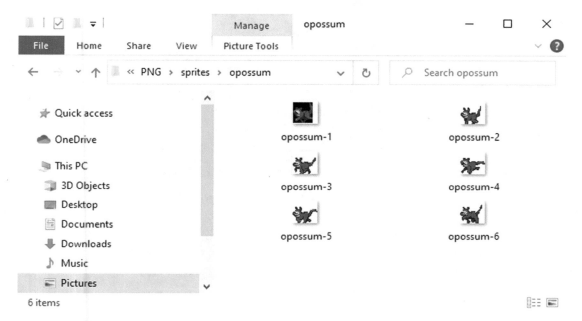

Figure 8-35. *Opossum enemy from the Sunny Land asset pack*

2. Let's create a separate folder for our enemy animation. Right-click the res:// folder, and select the New Folder option. Give the folder an appropriate name, such as enemy_animation, and click the OK button. Once it's created, drag and drop the enemy images from the FileSystem dock into this new folder. This is shown in Figure 8-36.

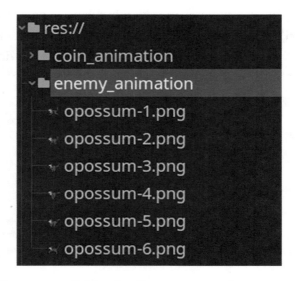

Figure 8-36. *Creating a new folder for the enemy sprites*

3. Now, create a new scene for the enemy by clicking the new scene button ➕ near the top of the 2D workspace. Click the new node button ➕ in the Scene dock to add a root node, search for KinematicBody2D, and click the Create button.

4. Next, add a CollisionShape2D node as a child of KinematicBody2D. To do this, select KinematicBody2D in the Scene dock, click the new node button ➕, search for *CollisionShape2D*, and click the Create button.

5. With the CollisionShape2D node selected in the Scene dock, expand the drop-down menu next to the Shape property in the Inspector dock, and select the New RectangleShape2D option.

6. Now, select KinematicBody2D in the Scene dock, click the new node button ➕, search for *AnimatedSprite*, and click the Create button. This adds AnimatedSprite as a child of KinematicBody2D, as shown in Figure 8-37.

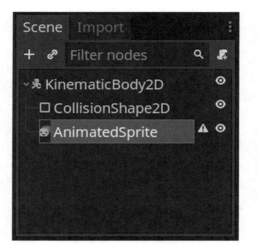

Figure 8-37. *Creating an AnimatedSprite as a child of KinematicBody2D*

7. Select AnimatedSprite in the Scene dock, and expand the drop-down menu next to the Frames property in the Inspector dock. Select the New SpriteFrames option, as shown in Figure 8-38.

Figure 8-38. *Creating a New SpriteFrames resource*

8. Click ▣ SpriteFrames in the Inspector dock next to Frames to open the SpriteFrames editor at the bottom of the interface.

9. As shown in Figure 8-39, click the "default" animation name in the SpriteFrames editor, and rename it to run.

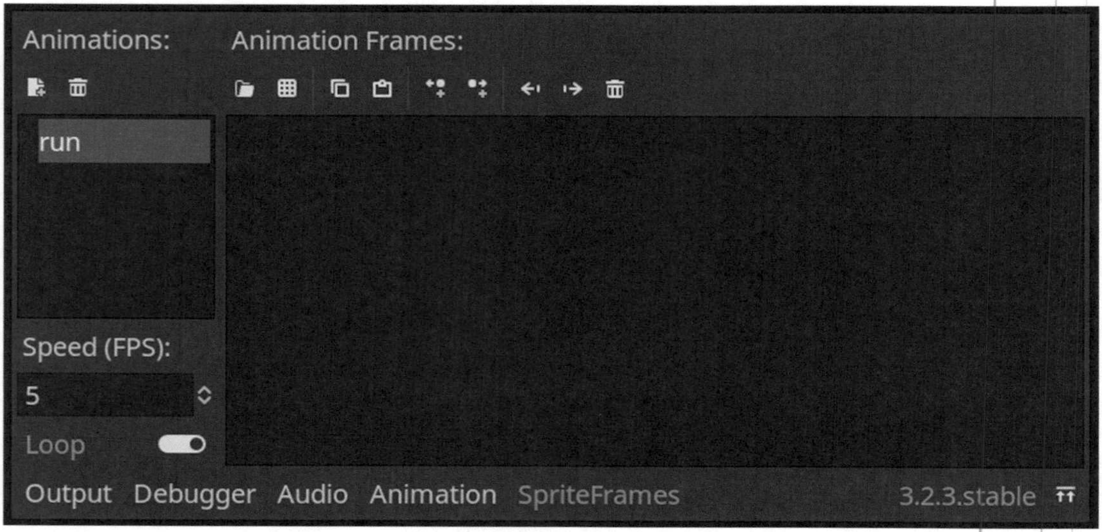

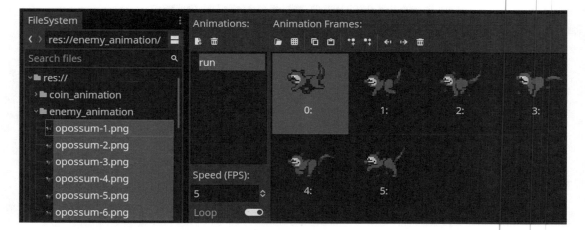

Figure 8-39. *Renaming the default animation to "run"*

10.   Now, drag and drop the enemy images into the SpriteFrames
editor, as shown in Figure 8-40.

Figure 8-40. *Creating the run animation for the enemy*

11.   With the AnimatedSprite node selected in the Scene dock, select
the Playing property in the Inspector dock. Now, you can see the
run animation of the enemy playing in the 2D workspace, at its
origin. We can change the speed of the animation by changing the
Speed Scale property in the Inspector dock of the AnimatedSprite.

12. Select the CollsionShape2D node in the Scene dock, and adjust it to fit the sprite as closely as possible, as shown in Figure 8-41. You can adjust the size and position of the CollisionShape2D by moving the orange vertices on its edges, as well as by changing its x and y Position property in the Inspector dock.

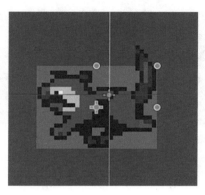

Figure 8-41. *Adjusting the CollisionShape2D to fit the enemy sprite*

13. Rename KinematicBody2D to Enemy, and save the scene as Enemy.tscn (Ctrl+Shift+S).

14. Now, open the main game scene, GameLevel.tscn, and select the root node, Game Level. Click the 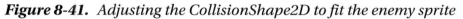 button and select Enemy.tscn in the Instance Child Scene window that pops up; then click the Open button, as shown in Figure 8-42. This creates an instance of the enemy in GameLevel.tscn.

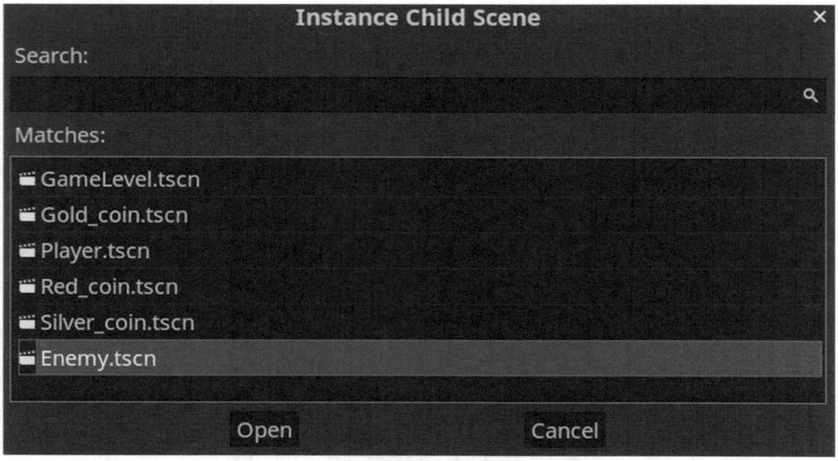

Figure 8-42. *Creating an instance of the enemy scene*

15.   The enemy is created at the origin in the workspace, but it's too small. Go back to Enemy.tscn, and select the Enemy node in the Scene dock. In the Inspector dock, expand the Transform property, and increase the x and y Scale to, say, 3 (to scale up the enemy size). Save the Enemy.tscn scene.

16.   If you now go back to GameLevel.tscn, you'll see that the size of the enemy is now proportional to our player. Drag and place the enemy on the platform in the game, as shown in Figure 8-43.

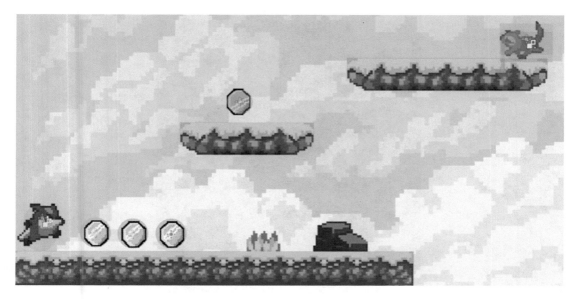

Figure 8-43. *Place the instance of the enemy in the game level*

17. Now, we can create multiple instances of the enemy and place them throughout the game level! Repeat step 14 every time you want to create a new instance of the enemy.

18. Next, we need to write a script for the enemy. Open Enemy.tscn and select the root node, Enemy; then click the new script button 📄 to generate a script.

19. In the Attach Node Script window, navigate to "No Comments" in the Template property's drop-down menu, and then click the Create button, as shown in Figure 8-44. A script called Enemy.gd is created in the FileSystem dock.

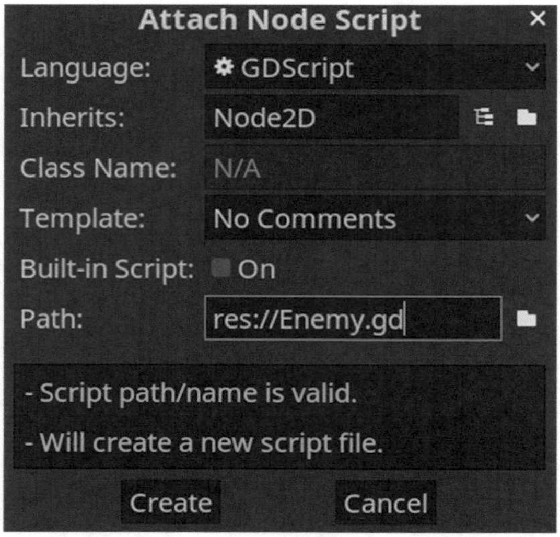

Figure 8-44. *Creating a script for the enemy called Enemy.gd*

20. Now, in the script Enemy.gd, replace the contents with the following code:

```
extends KinematicBody2D

var velocity = Vector2(0,0)
var speed = 100
var direction = -1

func _physics_process(_delta):
        velocity.x = speed * direction

if direction == -1:
            $AnimatedSprite.flip_h = false
        else:
            $AnimatedSprite.flip_h = true

        $AnimatedSprite.play("run")
        move_and_slide(velocity)
```

- Just as we saw in Chapter 5, `Vector2(x,y)` is used to define the initial velocity of our kinematic body (Enemy) in the x and y directions. Here, `velocity = Vector2 (0,0)` implies that the velocity of the enemy is initialized to 0, in both the x and y directions.

- `func _physics_process(_delta)` is a built-in physics function that we are using to play the enemy run animation, as well as to move the enemy left and right.

- The x velocity of the enemy, that is, the horizontal velocity, is equal to product of speed and direction. We use a variable called `direction` to determine whether the enemy is facing left or right. For facing left, we'll set direction to -1, and for facing right, we'll set the direction to +1. In this way, when the direction (which can be either -1 or +1) is multiplied with speed, the velocity is either a negative value or a positive value. A negative value of velocity implies the speed in the left direction, while a positive value implies the speed in the right direction.

- If direction is = -1, we don't flip the Animated Enemy sprite; hence, we set `$AnimatedSprite.flip_h = false`. Otherwise, if the direction is not -1, we flip it by setting `$AnimatedSprite.flip_h = true`.

- `$AnimatedSprite.play("run")` is used to continuously play the run animation for the enemy, while `move_and_slide(velocity)` is used to move the enemy according to the speed and direction.

If we play the main game scene by clicking the Play button (F5) ▶, we see the enemy running toward the left continuously, even after the platform ends, until it goes off the screen. But we don't want that. Instead, we want it to run back and forth along the platform. We also need a way to change the direction of the enemy every time it reaches either the left or right edge so that it doesn't go beyond the cliff. For doing this, we need a way to detect the edge of a cliff—through the use of raycasts.

TRY IT!

Creating an Enemy

1. Import images or a Sprite Sheet of an enemy character into the Godot project.

2. Create different animations for the enemy, such as running, walking, or flying.

3. Write a script for making the enemy walk across a platform in the game.

Detecting Ledges with a Raycast

In Godot, a raycast represents a line that can be used for detecting collisions along its path. It can be placed on the enemy sprite to collide with the ground until the enemy reaches the edge of a cliff. Once it does that, it won't collide with the ground anymore, and we can then use this detection mechanism to change the direction of the enemy. Let's understand this by diving right into the implementation of this scenario.

1. Open the Enemy scene, Enemy.tscn, and select the Enemy node (root node) in the Scene dock. Next, click the new node button ➕, and search for and add a RayCast2D node as the child node of Enemy, as shown in Figure 8-45. Then, save the scene (Ctrl+S on the keyboard).

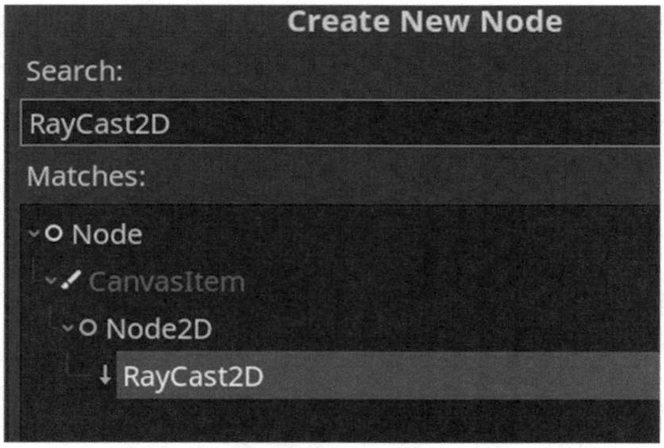

Figure 8-45. *Creating a RayCast2D node as a child of the Enemy node*

The RayCast2D gets added to center of the Enemy sprite in the workspace, as shown in Figure 8-46.

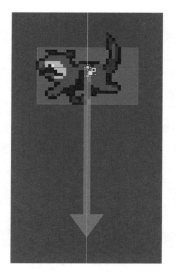

Figure 8-46. *The RayCast2D gets created in the workspace*

2. By default, it is disabled, and it can be enabled by selecting the
    RayCast2D node in the Scene dock and then checking the Enabled
    option in the Inspector node, as shown in Figure 8-47.

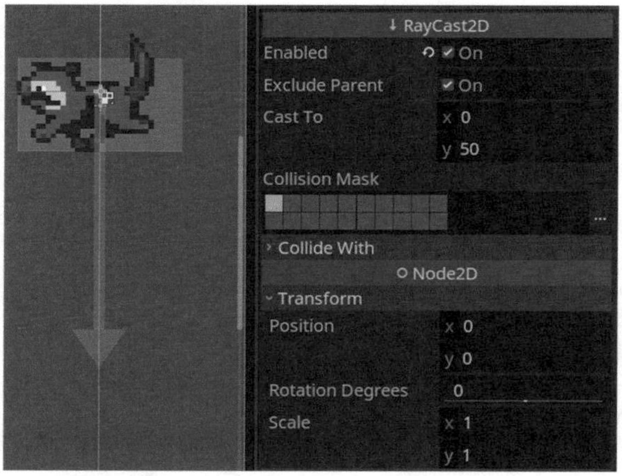

Figure 8-47. *Enabling the RayCast2D*

3. Now, let's move the RayCast2D toward the front part of the Enemy
    sprite so that it can detect the cliff when the enemy is moving
    toward it, as shown in Figure 8-48 (a). To do this, we can adjust
    the x value of the Position property, under the Transform tab in
    the Inspector. Let's change it to, say, -15. You can adjust this value
    until it is as close to the front of the Enemy sprite as possible.

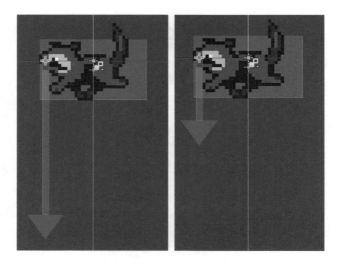

Figure 8-48. *(a) Moving the RayCast2D to the front of the Enemy sprite, (b) shortening the length of the RayCast2D*

4. Also, adjust the y value of the Cast To property so that it is close to the bottom edge of the Enemy sprite, while leaving some extra space. Let's change it to, say, 20. You can adjust this value until it as close to the bottom edge of the Enemy sprite as possible. The RayCast2D is shortened in length, as shown in Figure 8-48 (b). Save the scene (Ctrl+S on the keyboard).

5. Next, open the Enemy script, Enemy.gd, and add the following lines inside the _physics_process(_delta) function:

```
if $RayCast2D.is_colliding() == false:
    direction = direction * -1
    $RayCast2D.position.x *= -1
```

Now, your script with the proper indentations should look like the code shown here:

```
extends KinematicBody2D

var velocity = Vector2(0,0)
var speed = 100
var direction = -1
```

```
func _physics_process(_delta):
    velocity.x = speed * direction

    if direction == -1:
        $AnimatedSprite.flip_h = false
    else:
        $AnimatedSprite.flip_h = true

    $AnimatedSprite.play("run")
    move_and_slide(velocity)

    if $RayCast2D.is_colliding() == false:
        direction = direction * -1
        $RayCast2D.position.x *= -1
```

6. Now if we play the main game scene by clicking the Play button
   (F5) ▶, we can see the enemy going back and forth along the
   platform, without falling off! Once the enemy reaches one end of
   the platform, it turns and continues in the other direction.
   (The sprite is flipped horizontally.) This is shown in Figure 8-49.

Figure 8-49. *The enemy turns and continues in the other direction on reaching one end of the platform*

Colliding with the Enemy

Now that we have our enemy in the game scene, let's work on what should happen if our player runs into it. Let's implement a system where every time the player gets hit by the enemy, the player loses one life. If the player has no lives left, then it's "Game Over"!

1. Open Enemy.tscn, select the Enemy node, click the Add New Node button ![+], and add an Area2D as the child of enemy. Rename the Area2D node to CollisionChecker.

2. Next, add a CollisionShape2D as the child of the CollisionChecker node, and assign a RectangleShape2D to it from the Shape field in the Inspector dock. Your Scene dock should look like Figure 8-50.

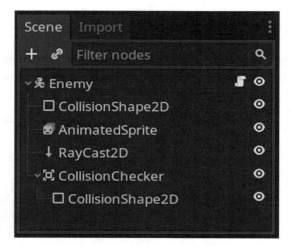

Figure 8-50. *Scene dock for the Enemy.tscn*

3. Adjust the CollisionShape2D of the CollisionChecker in the workspace so that it fits as closely to the enemy sprite as possible, as shown in Figure 8-51. You can change its position by changing the x and y Position properties in the Inspector dock under the Transform tab.

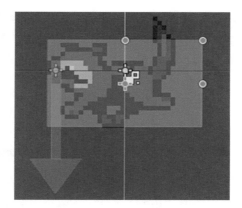

Figure 8-51. *Adjusting the size of the CollisionShape2D*

4. Now, select the CollisionChecker node in the Scene dock, and then head over to the Node dock. Double-click the body_entered signal and, in the Connect a Signal to a Method window, click the Connect button, as shown in Figure 8-52.

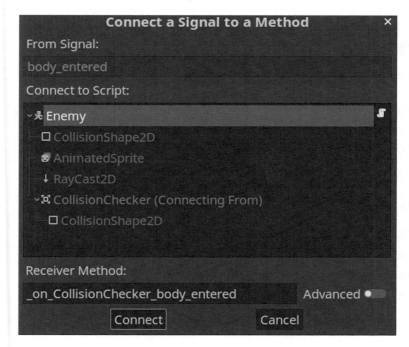

Figure 8-52. *Connect body_entered signal to enemy node*

5. Once you do that, the function _on_CollisionChecker_body_ entered(body) gets created inside the Enemy script, Enemy.gd. Inside this function, add the following lines of code:

```
print("enter enemy")
lives = lives - 1
if(lives == 0):
        get_tree().change_scene("res://GameLevel.tscn")
```

As seen in the last line, get_tree().change_scene() can be used for changing scenes. Whenever the player collides with the enemy, the number of lives reduces by 1. Once the number of lives becomes 0, we will reload the the main game scene, GameLevel. tscn. We can also load another scene called GameOver.tscn instead. Once we have a Game Over scene (we'll make it in the next chapter), we can replace GameLevel.tscn with GamerOver. tscn in the last line.

6. Declare a variable called lives at the top and initialize it to 3 as follows:

```
var lives = 3
```

This implies that the player has three lives in total. Every time it hits an enemy, it loses a life! Make sure to add multiple instances of the enemy throughout the game level. Your enemy script should now look like the one shown below:

```
extends KinematicBody2D

var velocity = Vector2(0,0)
var speed = 100
var direction = -1
var lives = 3
```

```
func _physics_process(_delta):
        velocity.x = speed * direction
        if direction == -1:
            $AnimatedSprite.flip_h = false
        else:
            $AnimatedSprite.flip_h = true

        $AnimatedSprite.play("run")
        move_and_slide(velocity)

        if $RayCast2D.is_colliding() == false:
            direction = direction * -1
            $RayCast2D.position.x *= -1

func _on_CollisionChecker_body_entered(body):
        print("enter enemy")
        lives = lives - 1
        if(lives == 0):
            get_tree().change_scene ("res://GameLevel.tscn")
```

Before playing the game scene, we need to tell Godot which objects in our game can collide with each other. If we don't do that, it might cause unwanted glitches and bugs in the game! Let's see how to do that with the help of collision layers and collision masks.

Collision Layer and Collision Mask

The Godot engine has properties called *collision layers* and *collision masks* for detecting whether two physics bodies are intersecting or in contact with each other at any given time.

- *Collision layers*: Determine the layers that an object exists in

- *Collision masks*: Determine the layers that the given object will scan for collisions

If you select any physics body node in the Scene dock, such as KinematicBody2D, and then expand the Collision property in its Inspector dock, you'll see two properties called Layer and Mask. This is shown in Figure 8-53.

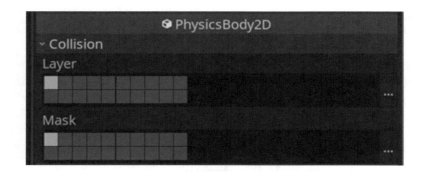

Figure 8-53. *Collision Layer and Mask properties*

There are different layers and masks (each represented by one square) that a physics object can be assigned to. A total of 20 layers are available in the editor, and you can set multiple masks for every layer. You can set a layer for a node by clicking the corresponding square. We can control which objects in our game can collide and thus interact with each other by setting various layers and masks for them. For example, in our game, we don't want the enemy to be able to collide and collect a coin, so we'll place the enemy in a different layer than the coin, and make sure that their masks are different. Let's see how this works in practice.

1. Navigate to Project ➤ Project Settings at the top of the interface. In the Project Settings window, in the General tab, scroll down and double-click 2d Physics under Layer Names. This is shown in Figure 8-54.

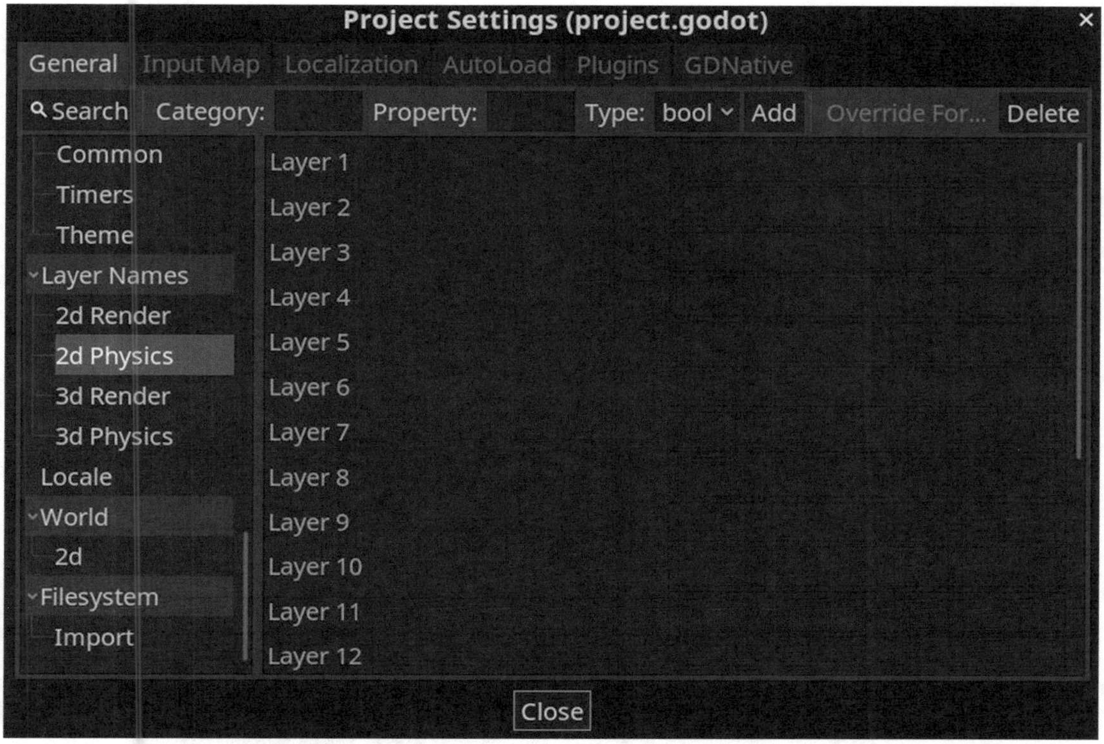

Project Settings (project.godot)   ✕

General   Input Map   Localization   AutoLoad   Plugins   GDNative

🔍 Search   Category: Property: Type: bool ∨ Add   Override For...   Delete

Common   Layer 1
Timers   Layer 2
Theme   Layer 3
∨ Layer Names   Layer 4
2d Render
2d Physics   Layer 5
3d Render   Layer 6
3d Physics   Layer 7
Locale   Layer 8
∨ World   Layer 9
2d   Layer 10
∨ Filesystem   Layer 11
Import   Layer 12

Close

Figure 8-54. *2D physics layers*

2. Here, we can name the different layers and assign them to various physics bodies that we have in our project. Let's name them as shown in Figure 8-55.

Layer 1   ↻ Player
Layer 2   ↻ Platform
Layer 3   ↻ Fall Area
Layer 4   ↻ Finish Level Area
Layer 5   ↻ Collectible
Layer 6   ↻ Enemy

Figure 8-55. *Renaming the 2D physics layers*

Now we can set the collision layers and masks for the different physics objects in our game. Let's set the layers and masks for the player, enemy, coins, fall area, and finish area.

Player

Open the Player scene (Player.tscn), and select the KinematicBody2D node. Set the collision layer and mask by clicking the three dots (...) next to them, as shown in Figure 8-56 (a) and 8-56 (b), respectively. This means the player only scans for collisions with other objects that are also placed in the Player layer.

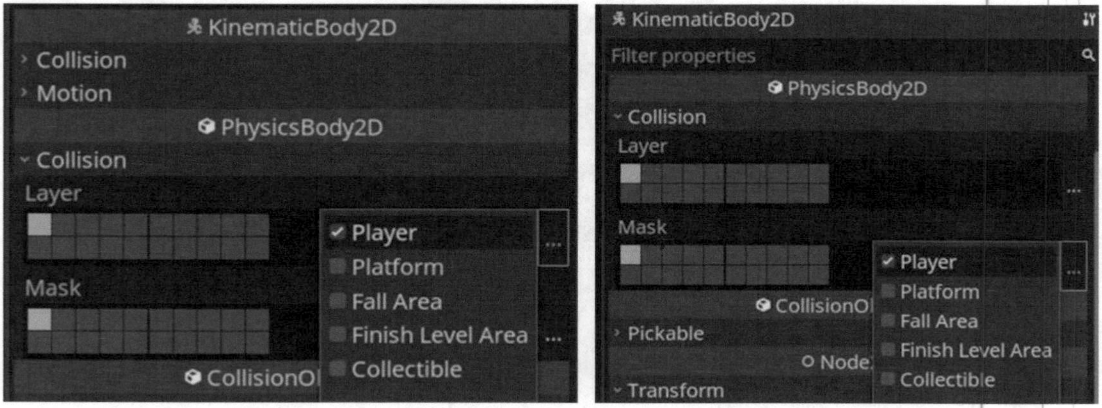

Figure 8-56. *(a) Setting the collision layer for the player, (b) setting the collision mask for the player*

Enemy

Open the Enemy scene, Enemy.tscn.

1. Select the Enemy node (root node) in the Scene dock, and then set the collision layer and mask, as shown in Figures 8-57 (a) and 8-57 (b), respectively.

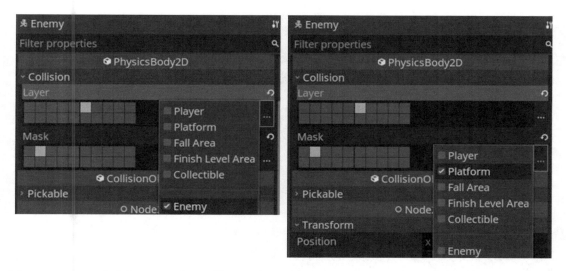

Figure 8-57. *(a) Setting the collision layer for the Enemy node, (b) setting the collision mask for the Enemy node*

2. Select the CollisionChecker node in the Scene dock, and set the collision layer and collision mask, as shown in Figure 8-58 (a) and 8-58 (b).

Figure 8-58. *(a) Setting the collision layer for the CollisionChecker node, (b) setting the collision mask for the CollisionChecker node*

Coin

Open the Coin scene, Gold_coin.tscn. Select the "Gold coin" node, and set the collision layer and mask, as shown in Figure 8-59 (a) and 8-59 (b).

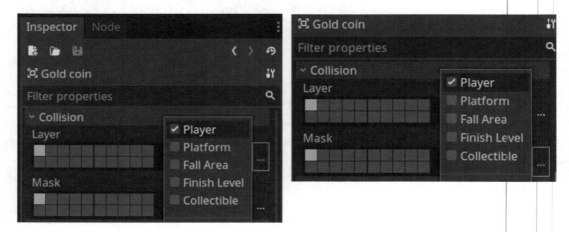

Figure 8-59. *(a) Setting the collision layer for the "Gold coin" node, (b) setting the collision mask for the "Gold coin" node*

Detecting Falls

If the player falls off the edge of the cliff, we can detect this when the player enters a certain area near the cliff, using the concept of signals. Let's see how to implement this.

1. In the main game scene, GameLevel.tscn, add a new node as a child of Game Level (the root node). Select Game Level in the Scene dock, and then click the new node button ➕. In the Create New Node window, search for *Area2D*, and then click the Create button. Rename the Area2D as **Fall Area**.

2. Fix the "Node configuration warning" next to Fall Area by adding a CollisionShape2D node as its child. Do this by selecting Fall Area in the Scene dock, then clicking the new node button ➕, and searching for CollisionShape2D; then click the Create button.

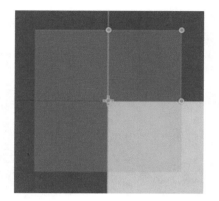

Figure 8-60. *The CollisionShape2D is created at the origin*

3. Select CollisionShape2D in the Scene dock, and then expand the drop-down menu next to the Shape property in the Inspector dock. Select the New RectangleShape2D option.

4. Now, as shown in Figure 8-60, the Fall Area is created at the origin on the workspace. Before moving it, bind it with its CollisionShape2D node by selecting Fall Area in the Scene dock and then clicking on the bind icon next to the lock icon on the 2D toolbar.

5. If you zoom into the workspace at the origin, you'll be able to see the CollsionShape2D with orange vertices on its edges. Drag these vertices to make the shape longer, and then move and place the Fall Area near the bottom of the cliffs in your game, as shown in Figure 8-61.

Figure 8-61. *Placing the Fall Area at the bottom of the cliffs*

When the player enters the Fall Area after falling off the cliff, the game will detect this. Let's see how to restart the game every time this happens.

Changing Scenes

Now, every time our player collides with an enemy or falls off a cliff, it loses a life, and the current game level restarts. Let's see how to change or restart a scene in Godot.

1. Select the Fall Area in the Scene dock, and then head over to the Node dock to see its associated signals, as shown in Figure 8-62.

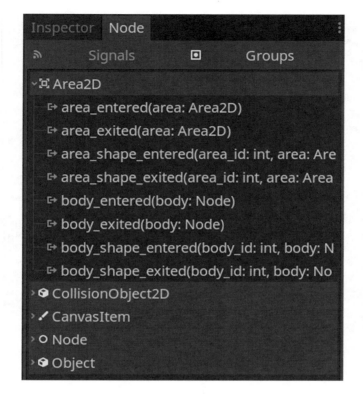

Figure 8-62. *Signals that can be emitted for the Area2D node*

2. Just as we did for the coins, double-click the body_entered
    signal. In the Connect a Signal to a Method window, select the
    KinematicBody2D node, and click the Connect button, as shown
    in Figure 8-63.

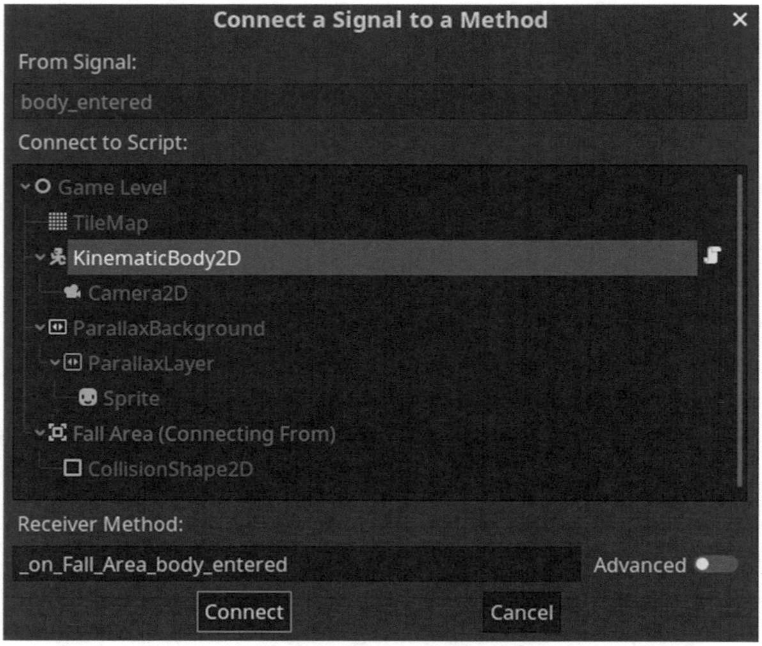

Figure 8-63. *Connect the body_entered Signal to the KinematicBody2D*

3. Once you do that, a function called _on_Fall_Area_body_
    entered(body) gets created and added at the bottom of the Player
    script, Player.gd. Modify the function as follows:

```
func _on_Fall_Area_body_entered(body):
        get_tree().change_scene("res://GameLevel.tscn")
```

4. We can create another Area2D in our main game scene and place
    it at the end of the level, such as on the door of the house, as
    shown in Figure 8-64. Every time the player enters this area, that
    is, "enters" the door of the house, the current game level finishes,
    and the next game level loads.

Figure 8-64. *An Area2D is placed on the door of a house object in the game*

5.   We can rename this Area2D to an appropriate name such as
Finish Level Area, as shown in Figure 8-65.

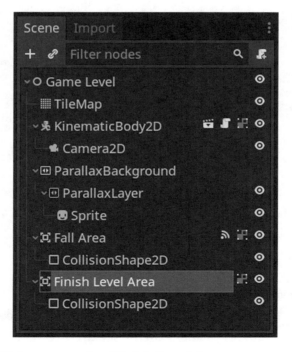

Figure 8-65. *Area2D is renamed to Finish Level Area*

6. Next, we need to add another signal to this area for switching scenes once it is entered. Select the Finish Level Area (the Area2D) node in the Scene dock, and then open the Node dock next to the Inspector dock. Double-click body-entered, select the KinematicBody2D node in the Connect a Signal to a Method window, and click the Connect button. This is shown in Figure 8-66.

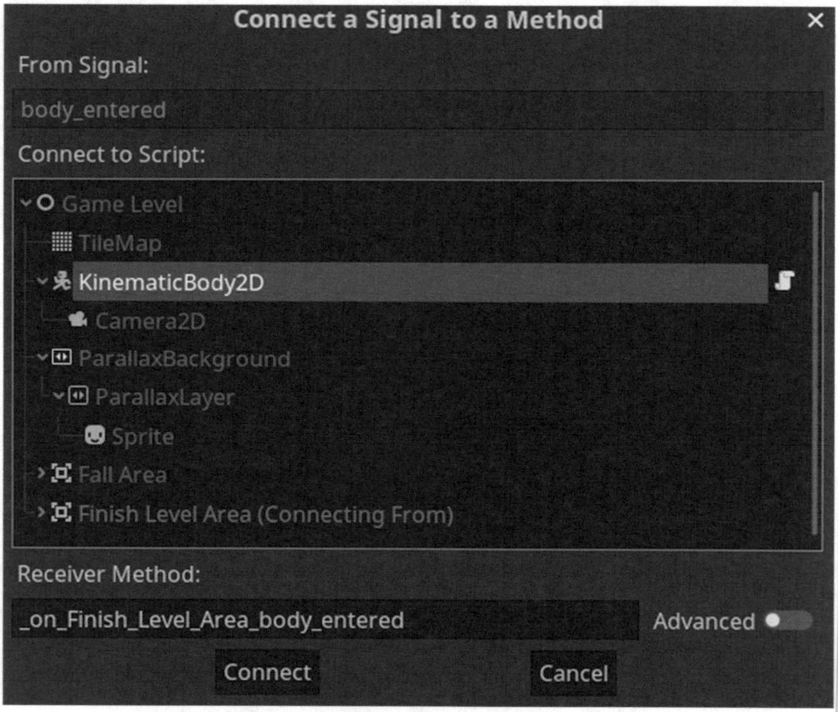

Figure 8-66. *Connecting the body_entered signal to the KinematicBody2D*

7. A function called _on_Finish_Level_Area_body_entered(body) is created in our Player script, Player.gd. Replace the pass in the function with the following line:

```
get_tree().change_scene("res://GameLevel.tscn")
```

Once the player reaches the house placed at the end of Level 1, the game reloads the current level. If we have another level designed in a scene called Level2.tscn, we can write that instead of GameLevel.tscn to load the scene corresponding to the next level.

Wins and Losses

1. Write scripts for keeping track of the score and lives of the player.

2. Create another game level, and load it every time the player completes the first game level.

Fall Area and Finish Level Area Collision

Since we want the Fall Area and the Finish Level Area to able to collide with only the player, we have to set their collision layer and mask properties accordingly. Open the main game scene GameLevel.tscn, and select the Fall Area node. Set the collision layer and mask according to Figure 8-67 (a) and 8-67 (b). Then, select the Finish Level Area node and do the same, as shown in Figure 8-68 (a) and 8-68 (b).

Figure 8-67. (a) Setting the collision layer for the Fall Area Node, (b) setting the collision mask for the Fall Area Node

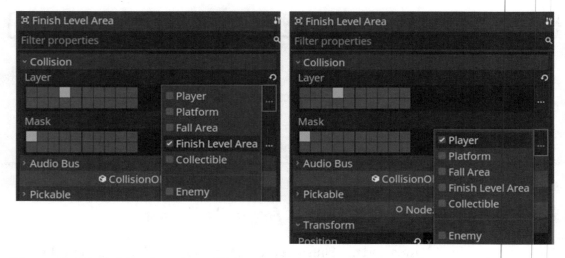

Figure 8-68. (a) Setting the collision layer for the Finish Level Area Node, (b) setting the collision mask for the Finish Level Area Node

Key Takeaways

In this chapter, we learned how to import and animate a collectible using the animation player. We also understood the concept of creating instances of objects in a scene. We wrote various scripts for implementing a coin collection and player life system, as well as for changing scenes if the player lost the current game level. We created an enemy that could independently move along a platform in the game and cause the player to lose a life on coming into contact with it. Moreover, we took a look at many various concepts such as signals, RayCast2D, collision masks and layers, and changing scenes.

PART IV

Game Enhancements and Export

CHAPTER 9

Game GUI

🤖 In this chapter, you'll learn how to use Godot's graphical user interface (GUI) components to design the main title screen and the Game Over screen. We'll also create a heads-up display (HUD) to display the player's score and lives. Lastly, we'll understand the process of adding music and sound effects to our game.

The GUI is essential to every game. It includes components that the player sees and can use for interacting with the game, such as the following:

- Game background

- Fonts for displaying text such as the game title

- Buttons such as Play, Pause, Quit

- Menus such as Settings/Options, Levels, Objectives

- Icons for connecting to the in-game store and various social media platforms

- Other screens such as Leaderboards and Achievements, Game Over/Win Screens

The GUI can be designed according to the theme and can greatly enhance the look of your game. The HUD is the part of the GUI that displays various aspects of the game such as the character's level, health, score, and remaining lives.

Now, let's jump right into the design of the GUI and HUD of our game!

© Maithili Dhule 2022
M. Dhule, *Beginning Game Development with Godot*, https://doi.org/10.1007/978-1-4842-7455-2_9

Creating the HUD

In the previous chapter, we created and added animated coins, as well as an enemy to our game level. When the player collects a coin or loses a life, we want the HUD to show this. Let's see how to create one.

1. Open Level 1 of the Game scene, i.e., GameLevel.tscn, by double-clicking it in the FileSystem dock.

2. Select the root node, Game Level, and click the ⊞ button to add a child node. Search for *CanvasLayer,* and click the Create button, as shown in Figure 9-1. This adds the node as a child of the Game Level node and is separate from the rest of the nodes in this scene. You can see this in Figure 9-2.

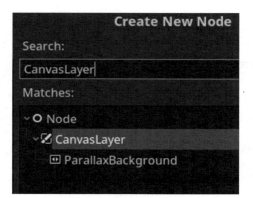

Figure 9-1. *Creating a new CanvasLayer node*

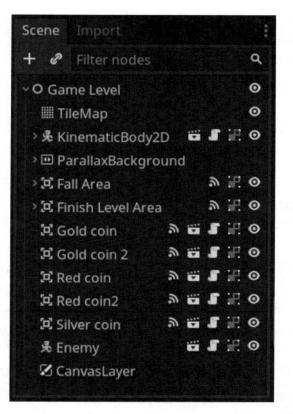

Figure 9-2. *The CanvasLayer node is added to the node hierarchy*

3. Now, we'll be adding the rest of the HUD components as children of the CanvasLayer node.

4. With the CanvasLayer node selected, add a TextureRect node and Label node as its children by clicking the **+** button in the Scene dock and then searching for the respective node in the Create New Node window, as shown in Figure 9-3 (a) and (b).

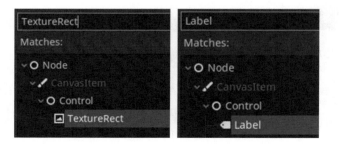

Figure 9-3. *(a) Adding a TextureRect node, (b) adding a Label node*

5. The TextureRect and Label nodes will be added as children of the
    CanvasLayer node, as shown in Figure 9-4 (the order of the nodes
    doesn't matter).

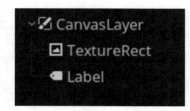

Figure 9-4. *The TextureRect and Label nodes are added as children of the*
CanvasLayer node

6. Now we will use the Label node that we added to the CanvasLayer
    to display the total score. But for displaying the text on the label,
    we need to first assign a custom font to label. For that, we will
    need to first import the custom font that we want to use into our
    Godot project by dragging and dropping them into the FileSystem
    dock, as shown in Figure 9-5.

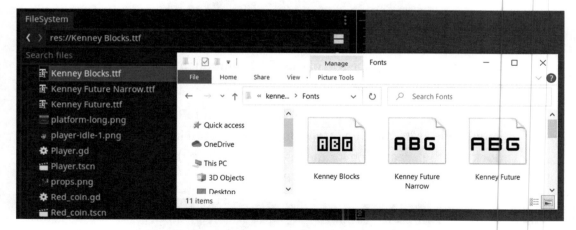

Figure 9-5. *Importing the fonts into the project*

We have imported three fonts called Kenny Blocks.ttf, Kenny Future Narrow.ttf
and Kenny Future.ttf into the project. You can download these, as well as other fonts,
from https://www.kenney.nl/assets/kenney-fonts.

7. With the Label node selected in the Scene dock, expand the Custom Fonts tab in the Inspector dock. Click the small arrow next to the "empty" field of the Font property, and select New DynamicFont, as shown in Figure 9-6.

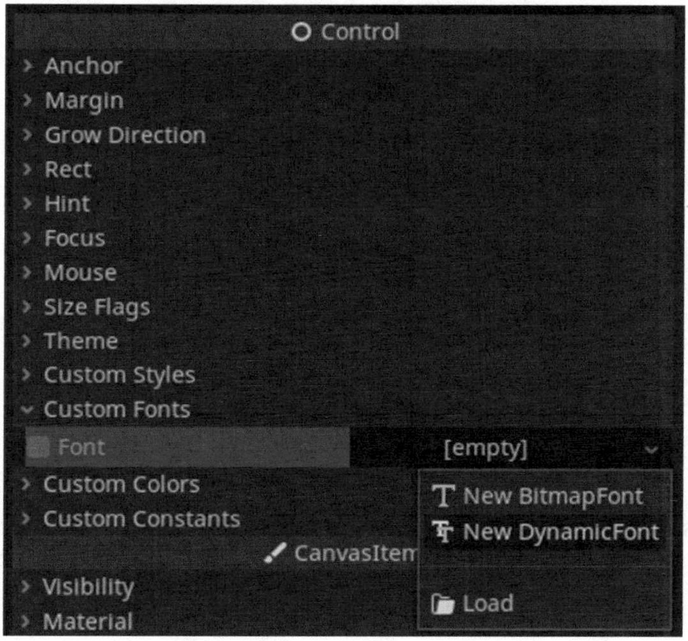

Figure 9-6. *Selecting New DynamicFont*

8. Then, click DynamicFont that appears in the Font property's field, as shown in Figure 9-7.

Figure 9-7. *Clicking DynamicFont in the Font property field*

9. This will open various property tabs such as Settings, Extra Spacing, Font, and Resource. Expand the Font property tab, and drag and drop the font you want to use, e.g., Kenny Future Narrow. ttf from the FileSystem dock into the Font Data property. Increase the size of the font to, say, 60, by changing the Size property on the Settings tab, as shown in Figure 9-8.

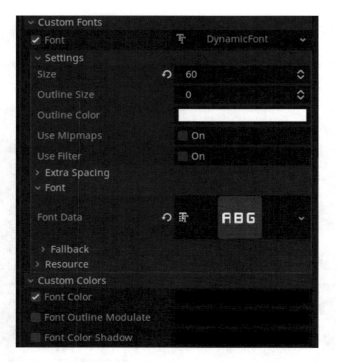

Figure 9-8. *Assigning a font and increasing its size*

10. To change the color of the font, expand the Custom Colors tab, and then click the black rectangle next to the Font Color property to open up a ColorPicker window, as shown in Figure 9-9. We'll select Black as our font's color.

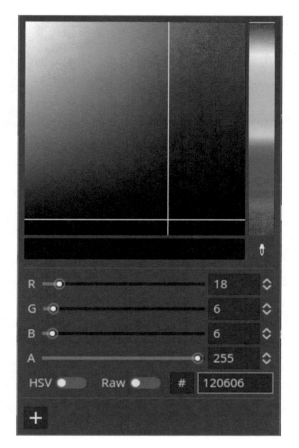

Figure 9-9. *The ColorPicker window*

Note You can click and drag your mouse anywhere in the colored window or in the color slider on the right, or you can adjust the value of the R (Red), G (Green), B (Blue), or A (Alpha, i.e., transparency) properties to select a certain color. You can also type in the hex value of a color—which is a numerical value that represents a color in the 32-bit color space.

---

11. In the Text property in the Inspector dock, enter the text **Score:** which will then appear in the workspace, as shown in Figure 9-10.

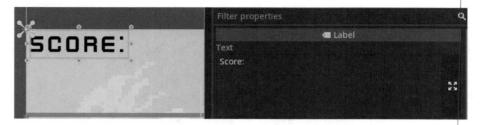

Figure 9-10. *Entering the text to be displayed by the label*

12. We can save this font resource for later use. Select the Label node in the Scene dock, and expand the Custom Fonts tab in the Inspector dock. Click the small arrow next to Dynamic Font **T DynamicFont** in the Font property, and select the Save option. Next, in the Save Resource As window that pops up, enter the filename (and .tres), e.g., **Mylabelfont.tres**, and click the Save button. Now, Mylabelfont.tres gets saved as a resource in the FileSystem dock and can be dragged and dropped into the Font field on the Custom Fonts tab for other components such as labels.

13. Next, let's add another label that will display the numerical value of the total score. Select the CanvasLayer node in the Scene dock, click the ➕ button, and then search for *Label* in the Create New Node window.

14. Let's rename this label as **ScoreValue**, as shown in Figure 9-11.

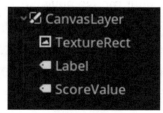

Figure 9-11. *Renaming the label as ScoreValue*

15.   Then, move it next to Score: in the workspace, and make it larger
by pulling on its orange vertices, as shown in Figure 9-12.

Figure 9-12. *Moving the label and making it larger*

16.   Now, just like we did for the Score: label, we will assign a custom
font to it. With the Score Value node selected in the Scene dock,
expand the Custom Fonts property in the Inspector dock, and
select DynamicFont from the drop-down menu. Then click
DynamicFont that appears in the Font property. Expand the Font
tab under Extra Spacing, and then drag and drop the Font file (.ttf)
from the FileSystem dock into the empty field next to Font Data.

17.   In the Text field in the Inspector dock, type in **00** for now.

HBoxContainer and VBoxContainer

We can make use of a GUI component called HBoxContainer to keep our labels aligned
to the top-left corner of the screen even if the window size changes. HBoxContainer
stands for Horizontal Box Container, and it arranges its child nodes horizontally, that is,
from left to right, in the GUI. Another type of container in Godot is called VBoxContainer,
or Vertical Box Container, which arranges its child nodes in a list, that is, from top to
bottom on the GUI.

Now, let's see how we can make use of the HBoxContainer for our labels.

1.   In the main game scene, GameLevel.tscn, select the CanvasLayer
node, and then add an HBoxContainer as its child. Expand the
HBoxContainer in the workspace so that it is large enough to hold
the two labels (displaying the score), as shown in Figure 9-13.

Figure 9-13. *Expanding the HBoxContainer*

2. Next, select the Label and ScoreValue nodes, and then drag and drop them onto the HBoxContainer so that it becomes their parent node. You can see this in Figure 9-14.

Figure 9-14. *Assigning Label and ScoreValue as child nodes of HBoxContainer*

3. Now, with the HBoxContainer selected in the Scene dock, expand its Margin property in the Inspector dock, and set its Left margin to a certain value, say 30, shown in Figure 9-15. This will ensure that there is some space between the top-left edge of the screen and the HBoxContainer.

Figure 9-15. *Moving the label and making it larger*

Creating a Script for the HUD

Now we need to create a simple script for this label for it to be able to change the value as the player's score increases.

1. Select the CanvasLayer in the Scene dock, and then click the new script ![icon] icon. In the Attach Node Script window that pops up, select No Comments in the Template field, and then click the Create button.

2. This will create and open up a script called `CanvasLayer.gd`.

3. If you have used a HBoxContainer for encapsulating the Label nodes, then type in the following script:

```
extends CanvasLayer

var score = 0

func _ready():
            $HboxContainer/ScoreValue.text = String(score)
```

4. In case you haven't used an HBoxContainer node, and if your ScoreValue label is a child of the CanvasLayer node, then type in the following script instead:

```
extends CanvasLayer

var score = 0

func _ready():
            $ScoreValue.text = String(score)
```

The script should look like the one shown earlier if in your node hierarchy the ScoreValue node is a child of CanvasLayer node.

Here, we are creating a variable called `score` and initializing it to 0. Now if you play the scene, you can see that the label will display this score as 0, as it converts the integer value to a `String` value.

Now we need a way to keep track of the score and increase it every time the player collects the coin. In the previous chapter, we used the player script (Player.gd) to keep track of the score, but now we will make the HUD calculate it instead. In Player.gd, we had three functions that increased the score by 1, 5, and 10 when a Gold, Red, or Silver coin was collected respectively. This is shown here:

```
func score_count_gold( ):
    score = score + 1
    print(score)
func score_count_red( ):
    score = score + 5
    print(score)
func score_count_silver( ):
    score = score + 10
    print(score)
```

Let's see how to use custom signals for making the HUD keep track of the score.

Custom Signals for Coin Collection

Follow these steps:

1. Open the player script, Player.gd. Declare three signals at the top of the script as follows:

   ```
   signal gold_coin_collected
   signal red_coin_collected
   signal silver_coin_collected
   ```

   These are customs signals defined by us that we can use, just like other signals.

2. Replace the contents of the score_count_gold(), score_count_red(), and score_count_silver() functions, as shown here:

   ```
   func score_count_gold( ):
       emit_signal("gold_coin_collected")
   ```

```
func score_count_red( ):
    emit_signal("red_coin_collected")

func score_count_silver( ):
    emit_signal("silver_coin_collected")
```

3. Now, open the script for the Gold coin, Gold_coin.gd. Recall how we created the following function in this script:

```
func _on_Gold_coin_body_entered(body):
    body.score_count_gold( )
    queue_free( )
```

This function detects when the player enters the coin and then calls score_count_ gold() declared in Player.gd. This function, score_count_gold(), then emits our custom signal gold_coin_collected every time a Gold coin is collected. Similarly, when a Red coin is collected, the red_coin_collected signal is emitted, and when a Silver coin is collected, the silver_coin_collected signal is emitted.

We can now use these signal to enable the HUD to calculate the total score.

4. Now that we've created a custom signal that is emitted every time the player collects a coin, we need to link it up with the instances of the coins that we have in our Game Level scene (GameLevel.tscn).

5. First, go ahead and delete all extra instances of the coins from the Scene dock, and keep only one instance each of the Gold, Red, and Silver coins. Figure 9-16 shows the Scene dock before and after deleting all the extra coin instances.

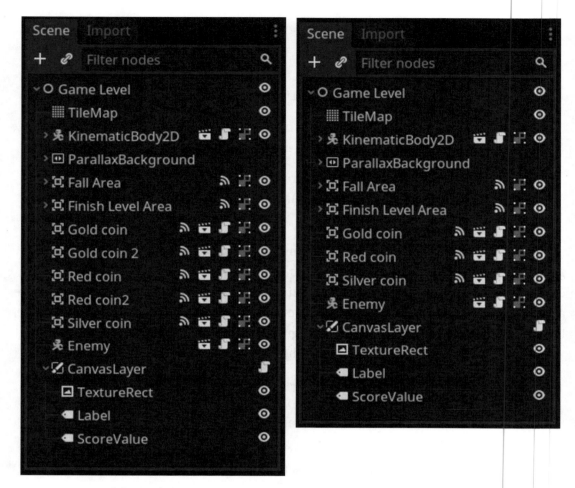

Figure 9-16. *(a) Before deleting extra instances of coins, (b) after deleting extra instances of coins*

6. Now, select the Player node in the Scene dock (In the main game scene GameLevel.tscn) (KinematicBody2D), and open the Node dock next to the Inspector dock. You'll see your custom signals, as shown in Figure 9-17.

Figure 9-17. *Custom signals appear in the Node dock*

7. Double-click gold_coin_collected(), and then select the
    CanvasLayer node in the Connect a Signal to a Method window,
    as shown in Figure 9-18, and click the Connect button.

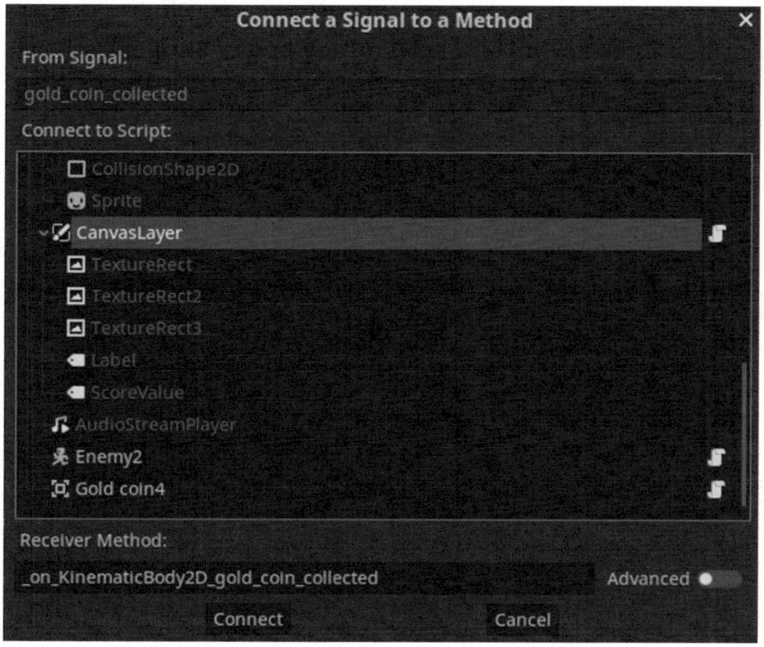

Figure 9-18. *Selecting the CanvasLayer node*

Note   It's important to choose the CanvasLayer script so that the
_on_KinematicBody2D_gold_coin_collected function is created in
CanvasLayer.gd and it can be used for calculating the total score.

---

8.   Once you click the Connect button, the HUD's script,
CanvasLayer.gd, opens, and a function called _on_
KinematicBody2D_gold_coin_collected is created inside it. In
this function, replace the pass with the following lines:

```
score = score + 1
_ready()
```

9.   Next, repeat steps 3 to 5 two more times, once for the Red coins
and another for collecting the silver coins, by selecting the
red_coin_collected() and silver_coin_collected() signals,
respectively.

Your script should now look like the one shown here:

```
extends CanvasLayer

var score = 0

func _ready( ):
    $ScoreValue.text = String(score)

func _on_KinematicBody2D_gold_coin_collected( ):
    score = score + 1
    _ready ( )

func _on_KinematicBody2D_red_coin_collected( ):
    score = score + 5
    _ready ( )

func _on_KinematicBody2D_silver_coin_collected( ):
    score = score + 10
    _ready ( )
```

Note   Recall that if in your node hierarchy, HBoxContainer is a parent of the ScoreValue node, then in under the _ready function, $ScoreValue will be replaced with $HBoxContainer/ScoreValue.

10. Now, go back to the Game scene, GameLevel.tscn. We can duplicate the Gold coin instances to create more Gold coins and place them in our game level. To do so, right-click the Gold coin node (instance) in the Scene dock, and click Duplicate, as shown in Figure 9-19 (or use the keyboard shortcut Ctrl+D).

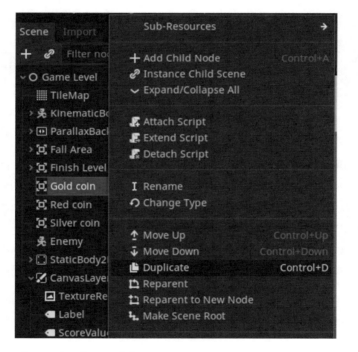

Figure 9-19. *Duplicating the Gold coin instance*

11. This creates a duplicated instance called "Gold coin2" in the Scene dock and copies and pastes the corresponding coin in the workspace, on top of the original gold coin. Move it around and place it next to the first one, as shown in Figure 9-20. We can do this multiple times to get more Gold coins in our game level. Do the same for the other two types of coins, that is, the Red and Silver coins.

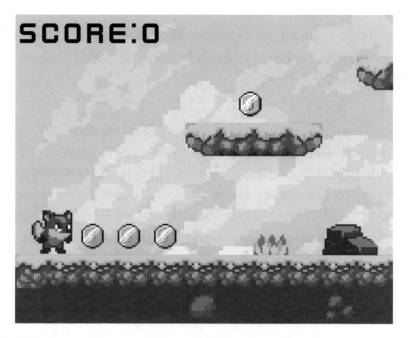

Figure 9-20. *Placing various coins around the game level*

12.   After placing all the coins, play the game scene. Now, every time
the player collects a Gold coin, the score increases by 1. Similarly,
the score increases by 5 every time a Red coin is collected, and by
10 every time a Silver coin is collected. As shown in Figure 9-20,
the score is initially 0. After collecting three Gold coins, the score
increases to 3, as shown in Figure 9-21.

Figure 9-21. *The score becomes 3 after collecting three Gold coins*

Displaying the Player's Lives

We can calculate and display the number of lives that the player has left in a similar way as we displayed the score. We'll display a red heart for every life that the Player has, just below the score in the HUD. Let's see the steps involved.

1. Select the TextureRect node (child node of CanvasLayer) in the Scene dock. Then, drag and drop the image of a heart from the FileSystem dock into the Texture property of the TextureRect node in the Inspector dock, as shown in Figure 9-22.

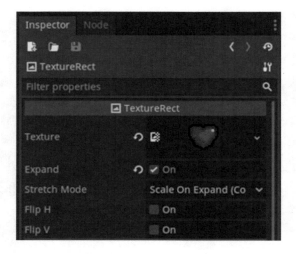

Figure 9-22. *Assigning the image of the heart to the Texture property*

We have used the heart image from the Collectibles & Buttons asset pack designed by Mihika Dhule. You can download it here: `https://mihikad.itch.io/collectibles-buttons`.

Note   If the heart image appears blurry on the workspace, select the image in the FileSystem dock, open the Import tab next to the Scene dock, deselect the Filter property under the Flags field, and click Reimport.

---

2. Move the heart image down and position it below the Score label in the workspace. To make the heart larger in size, select the Expand property of the TextureRect node in the Inspector dock, and then pull on the orange vertices on the TextureRect in the workspace. This is shown in Figure 9-23.

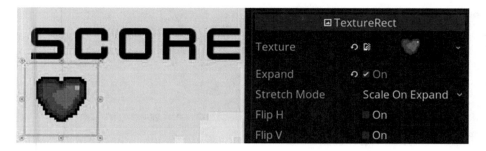

Figure 9-23. *Positioning the heart below the score and making it larger*

3. Now, duplicate the TextureRect node in the Scene dock two more times (Ctrl+D). In the workspace, move and position the three TextureRect nodes next to each other, as shown in Figure 9-24.

Figure 9-24. *Place the TextureRect nodes next to each other*

Note   To make it easier to align these nodes, you can use a container node as their parent, e.g., HBoxContainer. Alternatively, you can enable Smart Snap (Shift+S) to make placement easier.

---

4. Now, open the player script, Player.gd. At the top of the script, declare a variable called lives, initialize it to 3, and declare a custom signal called livescount as follows:

```
var lives = 3
signal livescount
```

5. Create a new function called func hit_enemy(), as follows:

```
func hit_enemy():
          lives = lives -1
          emit_signal("livescount")
```

6. Modify the functions _on_Fall_Area_body_entered and _on_ Finish_Level_Area_body_entered as follows:

```
func _on_Fall_Area_body_entered(body):
          get_tree().change_scene("res://GameOver.tscn")
```

```
func _on_Finish_Level_Area_body_entered(body):
          get_tree().change_scene("res://GameOver.tscn")
```

7. Create a new, temporary Game Over scene by clicking the New Scene ✚ button near the top of the workspace (or navigating to Scene ➤ New Scene from the toolbar at the top left of the interface). In this new scene, add a Control node as the root node by clicking User Interface, and save the scene as GameOver.tscn. This scene will act as a placeholder for the Game Over scene, and we will modify it later in the chapter.

8. Now, head over to the Game Level scene (GameLevel.tscn) and select the KinematicBody2D node (Player node). Next, open the Node dock, and double-click the livescount() signal. This was the custom signal that we created in the player script, Player.gd.

9. In the Connect a Signal to a Method window that pops up, select the CanvasLayer node, and click the Create button. This creates a function called _on_KinematicBody2D_livescount() in the script for the HUD (CanvasLayer.gd).

10. In this script, add the following lines to the _on_ KinematicBody2D_livescount() function:

```
     lives = lives - 1
     _ready()
```

11. At the top of the script, declare a variable called `lives`, and initialize it to 3.

12. Next, modify the _ready() function, as shown next, which shows the final script for the HUD. With these lines of code, we hide one of the hearts on the HUD when the player loses one life (has two lives left); then we hide two hearts when the player loses its second life (has one life left). If the number of lives becomes 0, then we load the Game Over screen.

```
extends CanvasLayer

var score = 0
var lives = 3

func _ready( ):
    $ScoreValue.text = String(score)
    if(lives == 2):
        $TextureRect3.hide( )
    elif(lives == 1):
        $TextureRect3.hide( )
        $TextureRect2.hide( )
    elif(lives == 0):
        get_tree().change_scene("res://GameOver.tscn")

func _on_KinematicBody2D_gold_coin_collected ( ):
    score = score + 1
    _ready ( )

func _on_KinematicBody2D_red_coin_collected ( ):
    score = score + 5
    _ready ( )

func _on_KinematicBody2D_silver_coin_collected ( ):
    score = score + 10
    _ready ( )

func _on_KinematicBody2D_livescount( ):
    lives = lives - 1
    __ready ( )
```

13. Now, go to the enemy scene, Enemy.gd, and replace the contents of the function _on_CollisionChecker_body_entered with the line shown here:

```
func _on_CollisionChecker_body_entered(body):
    body.hit_enemy( )
```

Turning the Player Red on Getting Hurt

Now, we can make the player turn transparent red in color every time it runs into the enemy and loses a life! We will turn it red in color as soon as it hits the enemy and then, one second later, change its color back to normal. This gives the effect of the player getting "hurt."

1. Open the Player scene Player.tscn, and add a child node called Timer as a child of KinematicBody2D (root node).

2. Next, select the Timer node in the Scene dock. You'll see in the Inspector dock that the default wait time is set to 1 second. We can change this according to the time we want to wait before changing the color back to normal after turning it red.

3. Open the Node dock next to the Inspector dock. Double-click the timeout() signal; then click the Connect button in the Connect a Signal to a Method window.

4. This creates a function called _on_Timer_timeout() in the Player script, Player.gd. In this function, type the following line:

```
set_modulate(Color(1,1,1,1))
```

This line is used for changing the color of the player. It's in the form set_modulate(Color(R,G,B,A)), where R stands for Red, G for Green, B for Blue, and A for the Alpha value. A value of 1 for all of them means that all the colors are present equally; hence, there is no change in color. We can change the color by modifying one or all of the first three values and make it more transparent by modifying the last (alpha) value.

5. Modify the function _hit_enemy, as shown here:

```
func hit_enemy( ):
    lives = lives - 1
    emit_signal("livescount")
    set_modulate(Color(1,0.3,0.3,0.6))
    $Timer.start( )
```

By doing this, we are setting the R (Red value) to the maximum, while reducing the G (Green) and B (Blue) color content, which gives our character a reddish hue whenever it collides with the enemy. As shown in Figure 9-25, the first time the player collides with the enemy, it loses one life and turns red in color. After a wait time of one second, the player's color goes back to normal.

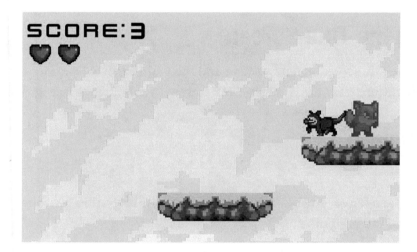

Figure 9-25. The player turns red on colliding with the enemy

Once you design the Win screen of the game and save it as WinScreen.tscn, you can replace GameOver.tscn with WinScreen.tscn in the function _on_Finish_Level_Area_body_entered( ). This will load Win screen once the player finishes the game level.

TRY IT!

Creating the Game HUD

1. Import HUD components such as custom fonts and icons to represent the player health (such as hearts) into the project.

2. Design a HUD to calculate and display the player's score and health.

3. Give the player four lives at the start of the game, and modify the Player, Enemy, and HUD scripts to make the player lose one life on colliding with the enemy.

4. Make the player turn blue for two seconds after colliding with the enemy.

Creating the Title Screen

We'll create the title screen in a new scene and then add various UI nodes for the background, buttons, text, and images. Let's start with creating the background.

Background

Follow these steps:

1. Create a new scene by clicking the New Scene ⊞ button near the top of the 2D toolbar.

2. In the Scene dock, click the User Interface option shown in Figure 9-26 (a) to create a Control node as the root node of the scene, as seen in Figure 9-26 (b). All the UI elements will be child nodes of this Control node.

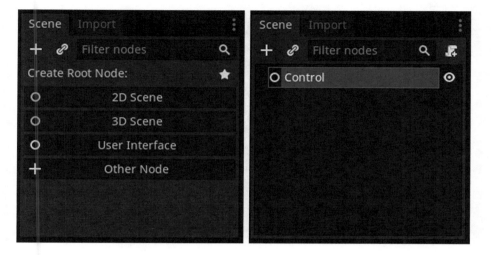

Figure 9-26. *(a) Creating a User Interface node as a root node, (b) creating a Control node*

3. In the Scene dock, select the Control node and click the ➕ button to add a child node to it. In the Create New Node window, search for the ColorRect node and click the Create button. You can see this in Figure 9-27.

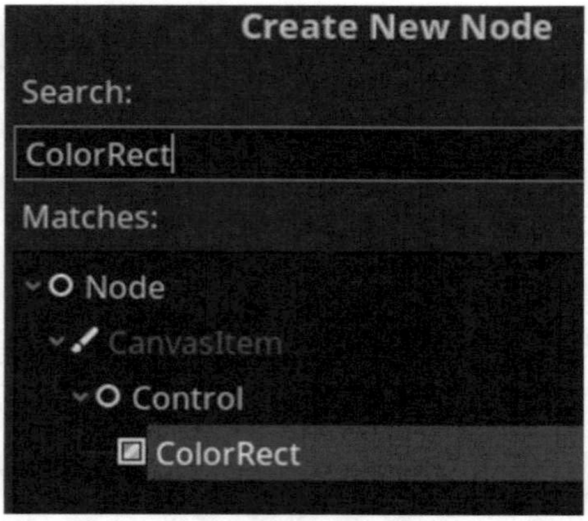

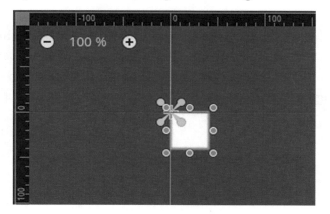

Figure 9-27. *Creating a ColorRect node*

As shown in Figure 9-28, a white rectangle with orange vertices is created on the 2D workspace, with its top-left corner coinciding with the origin.

Figure 9-28. *The ColorRect is created near the origin*

4. Select the ColorRect node in the Scene dock, and expand the Margin property in the Inspector dock. Then, set the all the margins (Left, Top, Right, and Bottom) to 0. Expand the Anchor tab, and set the Bottom and Right Anchors settings to 1. This is shown in Figure 9-29. This ensures that the ColorRect will always cover the entire game window, no matter what size it is.

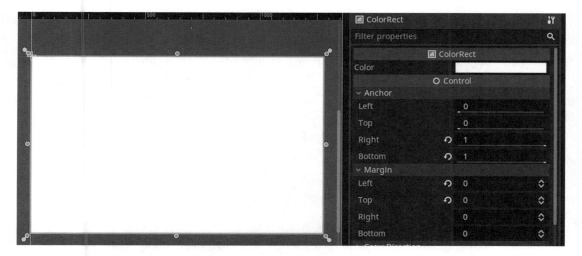

Figure 9-29. *Setting the margins and anchors of the ColorRect*

5.   To change the color of the rectangle, click the white rectangle
      next to the Color property in the Inspector dock, as shown in
      Figure 9-29. A Color Picker window pops up where you can select
      a particular color. Use the sliders to pick a color that you want to
      set the Background to, such as the one shown in Figure 9-30.

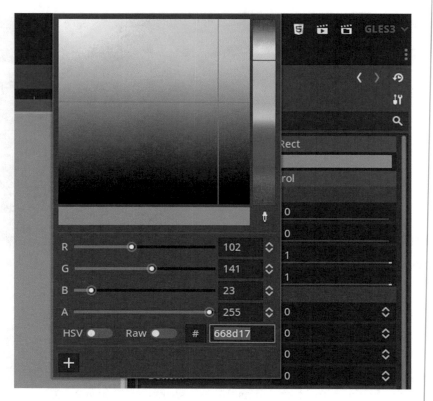

Figure 9-30. *Picking a color for the background using the ColorPicker*

Note   You can also find a particular color in the Color Picker window by typing in its particular hex value or by adjusting the R (Red), G (Green), and B (Blue) sliders. The A, that is, "Alpha" value slider, can be adjusted to change the transparency of the color.

---

6. Click anywhere in the workspace to exit the Color Picker.

Adding Text

Next, let's add the title of our game.

1. Previously, we saw how to add a UI component called HBoxContainer for keeping our labels aligned with the game window. Let's add a similar component called CenterContainer for aligning our title with the top of the screen. Select the Control node and then add a CenterContainer node as its child. You can either search for the CenterContainer in the Create New Node window, or navigate to it under this path: Node ➤ CanvasItem ➤ Control ➤ Container ➤ CenterContainer.

2. Now, select the CenterContainer in the Scene dock, click the green Layout icon on the 2D toolbar, and select the Center Top option, as shown in Figure 9-31.

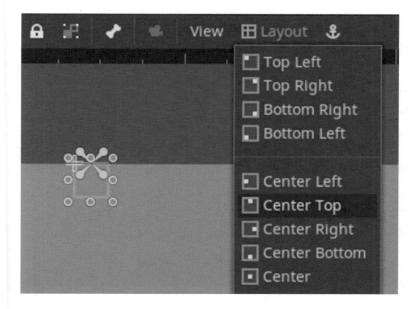

Figure 9-31. *Aligning the Center container to the center top of the ColorRect*

3. Next, expand the Anchor property of the CenterContainer, and set the Left and Right Anchors to 0 and 1, respectively, and the Top and Bottom anchors to 0, as shown in Figure 9-32.

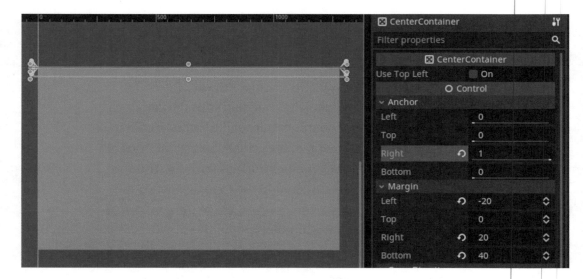

Figure 9-32. *Setting the anchors of the ColorRect*

4. Select the CenterContainer node in the Scene dock and then add a label as its child node. You can either search for the Label node in the Create New Node window, or navigate to it under this path: Node ➤ CanvasItem ➤ Control ➤ Label. Then, expand the Custom Fonts tab, and click the small arrow next to the empty Font property. Click Load, select the saved Font Resource from the Open a File window, and click Open. If you haven't saved any font resource, you can create a new one (Select New DynamicFont under the Font property of Custom Fonts). Then, click on the DynamicFont, and drag and drop a font file (.ttf) from the FileSystem dock into the Font Data field in the Inspector dock.

5. Now, with the DynamicFont option selected (it appears blue), expand the Settings tab and change the Size and Outline Color properties. This changes how your title will appear on the top of the screen. You can change the Font Color property under the Custom Colors tab.

6. Type the text you want the label to display, that is, the title of the game, in the Text field of the Inspector dock (e.g., My Game). Your title should now appear in the ColorRect, as shown in Figure 9-33.

Note that the Display Window size has been set to 1280 x 800 in Figure 9-33. You can change the window size by navigating to Project ➤ Project Settings ➤ Display ➤ Window, then changing the Width and Height properties under Size.

Figure 9-33. *The game title is created in the workspace*

Adding a Panel

Next, let's add a colored panel as a small background for the buttons.

1. Select the Control node and add a Panel node as its child. You can navigate to this path: Node ➤ CanvasItem ➤ Control ➤ Panel. Now, with the Panel node selected in the Scene dock, click the green Layout button on the 2D toolbar and choose the Bottom Wide option, as shown in Figure 9-34.

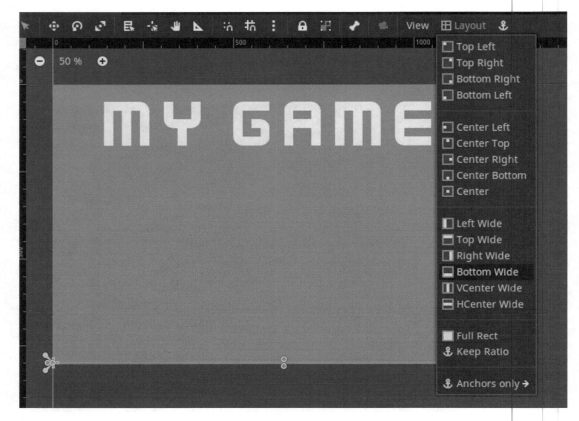

Figure 9-34. *Setting the layout of the panel as Bottom Wide*

2. Then, expand the panel upward by pulling its top middle orange
    vertex, until the panel covers the lower part of the screen. Next,
    select the green Layout button again on the 2D toolbar, and select
    the Keep Ratio option. This sets the anchors to all the vertices of
    the panel, as shown in Figure 9-35. You can also manually set the
    anchor values as shown.

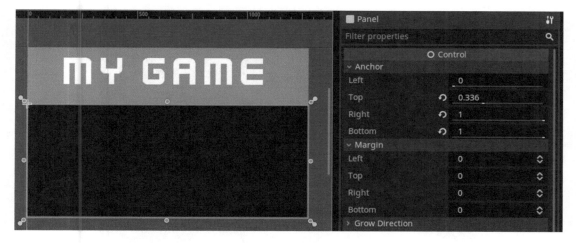

Figure 9-35. *Expanding the panel upward*

3. To change the background color of the panel, expand the Custom Styles tab in the Inspector dock, and then click the drop-down menu next to the Panel property and select the New StyleBoxFlat New StyleBoxFlat option, as shown in Figure 9-36.

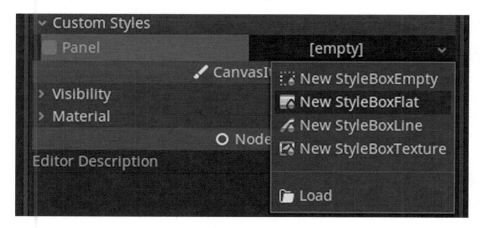

Figure 9-36. *Creating a new custom style called StyleBoxFlat*

4. Next, click StyleBoxFlat StyleBoxFlat that appears in the field next to the Panel property. On doing so, the Preview, Bg (Background) Color, Draw Center, and Corner Detail properties are visible, as shown in Figure 9-37.

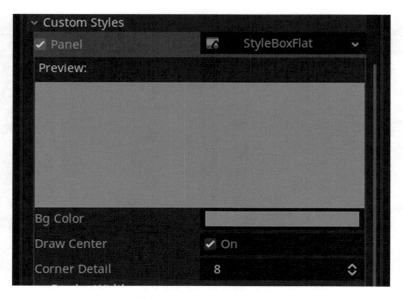

Figure 9-37. *The properties of the StyleBoxFlat custom-styled panel*

5. To change the background color of the panel, click the gray
    rectangle next to the Bg Color property, which will open a
    ColorPicker window. Pick a color in this window, and the color
    will automatically be assigned to the panel in the workspace. For
    example, as shown in the Figure 9-38, we've picked a dark green
    color for the panel.

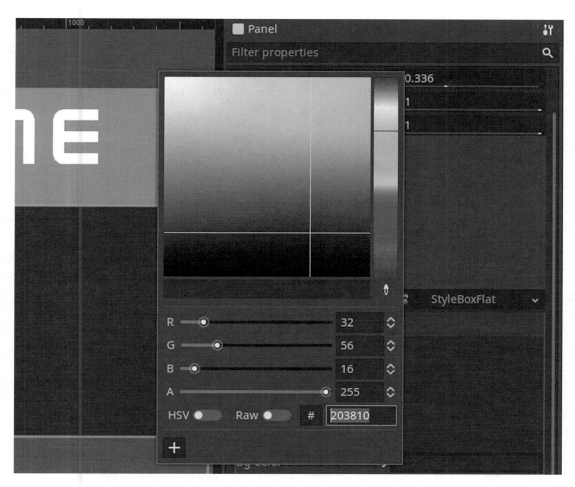

Figure 9-38. *Choosing a color for the panel*

6. If you want to give the panel rounded edges, expand the Corner Radius property under Custom Styles, and adjust the values of Top Left, Top Right, Bottom Right, and Bottom Left fields. The higher the value, the more rounded the corresponding corner of the panel will be.

Adding Buttons

Now, let's add some buttons to the title screen!

1. Select the Control node in the Scene dock, and then add a button as its child node. See Figure 9-39.

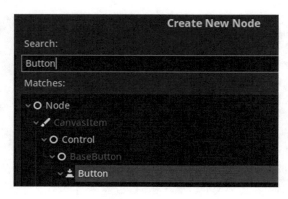

Figure 9-39. *Creating a Button node*

2. Now, select the Button node in the Scene dock, move it to the center of the screen, and make it larger by dragging on its edges. Then, click the green Layout button on the 2D toolbar and select Keep Ratio. This makes the anchors appear on all the corners of the button, as shown in Figure 9-40. You can enable Smart Snap and Grid Snap options (on the toolbar) to make placement easier.

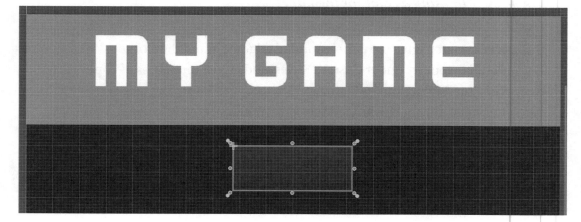

Figure 9-40. *Positioning and resizing the button*

3. Now, let's assign a font for the text that the button will display. With the Button node selected in the Scene dock, expand the Custom Fonts property in the Inspector dock. Click the small arrow in the field next to the Font property, and select the New DynamicFont 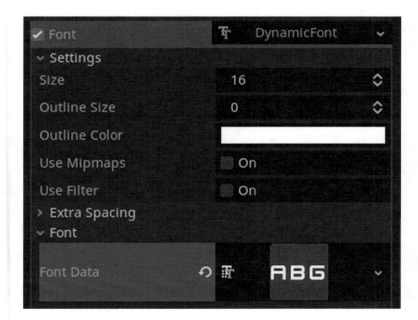 New DynamicFont option.

4. Now, click the DynamicFont DynamicFont option next to Font, as shown in Figure 9-41. This opens up the Settings, Extra Spacing, Font, and Resource properties.

5. As shown in Figure 9-41, expand the Font and Settings properties. In the "empty" field next to Font Data, drag and drop the imported font, e.g., Kenny Future.ttf from the FileSystem dock. Now, the text on our button will have this font. You can change various properties of the font such as its Size, Outline Size (thickness of colored-outline), and Outline Color from the Settings menu shown.

Figure 9-41. *Expanding the Settings and Font properties of the Custom Fonts tab*

6. Type in the name of the first button, e.g., Play, in the Text property in the inspector. This text will appear on the button in the workspace. Make the text larger by increasing the Size property under the Settings of the DynamicFont (under Custom Fonts). To make the button transparent so that only the text is visible, turn on the Flat property, as shown in Figure 9-42.

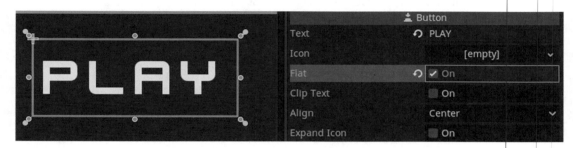

Figure 9-42. *Typing Play in the Text field*

7. You can also give the text an outline color by clicking the white rectangle next to the Outline Color property under the Settings tab and then picking a color in the ColorPicker. Then, make the colored outline visible by increasing the Outline Size property. As shown in Figure 9-43, a light green outline with a size of 3 is assigned for the Button text.

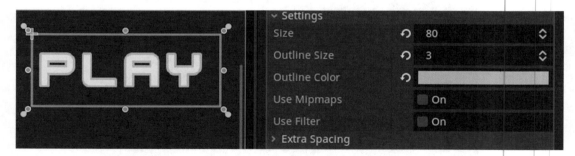

Figure 9-43. *Setting a light-green outline color for the button's font*

8. To create another button, we can just copy the first one. Select the Button node in the Scene dock and then click Ctrl+D on your keyboard. This copies and pastes a button on top of the original Play button in the workspace. Let's go ahead and repeat

this three times for creating three more buttons. Then, arrange them in a vertical line, as shown in Figure 9-44. Rename the four button nodes in the Scene dock accordingly, such as PlayButton, HowToPlayButton, Settings, and Quit.

Figure 9-44. *Four buttons are created*

9. To change the text displayed by a button in the workspace, select its corresponding node in the Scene dock, and then type in the name in the **Text** field in the Inspector dock. As shown in Figure 9-44, we've named the four buttons in the workspace as Play, How to Play, Settings, and Quit. Note that you might need to set the Keep Ratio property (under the Layout button on the toolbar) again for each of the new buttons.

There are many properties that you can set for a button in the Inspector. Here are some examples:

- *Disabled*: Turning it on makes the button unclickable.

- *Toggle Mode*: This makes the button change its state from pressed to unpressed (and vice versa) every time it is clicked.

- *Button Mask*: This controls which mouse button (left, right, middle) can be used to click the button.

- *Pressed*: If this property is turned on, the button is considered to be pressed down by default.

- *Action Mode*: This is used to determine when the button is considered clicked, meaning during the release of the mouse button or when it is just clicked (before its release).

10. We can also make the font on the button change color every time it is clicked or when we hover over it using our mouse. Click the button in the workspace (or select its node in the Scene dock) and then select the Font Color Hover and Font Color Pressed properties under the Custom Colors tab to set each respective property. To change the color, click the black rectangle and choose a color. This is shown in Figure 9-45. We can do this for all of the buttons by repeating this step for all of them.

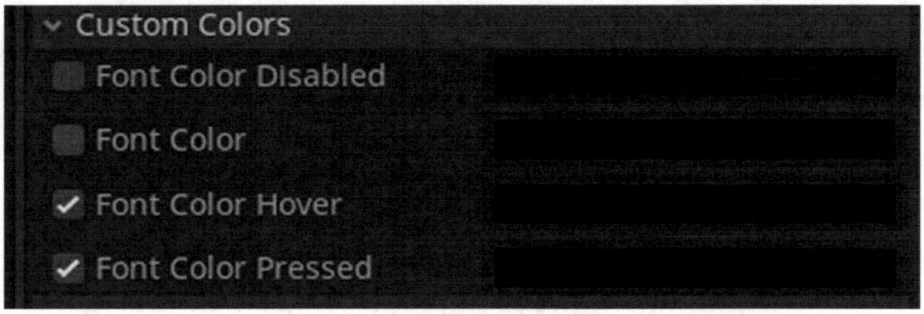

Figure 9-45. *Set the Font Color Hover and Font Color Pressed properties*

Note   The "Hover" or "Pressed" color can be changed by clicking the black rectangle next to the corresponding properties and then choosing the color in the ColorPicker window.

11. Save the scene (Ctrl+S or Ctrl+Shift+S), giving it a suitable name such as TitleScreen.tscn.

12. Now, play the scene by clicking the Play Scene button (F6). When you hover over each button, the color of the font changes to the one set for the Font Color Hover property, as shown in Figure 9-46.

Figure 9-46. *On hovering over the button, the Hover Color is visible*

Attaching a Script to a Button

If you click any of the buttons in the scene that's playing, nothing happens! This is because we need to tell Godot what to do when the button is pressed. For this, we need to add a script to the button. Let's start with the Play button.

1. Select the Play button's node in the Scene dock (PlayButton), and click the icon to attach a script to it.

2. In the Attach Node Script window, set Template to No Comments to remove the default comments in the script, and then click the Create button. As shown in Figure 9-47, the script is saved after the node name—PlayButton.gd.

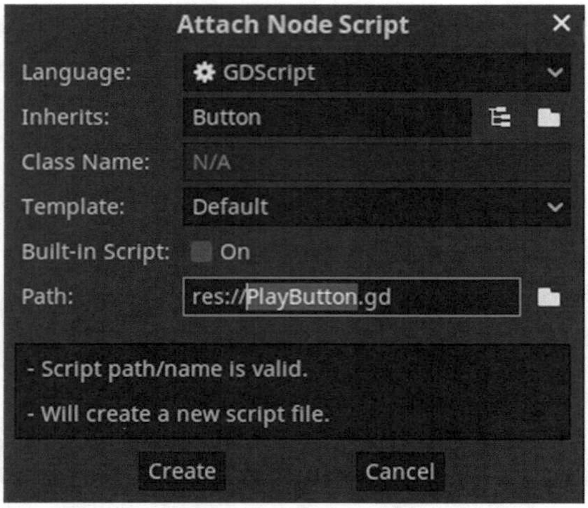

Figure 9-47. *Creating a script for the Play button called PlayButton.gd*

3. Once the script opens, we can delete func _ready(), and pass since it is not needed.

4. Now, in the Scene dock, select the PlayButton node and click the Node dock next to the Inspector dock. Double-click the pressed() signal, and in the Connect a Signal to a Method window, click the Connect button. You can see this in Figure 9-48. This creates a function called _on_PlayButton_pressed in the script PlayButton.gd.

Figure 9-48. *Connecting the pressed() signal to the script PlayButton.gd*

5. In this function, replace the "`pass`" with the following line:

```
get_tree().change_scene("res://GameLevel.tscn")
```

The code should look as follows:

```
extends Button

func _on_PlayButton_pressed():
    get_tree().change_scene("res://GameLevel.tscn")
```

This will ensure that when the play button is clicked, the main game level, GameLevel.tscn, will be loaded.

6. We can implement the scripts for the other buttons after connecting the pressed() signal to them in a similar way. For example, if we have a game scene designed for "How To Play" called HowToPlay.tscn, we can connect the pressed() signal to the HowToPlayButton node's script. Then, in this button's script, we can type in the following line of code:

```
extends Button

func _on_HowToPlayButton_pressed():
        get_tree().change_scene("res://GameLevel.tscn")
```

7. Similarly, after connecting the QuitButton node to the pressed()
    signal, a function called _on_QuitButton_pressed is created
    in the script QuitButton.gd. Since we want to exit the game on
    pressing the Quit button on the title screen, we can type in the
    following line of code in the _on_QuitButton_pressed function:

```
get_tree().quit()
```

The script for the Quit button should look like the one shown here:

```
extends Button

func _on_QuitButton_pressed():
        get_tree().quit()
```

As shown in Figure 9-49, we have our title screen!

Figure 9-49. *The main title screen*

Now that we have our title screen, we need to set this as the main scene in the game so that this scene is the first one that the player sees once he starts the game. To do that, right-click `TitleScreen.tscn` in the FileSystem dock, and select the ⬚ Set As Main Scene Set As Main Scene option.

Adding an Image to the Title Screen

We can enhance our title screen further by adding images to it! Let's see how to do that.

1. Select the Control node in the Scene dock and click the ➕ button to add a child node. Search for the *TextureRect* node in the Create New Node window, and click the Create button.

2. The TextureRect is created on the workspace near the origin. We can assign an image to it by selecting the TextureRect node in the Scene dock and then dragging and dropping an image from the FileSystem dock into the Texture field in the Inspector dock.

3. An example of a title screen with the images is shown in Figure 9-50.

Figure 9-50. *Final title screen with images*

4. Make sure to set the correct anchors for each image, e.g., by setting the Keep Ratio layout option that we saw earlier.

The Game Over Screen

Previously, we created an empty scene called GameOver.tscn, with the Control node as a placeholder. We can design the Game Over screen in this scene, in the same way that we designed the Main Title Screen. Figure 9-51 shows an example of a Game Over screen.

Figure 9-51. *The Game Over screen*

TRY IT!

Designing the Game GUI

1. Design the title screen and Game Over screen with the help of a ColorRect, Buttons, Panels, and Images.

2. Create various buttons for playing and quitting the game, accessing the Settings page, How to Play Screen, etc.

Adding Music to the Game

Godot supports three types of music file formats: `.wav`, `.ogg`, and `.mp3`. We can download music and sound effect files from online sources in any of these three formats. To import the music/sound files into the Godot project, you can drag and drop it into the FileSystem dock from any file on your computer. Now, let's add music to the title screen.

1. Open the title screen scene, `TitleScreen.tscn`.

2. Select the Control node in the Scene dock and click the ➕ button to create a child node. Search for *AudioStreamPlayer* in the Create New Node window and click the Create button. You can see this in Figure 9-52.

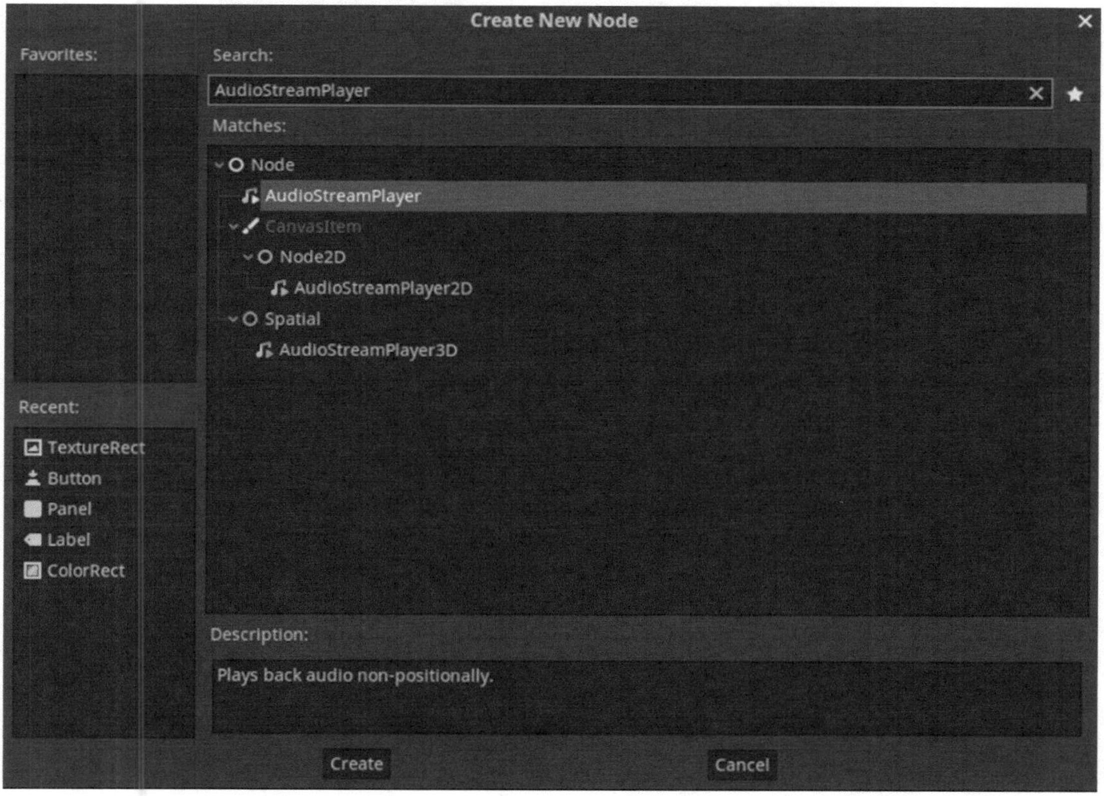

Figure 9-52. *Creating an AudioStreamPlayer node*

The AudioStreamPlayer gets added to the node hierarchy as a child of the Control node.

3. With the AudioStreamPlayer node selected in the Scene dock, drag and drop the music file (`.ogg` file) from the FileSystem dock into the Stream property in the Inspector dock.

4. Next, set the AutoPlay property to On, as shown in Figure 9-53. Now, when you play this scene, the music will automatically play for the title screen on playing the game scene. To stop playing the audio continously in a loop, select the file in the FileSystem dock, open the Import dock next to the Scene dock, uncheck Loop, and click on Reimport.

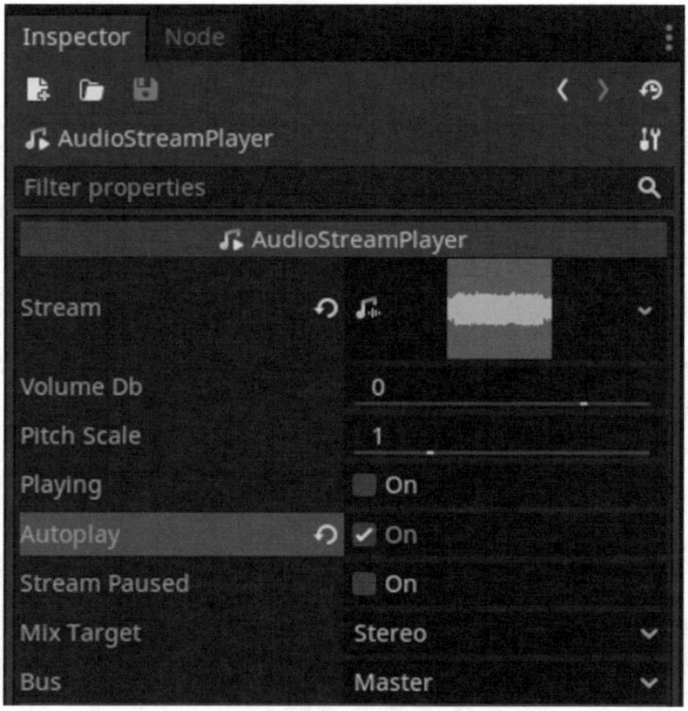

Figure 9-53. Dragging and dropping the music file into the Stream property in the Inspector dock

---

Note   The volume and pitch of the music can be changed by adjusting the Volume Db and Pitch Scale properties in the Inspector dock.

Adding Sound Effects

Sound effects can enhance the game, making it more delightful to play! We can play sound effects during every time the player jumps, collects a coin, defeats the enemy, finishes the level, or loses the game.

Let's see how to add sound effects for jumping and collecting a coin to our game.

Jumping

Let's add a sound effect that plays every time the player jumps.

1. Open the player scene (`Player.tscn`) by double-clicking it in the FileSystem dock.

2. Select the root node of the scene (KinematicBody2D) and click the ➕ button to add a child node. Search for *AudioStreamPlayer* in the Create New Node window, and click the Create button.

3. The AudioStreamPlayer node is created as a child of KinematicBody2D, as shown in Figure 9-54.

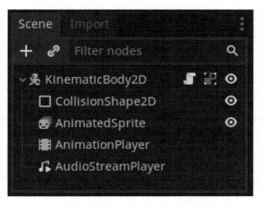

Figure 9-54. *The AudioStreamPlayer is created as a child of KinematicBody2D*

4. Select the AudioStreamPlayer node in the Scene dock, and then drag and drop the sound effect from the FileSystem into the Stream property in the Inspector dock. Since we don't want the sound to play continuously on a loop, let's disable looping. Select the sound in the FileSystem dock, then under the Import Settings next to the Scene dock, uncheck Loop and click the Reimport button.

5. Now, open the Payer script (Player.gd), and, within the `Input.is_action_just_pressed("Jump")` and `is_on_floor()` statement, after the line `$AnimatedSprite.play("jump")`, type in the following line:

```
$AudioStreamPlayer.play()
```

Your `_physics_process(_delta)` function should look like the one shown here:

```
func _physics_process(_delta):
    if Input.is_action_just_pressed("jump") and is_on_floor():
        velocity.y = -1000
        $AnimatedSprite.play("jump")
        $AudioStreamPlayer.play( )
    if Input.is_action_pressed("left_arrow"):
        velocity.x = -300
        $AnimatedSprite.play("run")
        $AnimatedSprite.flip_h = true
    if Input.is_action_pressed("right_arrow"):
        velocity.x = 300
        $AnimatedSprite.play("run")
        $AnimatedSprite.flip_h = false
    else:
        $AnimatedSprite.play("idle")
    if not is_on_floor_( ):
        $AnimatedSprite.play("jump")
```

Coin Collected

Follow these steps:

1. Open the scene of one of the coins, e.g., Gold_coin.tscn. In the Scene dock, select the root node (Gold coin), and click the ➕ button to add a child node. Search for AudioStreamPlayer in the Create New Node window, and click the Create button.

2. The AudioStreamPlayer is then created as a child of the root node and appears in the Scene dock. Double-click it, and rename it to CoinCollectSound, as shown in Figure 9-55.

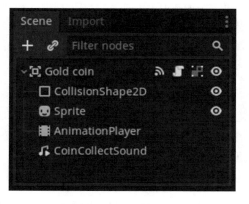

Figure 9-55. *Renaming the AudioStreamPlayer to CoinCollectSound*

Now, with the CoinCollectSound node selected in the Scene dock, drag and drop the sound effect (e.g., `CoinCollect.ogg`) into the Stream property in the Inspector dock.

3. Next, open the script for the Gold Coin (`Gold_coin.gd`) by double-clicking it in the FileSystem dock.

4. In the function _on_Gold_coin_body_entered, add the following line:

```
$CoinCollectSound.play()
```

Your code should look like the one shown here:

```
extends Area2D

func _ready( ):
    $AnimationPlayer.play("Rotate_Coin")

func _on_Gold_coin_body_entered(body):
    $CoinCollectSound.play( )
    body.score_count_gold( )
    queue_free( )
```

But now if you play the game scene, you'll notice that the sound doesn't play when you collect the Gold coin! This is because the line queue_free() deletes the coin object before you can play the sound!

We can fix this by adding a short animation to the coin before deleting it, which gives the sound some time to play. We'll make the coin move up and down, that is, effectively "bounce" in position for a short while before disappearing when the player collects it. Let's see how to do that.

1. In the same scene (Gold_coin.tscn), select the root node (Gold coin), and click the ➕ button to add a child node. In the Create New Node window, search for *AnimationPlayer* and click the Create button. This gets added to the node hierarchy as AnimationPlayer2, as shown in Figure 9-56.

Figure 9-56. *Creating a second AnimationPlayer for the coin bounce animation*

2. When you click the AnimationPlayer2 node in the Scene dock, the Animation panel should open up at the bottom of the interface. Click the Animation button as shown in the Figure 9-57, and select the New ▊New option to create a new animation track.

Figure 9-57. *Clicking the Animation button and selecting the New option for creating a new track*

3. In the Create New Animation window that pops up, enter the animation name such as **coin_bounce**, and click the OK button.

4. Change the timescale next to the ⏱ icon to 1 second, and make sure that the blue marker is at the 0-second position, as shown in Figure 9-58.

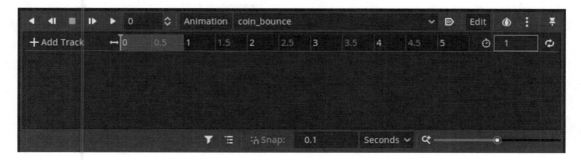

Figure 9-58. *Changing the timescale to 1 second*

5. Now, since we will be creating an animation for the coin's sprite, select the Sprite node in the Scene dock. This will show all the properties in the Inspector docks that we can animate. For making the coin bounce, we will animate its Position property.

6. Under the Transform tab in the Inspector dock, click the key 🔑 icon next to the Position x and y values.

7. A window pops up asking you for confirmation to create a new track for the Position property. Click the Create button. A key is inserted at the 0th second position on the timeline, as shown in Figure 9-59.

Figure 9-59. *The key is inserted at the 0 seconds position in the timeline*

8. Now, move the blue cursor to the 0.5 seconds position by clicking the line near 0.5 on the timeline, as shown in Figure 9-60.

Figure 9-60. *Moving the blue cursor to the 0.5-second position*

9. Select the Sprite node in the Scene dock, and change the y value of the Position property to -15, to move the coin's sprite slightly upward in the workspace. Then, click the key icon next to the Position property to add another key at the 0.5 second mark on the timeline, as shown in Figure 9-61.

Figure 9-61. *Adding another key with a different y position at the 0.5-second position*

10. Now, move the blue marker to the 1-second mark on the timeline. Select the Sprite node in the Scene dock again, and this time, change the y value of the Property back to 0. Then, click the key icon to add this position as a key to the timeline, as shown in Figure 9-62.

Figure 9-62. *Adding a third key at the 1-second position*

We now have our coin bounce animation, where the coin bobs up and down. Next, we need to modify the coin's script (Gold_coin.gd) for playing this animation.

11. Open Gold_coin.gd, and delete the line queue_free() from the function _on_Gold_coin_body_entered. In the same function, type in the following line:

```
$AnimationPlayer2.play("coin_bounce")
```

Your script should look like the one shown here:

```
extends Area2D

func _ready( ):
    $AnimationPlayer.play("Rotate_Coin")

func _on_Gold_coin_body_entered(body):
    $CoinCollectedSound.play( )
    $AnimationPlayer.play("coin_bounce")
    body.score_count_gold( )
```

Now, this coin animation will play every time the player collects a Gold coin. Since we want the coin to disappear after the bounce animation stops playing, we can use a signal to do that.

12. Select the AnimationPlayer2 node in the Scene dock and then
    open the Node dock next to the Inspector dock. Double-click the
    animation_finished signal, and a Connect a Signal to a Method
    window will pop up, as shown in Figure 9-63.

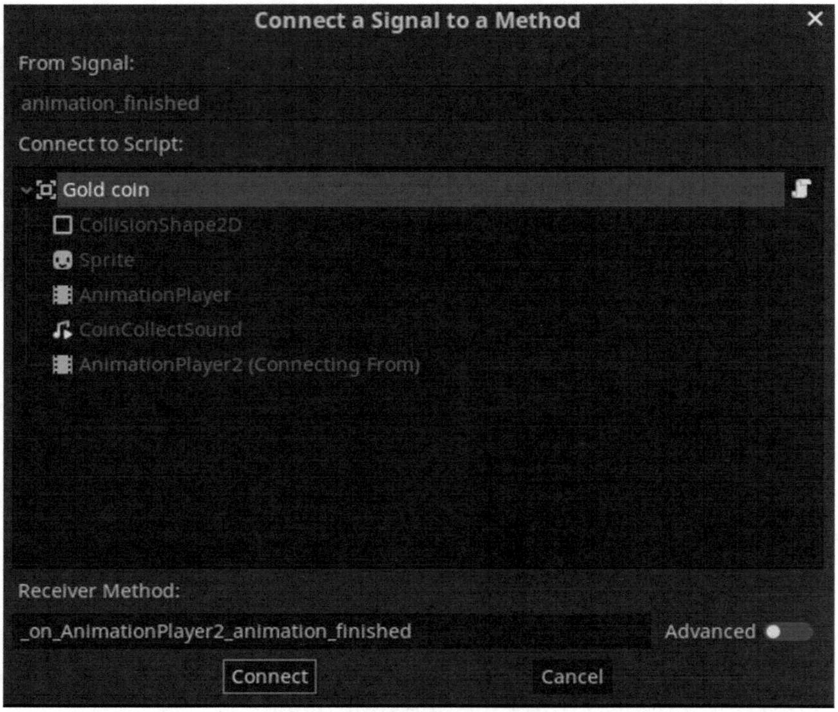

Figure 9-63. *Connecting the animation_finished signal to the Gold_coin.gd*

13. Click the Connect button, and a new function is created in the
    Gold coin's script (Gold_coin.gd) called _on_AnimationPlayer2_
    animation_finished. In this function, replace the "pass" with
    queue_free(). Your script should look like the one shown here:
    (We can remove the custom collected_coin signal from the script)

```
extends Area2D
```

```
func _ready( ):
     $AnimationPlayer.play("Rotate_Coin")
```

```
func _on_Gold_coin_body_entered(body):
     $CoinCollectSound.play( )
```

```
$AnimationPlayer2.play("coin_bounce")
body.score_count_gold()

func_on_AnimationPlayer2_animation_finished(coin_bounce):
    queue_free( )
```

If you now play the main game scene by clicking the ▣ button, every time the player collects a Gold coin, the coin will bounce up and down for 1 second and then disappear. At the same time, we'll hear the CoinCollect sound effect. We can apply the same procedure for other coins and collectibles in our game (e.g., Silver coin and Red coin).

There's still one issue—if the player goes back into the coin when the coin animation is playing, the player can collect the same coin multiple times! We can solve this in many ways—one way is to make the coin animation last for a very short time (by changing the animation duration).

TRY IT!

Adding Music and Sound Effects

1. Import music and sound effect files into your project.

2. Add music to the Title screen and game level.

3. Add sound effects for jumping and collecting a coin.

Key Takeaways

In this chapter, we used Godot's GUI components to design various game screens, such as the main title screen and the Game Over screen. We saw how to add a colored background, buttons, panels, and images to a scene, and we created text with custom fonts. With the help of imported fonts and a heart image/icon, we created a HUD to calculate and display the player's score, as well as the remaining lives after enemy collision. Further, we saw how to add music and sound effects to different scenes in the game.

CHAPTER 10

Publishing Your Game

This chapter wraps up the beginning of our game development journey with Godot. We'll learn about key features that can enhance our game, such as a global variable system for keeping track of the player score and lives, a fireball system for shooting enemies, and touchscreen buttons for mobile games. We'll walk through the steps for exporting our game for three platforms: mobile (Android), PC (Windows), and browser (HTML5). Finally, you will look at some exciting ways to publish and monetize your game.

You finally did it! You created your very first 2D platformer in Godot! You've learned so much, including animating the character, designing the game world using TileMaps, adding enemies that can hurt the player, and adding different coins that the player can collect. We created a title screen and a heads-up display (HUD) for our game that calculated and displayed the total score as well as the number of lives the player has left. We also made the game even more fun to play by adding music and cool sound effects!

Now it's time for you to share your game for the world to see. We'll soon explore the techniques for exporting your game to various platforms, such as PC (Windows), mobile (Android), and browser (HTML).

But first, let's look at some possible ways you can upgrade your game to enhance the player's experience.

Game Enhancements

The process of designing and developing a game is iterative—you can always find something to fix or improve! That's the reason why many developers often release updates and patches even after the game comes out in the market. Let's see some updates we can make for our game.

323

© Maithili Dhule 2022
M. Dhule, *Beginning Game Development with Godot*, https://doi.org/10.1007/978-1-4842-7455-2_10

Creating Global Variables

In the previous chapters, we designed a single level of our platformer. You saw how to reload the current game level or go to another game screen (such as a Game Over screen) if the player fell off a cliff or reached the end of the level. But in a real platformer, we might have multiple levels, and we will want to keep track of player variables such as the total score and the number of lives left throughout the game. In such a case, the current values of the score and lives should be carried over from one level to the next (or updated accordingly during the reload of the current game level).

This can be achieved through the concept of singletons and autoloads. Since we want the variables `score` and `lives` to be common across all the scenes of the game, we can create a single global script for storing and accessing their values throughout the game. Let's see how to implement a global variable system.

1. Right-click near the blank space at the bottom of your FileSystem dock and click the New Script 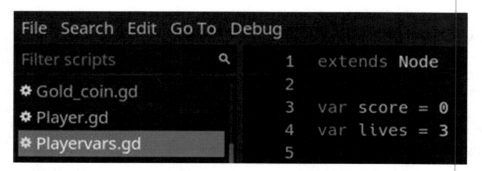 option. In the Create Script window, name this script `Playervars.gd`, and then click the Create button.

2. Double-click on the script in the FileSystem dock. Then, modify the script so that it looks like the one shown here:

```
extends Node

var score = 0
var lives = 3
```

We have declared two variables called `score` and `lives` and initialized them to 0 and 3, respectively. Here, `score` represents the player's total score, and `lives` represents the number of lives left. See Figure 10-1.

Figure 10-1. *Creating a new script called Playervars.gd*

3. Click the File tab shown in Figure 10-1, and click Save (keyboard shortcut Ctrl+Alt+S).

4. Now, navigate to Project ➤ Project Settings from the toolbar at the top of the interface, and open the AutoLoad tab shown in Figure 10-2.

5. Click the file ▣ icon next to the Path: field, and select Playervars.gd in the Open a File window. As shown in Figure 10-2, the path to the script gets added to the **Path** field, and its name, Playervars, is assigned to the **Node Name** field.

Figure 10-2. *Autoloading the Playervars.gd script*

6. Click the Add button next to the Node Name field. Your Project Settings should now look like Figure 10-3. Make sure that under the Singleton field, the Enable field is checked. We've created a Singleton called **Playervars**, which will be "autoloaded" for every scene in the game. This means that our Playervars.gd script can be accessed from any scene in the project using the node name **Playervars**. Close the Project Settings.

Project Settings (project.godot)			✕

General   Input Map   Localization   **AutoLoad**   Plugins   GDNative

Path: 📁 Node Name: Add

Name	Path	Singleton	
Playervars	res://Playervars.gd	✔ Enable	📁 ↑ ↓ 🗑

Close

Figure 10-3. *Adding Playervars to the AutoLoad list and enabling Singleton*

7. Now, open CanvasLayer.gd, the script we created for the HUD in the main game scene. In this script, delete the declarations for the score and lives variables at the top.

8. In the rest of the script, replace score with Playervars.score, and replace lives with Playervars.lives. This means we will be using and updating the scores and lives variables declared in the Playervars.gd script, instead of using local declarations in the CanvasLayer.gd script. Note: We need to replace lives with Playervars.lives and replace score with Playervars.score throughout the entire project!

9. Also, add a $TextureRect3.hide() line inside the elif (Playervars.lives == 1) statement in the _ready() function. This will ensure that when the player has only one life left, that is, when the player loses two lives, only the leftmost heart icon on the HUD (TextureRect1) is visible, while the other two heart icons are hidden, as shown in Figure 10-4 (b).

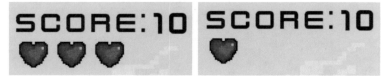

Figure 10-4. *(a) Three lives left, (b) one life left*

10. Your CanvasLayer.gd script should now look like the one shown here:

```
extends CanvasLayer

func _ready():
    ScoreValue.text = String(Playervars.score)
    if(Playervars.lives == 2):
        $TextureRect3.hide()
    elif(Playervars.lives == 1):
        $TextureRect3.hide()
        $TextureRect2.hide()
    elif(Playervars.lives == 0):
        get_tree().change_scene("res://GameOver.tscn")

func _on_KinematicBody2D_gold_coin_collected():
    Playervars.score = Playervars.score + 1
    _ready()

func _on_KinematicBody2D_red_coin_collected():
    Playervars.score = Playervars.score + 5
    _ready()

func _on_KinematicBody2D_silver_coin_collected():
    Playervars.score = Playervars.score + 10
    _ready()

func _on_KinematicBody2D_livescount():
    Playervars.lives = Playervars.lives - 1
    _ready()
```

Note   If in your Scene dock ScoreValue is a child node of HBoxContainer, then $ScoreValue.text will be replaced with $HBoxContainer/ScoreValue in the first line of the _ready() function.

11. Now, open the player script Player.gd, and modify the _on_Fall_ Area_body_entered() function, as shown here:

```
func _on_Fall_Area_body_entered(body):
        Playervars.lives = Playervars.lives - 1
        get_tree().change_scene("res://GameLevel.tscn")
```

Note   We don't need to calculate Playervars.lives in the hit_enemy() function of the player, since we are already updating it in the Canvas.gd script using our custom livescount signal.

Now, whenever you go to another game level and the scene changes or when the current scene reloads after falling off a cliff, the score and lives properties will be calculated throughout the game! Also, if the player's lives become 0, the CanvasLayer.gd script will load the Game Over screen.

Defeating the Monsters

So far, in our game, we don't have a way for our player to defeat the enemy. We can implement a system where the player can shoot fireballs at the enemy, making it disappear every time the fireball hits it. Let's take a look at the steps involved.

1. Create a new scene called Fireball, and create an Area2D node as the root node (rename it to Fireball). Add a sprite and a CollisionShape2D as child nodes, as shown in Figure 10-5. Select the CollisonShape2D and assign it a rectangular collision shape in the Inspector dock.

Figure 10-5. *Scene dock of the Fireball.tscn*

328

2. Select the Sprite node, and drag and drop the image you want to use for the fireball into the Texture field in the Inspector dock. Then, make the sprite as well as the CollisionShape2D larger. As shown in Figure 10-6, we've loaded the same heart image in the Texture field that we used when creating the game HUD in the previous chapter. (You can import another image into your Godot project and use that as the texture instead.)

Figure 10-6. *Loading the heart image into the Texture field*

3. Now, select the Fireball (root) node and click the ▦ bind icon next to the lock icon on the 2D toolbar to make its children nonselectable. Then, with the Fireball node selected, click the 📄 icon in the Scene dock to attach a script. Click the Create button in the Attach Node Script window, and a script called Fireball.gd is created and opened.

4. Replace the contents of the Fireball.gd script with the code shown here:

```
extends Area2D

func _physics_process(_delta):
    position.x = position.x + 1000 * (_delta)
```

5. This code will continuously increase the x position of the fireball by 1,000 units, effectively moving it across the screen from left to right. Increasing this value will move the fireball faster, while decreasing will make it move slower. Note that we are multiplying this increment value by the delta value to prevent changes in the gameplay in case your game's FPS is changed.

Now, we need to make the fireball as well as the enemy disappear every time the fireball collides with it.

6. Select the Fireball node (root node), and open the Node dock next to the Inspector dock. Double-click the area_entered signal; then click Connect in the Connect a Signal to a Method window. This creates a function called _on_Fireball_area_entered() in the Fireball.gd script. Replace the pass with queue_free(), as shown here:

```
func _on_Fireball_area_entered(area):
    queue_free()
```

7. Now open the Input Map tab of the Project Settings. Add an action called shoot, and assign a keyboard key to it, such as the F keyboard key, as shown in Figure 10-7. This will be the key that the player has to press to shoot a fireball. Close the Project Settings.

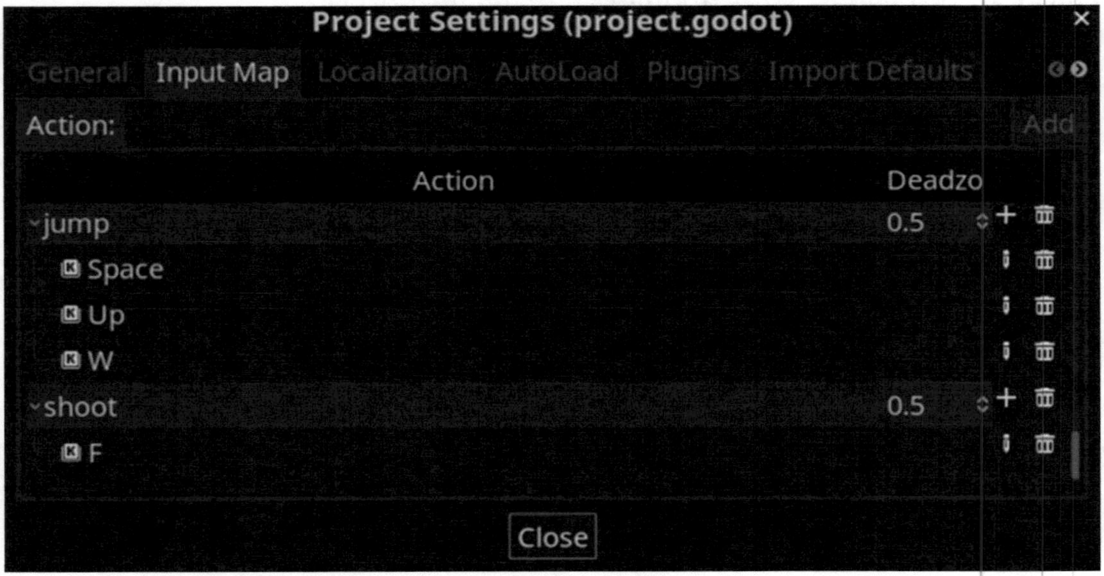

Figure 10-7. Adding a shoot action keyboard key in the input map

8. Open the player scene (Player.tscn), and then add a Position2D as a child node of the player (KinematicBody2D), as shown in Figure 10-8.

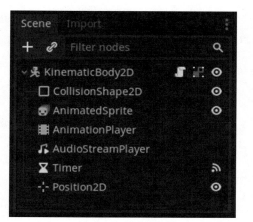

Figure 10-8. *Adding a Position2D node as a child of the KinematicBody2D*

9. Select the Position2D node in the Scene dock, and adjust the
    Position2D in the workspace so that it is slightly in front of
    the player by changing the x and y position properties on the
    Transform tab in the Inspector dock, as shown in Figure 10-9.
    This is where all the fireballs will come from when the player
    shoots them.

Figure 10-9. *Adjusting the Position property of Position2D*

10. Now open the Player script (Player.gd), and modify it for preloading Fireball.tscn, as shown here:

```
extends KinematicBody2D

var velocity = Vector2(0,0)
var gravity = 2000

signal gold_coin_collected
signal red_coin_collected
signal silver_coin_collected

signal livescount
const FIREBALL = preload("res://Fireball.tscn")
```

11. Modify the _physics_process(_delta) function, as shown next. Whenever the keyboard key for the shoot function (F key) is pressed, an instance of the Fireball scene will be created and added as a child of the Player node. The position of the fireball is also set to the position we defined for the Position2D node in Player.tscn.

```
func _physics_process(_delta):
    if Input.is_action_just_pressed("jump") and is_on_floor():
        velocity.y= -1000
        $AnimatedSprite.play("jump")
        $AudioStreamPlayer.play()
    if Input.is_action_pressed("left_arrow"):
        velocity.x = -300
        $AnimatedSprite.play("run")
        $AnimatedSprite.flip_h = true
    elif Input.is_action_pressed("right_arrow"):
        velocity.x = 300
        $AnimatedSprite.play("run")
        $AnimatedSprite.flip_h = false
    else:
        $AnimatedSprite.play("idle")
```

```
    if not is_on_floor():
        $AnimatedSprite.play("jump")

    if Input.is_action_just_pressed("shoot"):
        var fireball = FIREBALL.instance()
        get_parent().add_child(fireball)
        fireball.position = $Position2D.global_position

    velocity.y  = velocity.y + gravity *(_delta)
    move_and_slide(velocity, Vector2.UP)
    velocity.x = lerp(velocity.x,0,0.1)
```

12. Open Enemy.tscn. Select the root node Enemy
    (KinematicBody2D) and add an Area2D as a child to it (rename
    it FireballCollisionChecker). Add a CollisionShape2D as a
    child node of FireballCollisionChecker, and assign it a circular
    collision shape in the Inspector dock (Shape property). Your node
    hierarchy should look like Figure 10-10.

Figure 10-10. *Adding an Area2D node (FireballCollisionChecker) as a child of the*
Enemy node

13. Now, select the CollisionShape2D node (child node of FireballCollisionChecker node) in the Scene dock. Then, adjust the size of the circular collision shape in the workspace and its position by changing the x and y Position properties on the Transform tab in the Inspector dock. Move it as close to the front part of the enemy as possible. This is shown in Figure 10-11.

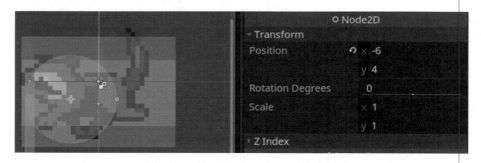

Figure 10-11. *Adjusting the size and position of the CollisionShape2D*

14. When the fireball enters this circular collision shape, the enemy will be "hit." We will use a signal to detect this and to delete the enemy node subsequently. With the FireballCollisionChecker selected in the Scene dock, open the Node dock next to the Inspector dock, and double-click the area_entered() signal. Click the Connect button in the Connect a Signal to a Method window (where the Enemy node is selected).

15. A function called _on_FireballCollisionChecker_area_ entered() is created in the Enemy script, Enemy.gd. Replace the pass in this function with queue_free, as shown here:

```
func _on_FireballCollisionChecker_area_entered(area):
    queue_free()
```

This implies that whenever an area (the fireball) enters the FireballCollisionChecker's CollisionShape2D node, it will signal the Enemy script to delete the Enemy node. But one important step still remains- setting up the correct collision masks and collision layers so that only the fireball can collide with the FireballCollisionChecker in the game.

16. Open the Project Settings (Project ➤ Project Settings), and navigate to the 2d Physics settings under the Layer Names tab. As shown in Figure 10-12, we had assigned different collision layers (1 to 6) to various collidable objects in our game. In the next empty layer, e.g. Layer 7, enter **Fireball** and then close the Project Settings. Click Save (Ctrl+S).

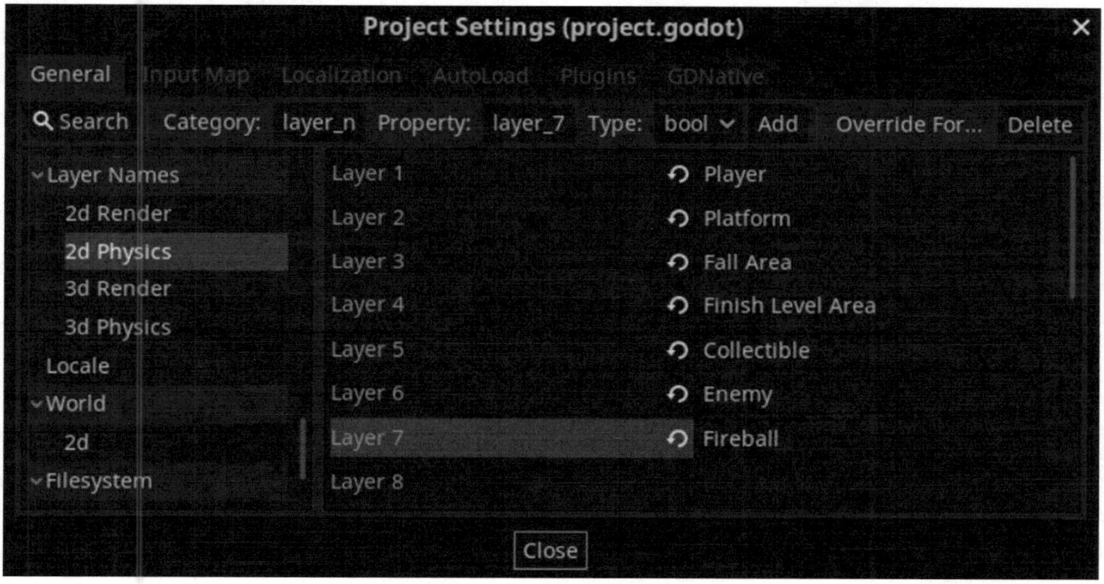

Figure 10-12. *Adding a collision layer for the Fireball*

17. In Enemy.tscn, select the FireballCollisionChecker node in the Scene dock and then expand the Collision tab in the Inspector dock. Now, click the three dots (…) next to the Layer property and unselect the Player layer, as shown in Figure 10-13 (a). We don't need to set a layer for the FireballCollisionChecker as long as we set its mask to monitor collisions with the fireball. For the Mask property, unselect the Player layer and select the Fireball layer, as shown in Figure 10-13 (b).

Figure 10-13. (a) Assigning the fireball mask for the FireballCollisionChecker, (b) assigning the fireball layer and mask for the Fireball

18. Now, we have to set the Layer and Mask properties for the fireball. Open the Fireball.tscn, and select the root node fireball. Expand the Collision tab in the Inspector dock; then for the Layer property, unselect the Player layer and set the Fireball layer, as shown in Figure 10-13 (b). Next, do the same for the Mask property, as shown in Figure 10-13 (b). It's important that the FireballCollisionChecker and Fireball are on different layers so that two fireballs won't collide with and delete each other.

That's it! Now when you play the game, you'll be able to shoot the enemy by pressing the F key button, which will make the enemy disappear.

Adding Touchscreen Buttons

Before you export your game to mobile, you can add touchscreen buttons to your game for controlling the player's left, right, and jump motions. This can be done in a few simple steps.

1. Download images of the buttons you want to use, and import them into your project. We'll be using the Up, Left, and Right Buttons from an asset pack designed by Mihika Dhule. (You can download it here: `https://mihikad.itch.io/collectibles-buttons`.)

2. Open the Game Level scene `GameLevel.tscn`, and select the CanvasLayer node that we created as the parent node for the Score Label and Health Heart icons.

3. Add a CenterContainer node as a child of CanvasLayer, and set its Layout option as Bottom Wide (Under the green Layout button on the 2D toolbar). Next, expand it so that it fills the bottom portion of the game screen where you want to place the buttons, as shown in Figure 10-14.

Figure 10-14. *Expand the CenterContainer to fill the bottom portion of the game screen*

4. Next, add three TouchScreenButton nodes as children of the CenterContainer node, as shown in Figure 10-15 (a). Rename them as Left, Right, and Jump, respectively, as shown in Figure 10-15 (b).

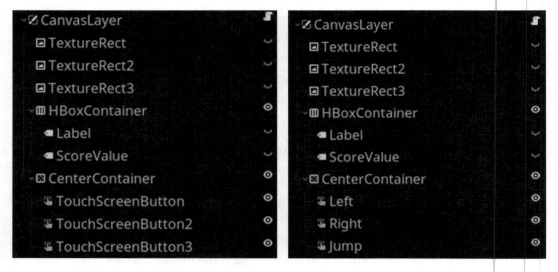

Figure 10-15. *(a) Adding TouchScreenButton nodes as children of CenterContainer, (b) renaming the TouchScreenButton nodes to Left, Right, and Jump*

5. Now, select one of these TouchScreenButton nodes in the Scene dock, and then drag and drop its corresponding image from the FileSystem dock into the Normal property in the Inspector dock. For example, as shown in Figure 10-16, we've assigned the image of the Left Arrow button to the Normal field of the Left node.

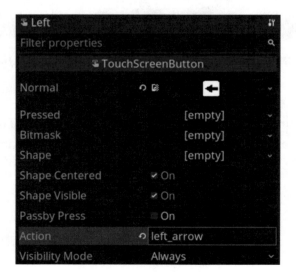

Figure 10-16. *Typing in left_arrow in the Action property*

6.   In the Action property of the Left TouchScreenButton button, type in **left_arrow**, as shown in Figure 10-16. Similarly, type in **right_arrow** for the Right TouchScreenButton button, and jump for the Jump TouchScreenButton button. Recall that we had added these actions for the keyboard key presses on the Input Map tab of the Project Settings.

7.   In the Project Settings, under the General tab, open the Pointing properties under Input Devices. Make sure that the Emulate Mouse From Touch option is enabled, as shown in Figure 10-17. This simulates a mouse click every time you touch or tap on the screen on your phone.

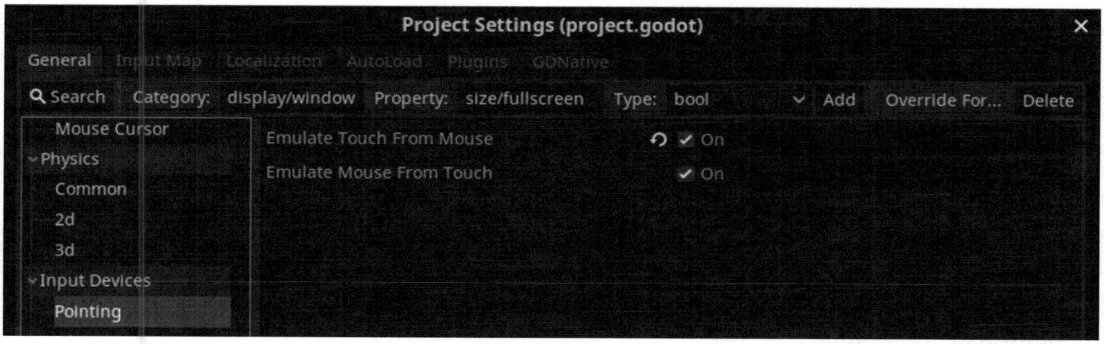

Figure 10-17. *Make sure the Emulate Mouse from Touch option is enabled*

Note   You can optionally also choose the Emulate Touch From Mouse option as well, if you want to simulate a touch or a tap on the screen, every time you click the mouse button on your computer screen.

---

8.   Resize, position, and place these buttons on the CenterContainer in the workspace where you want them to appear in the game.

9.   That's it, your touchscreen buttons are ready! When you play the game, you can see the buttons appear on the bottom portion of the game, as shown in Figure 10-18.

Figure 10-18. *Touchscreen buttons added to the game screen*

Note   The scale and position of the button may change according to your screen resolution.

TRY IT!

Upgrading Your Game

1. Create a global script called Globalvars.gd, and add it to the AutoLoads list.

2. Declare two variables, called score and lives in this script, and initialize them to 0 and 4, respectively. Modify the HUD (CanvasLayer) to initially display five heart icons.

3. Modify the score and lives variables in the Player and Enemy scripts to access the variables declared in Globalvars.gd instead.

4. Create a fireball system to defeat the enemy.

Exporting Your Game

Once you're happy with your project, you can export your game to (make it playable on) various platforms. But first, you need to install Godot's export templates. This can be done via the interface itself.

Downloading Export Templates

Follow these steps:

1. Navigate to Editor ➤ Manage Export Templates at the top left of the interface, as shown in Figure 10-19.

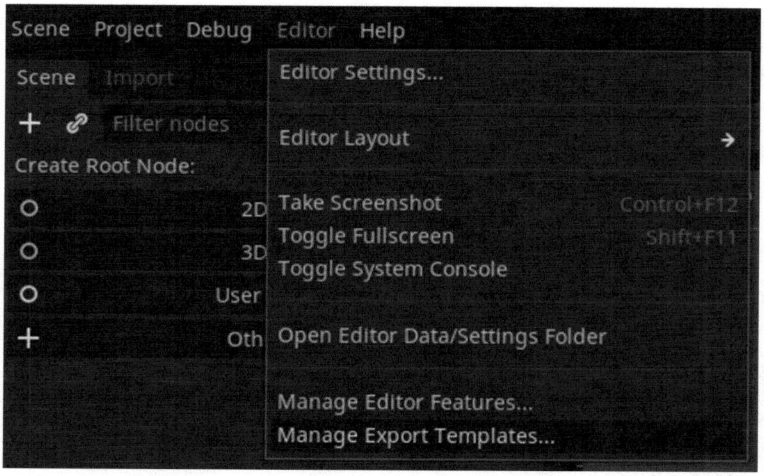

Figure 10-19. *Click the Manage Export Templates option*

2. In the Export Template Manager, you'll see that your export templates are missing, as shown in Figure 10-20 (a). Once you click Download, you can select a mirror link that lets you download the required templates from the Godot website into your project, as shown in Figure 10-20 (b). Once you click this link, the downloading will start, as shown in Figure 10-21 (a).

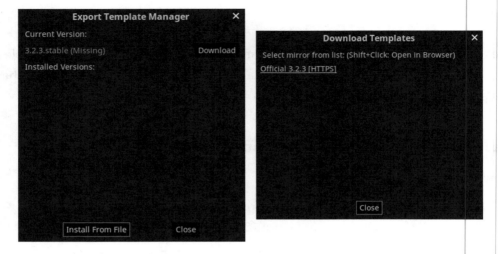

Figure 10-20. *(a) Export templates are missing, (b) clicking the mirror link to download the templates from the Godot website*

3. Once the Export templates have been downloaded, you should see Figure 10-21 (b).

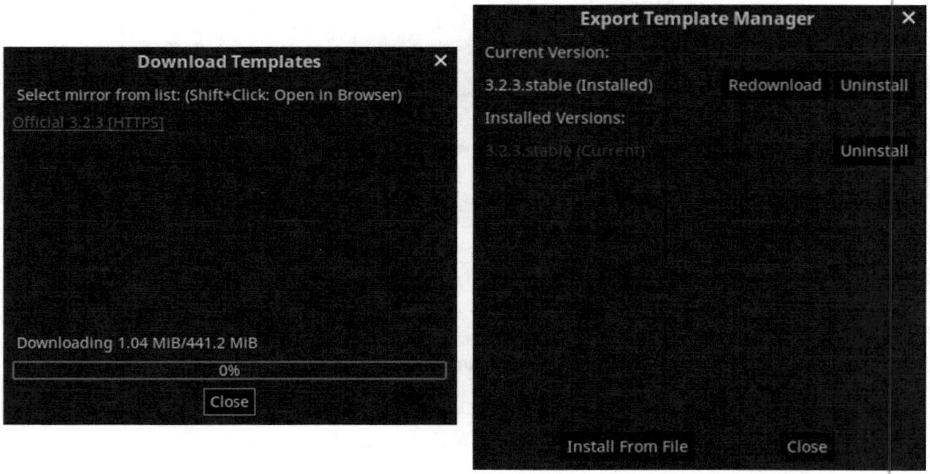

Figure 10-21. *(a) The download of the export templates starts. (b) The export templates are successfully downloaded and installed*

Now you're ready to start exporting your game to different platforms!

Exporting to PC (Windows)

Follow these steps:

1. From the toolbar at the top of the interface, navigate to Project ➤ Export, as shown in Figure 10-22.

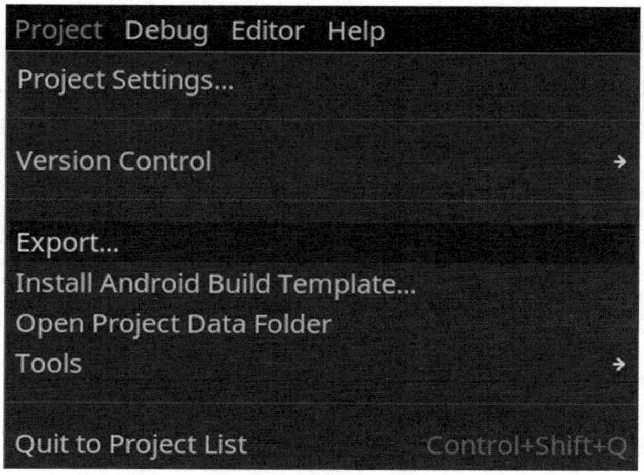

Figure 10-22. *Opening the Export window*

2. Click the Add button on the Export window that opens up, as shown in Figure 10-23. Click the Windows Desktop icon.

Figure 10-23. *Adding a Windows Desktop export preset*

3. The Windows Desktop option gets loaded into the Presets list. As shown in Figure 10-24, you can change various features related to this preset. Make sure to keep the Runnable button on, and then click the Export Project button.

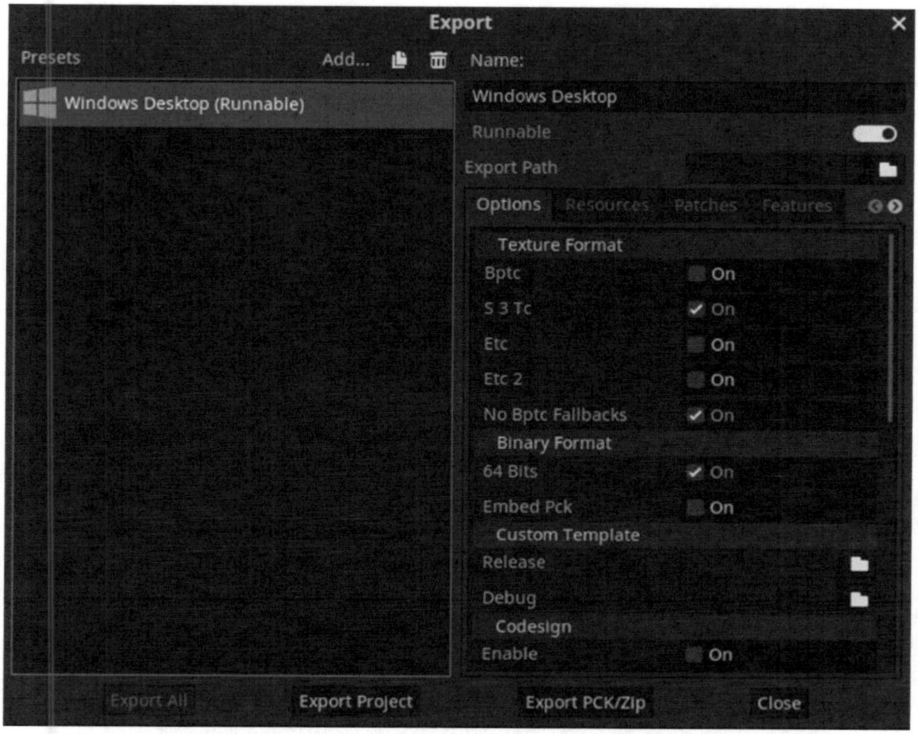

Figure 10-24. *The Windows Desktop preset is added*

4.   Once you do that, a Save a File window opens. Navigate to the
     path where you want to save your exported game, and give it a
     name in the File field, as shown in Figure 10-25. Once you click
     the Save button, your game gets successfully exported to your
     specified path. Note that the Export With Debug option should be
     disabled when you export your game for the final release.

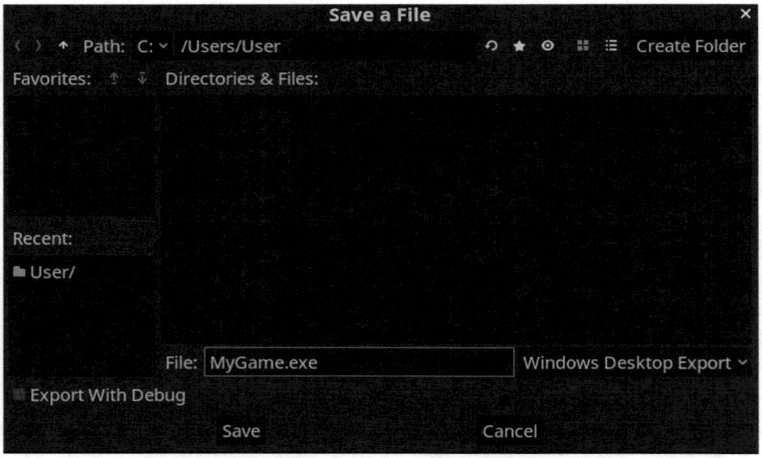

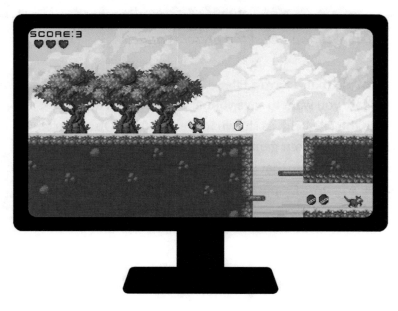

Figure 10-25. *Specifying the name and path of the export file*

5. Navigate to the path where the game is saved on your computer, and double-click the game to start playing it on Windows! See Figure 10-26.

Figure 10-26. *Author's depiction of the game being played on the PC*

Exporting to Mobile (Android)

We can export to Android by creating an Android Application Package (APK) file for our game. For doing so, we need to first ensure that we have the correct setup files that are required, as given in the official Godot documentation.[1] Moreover, the process is slightly different in case of exporting with Godot version 3.2.3 or Godot version 3.3 or above. Let's look at the Export process for Godot 3.2.3.

1. Download and install Android Studio version 1.4 or later, and run it. You can download the latest version here: `https://developer.android.com/studio`.

2. Ensure that the packages given here are installed:

    -   Android SDK Platform-Tools version 30.0.5 or later

    -   Android SDK Build-Tools version 30.0.3

    -   Android SDK Platform 29

    -   Android SDK Command-line Tools (latest)

    -   CMake version 3.10.2.4988404

    -   NDK version 21.4.7075529

3. Download and install a Java Development Kit (JDK). Godot recommends using OpenJDK 8, which can be downloaded from `https://adoptopenjdk.net/`. You can also choose to download and install the latest version from the same site, `jdk-16.0.2`.

4. Create a `debug.keystore` key:

    -   Run the Command Prompt as Administrator.

    -   Change the directory (`cd ..` to go back one level) to the `bin` directory of the JDK. For example, if you downloaded and installed `jdk-16.0.2`, navigate to `C:\Program Files\Java\jdk-16.0.2\bin` at the CMD prompt.

    -   Copy and paste the following command, and then press Enter:

- keytool -keyalg RSA -genkeypair -alias androiddebugkey -keypass android -keystore debug.keystore -storepass android -dname "CN=Android Debug,O=Android,C=US" -validity 9999 -deststoretype pkcs12

- A file called debug.keystore should be created in your bin folder (C:\Program Files\Java\jdk-16.0.2\bin\debug.keystore).

5. In the Godot interface, navigate to Editor ➤ Editor Settings (at the top left), and open the Android settings found under Export on the General tab. As shown in Figure 10-27, enter the path to the Debug Keystore (same as in the previous step).

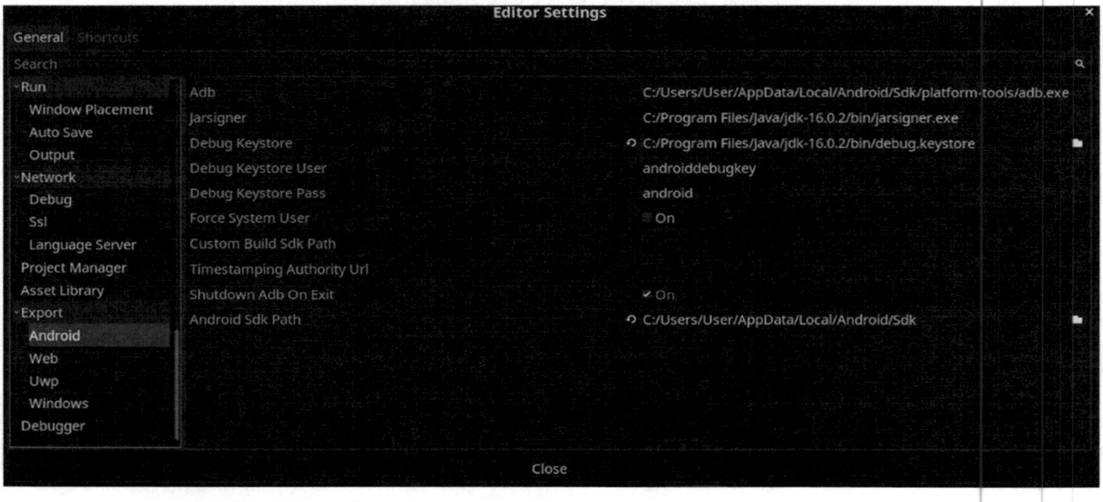

Figure 10-27. *Editor settings for Android export*

Note   Your Editor Settings will look different from Figure 10-27 if you are using a different version of Godot. If the Adb and Jarsigner fields are missing, then there is no need to enter their paths. But we need to do that if we are using Godot 3.2.3.

---

6. Fill in the Adb, Jarsigner, and Android SDK Path fields with the respective paths given here (replace UserName with your Windows account name):

    - `C:/Users/UserName/AppData/Local/Android/Sdk/platform-tools/adb.exe`

    - `C:/Program Files/Java/jdk-16.0.2/bin/jarsigner.exe`

    - `C:/Users/UserName/AppData/Local/Android/Sdk`

7. Close the Editor Settings, and navigate to Editor ➤ Manage Export Templates at the top left of the interface. Your Export Template Manager should look like the one shown in Figure 10-28 if you've downloaded the export template as explained previously. If you haven't done so, you can just click the Download button in your Export Template Manager to download the templates.

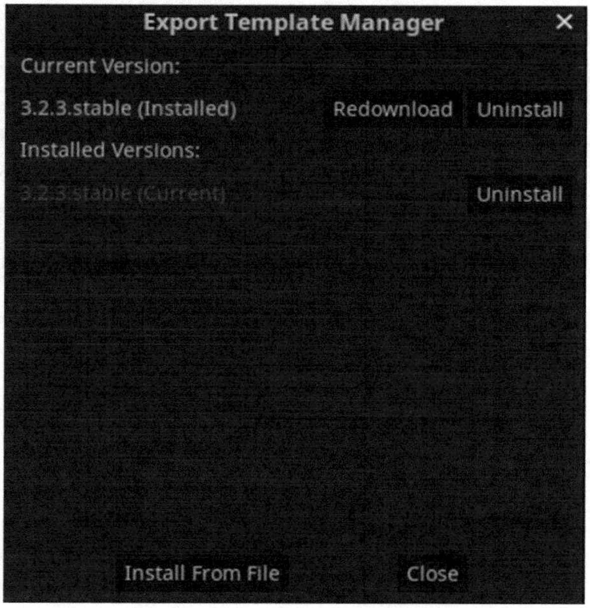

Figure 10-28. *The Export Template Manager after installing the Export Templates*

8.   Next, navigate to Project ➤ Export from the Project tab at the top-left corner of the interface. Click the Add button and select the Android option, as shown in Figure 10-29.

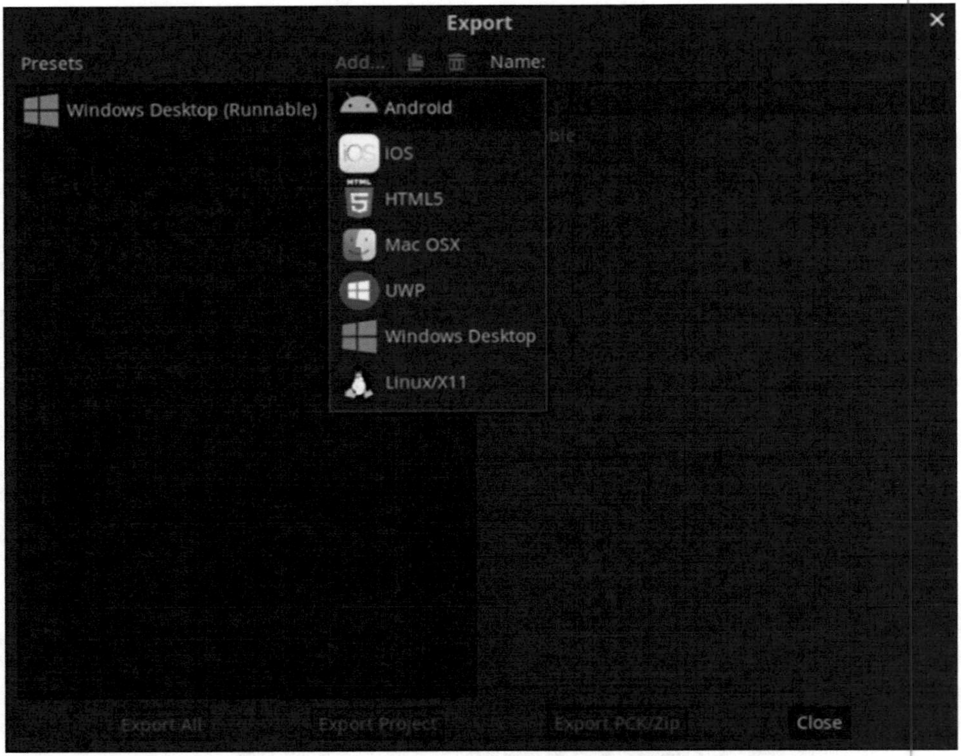

Figure 10-29. *Adding an Android export preset*

Note   If you've already created an export for Windows Desktop, its corresponding preset will be already be added to the Presets list.

9. An Android export preset will be added to the Presets list, as shown in Figure 10-30. You can change various features related to this export in the window. Click the Export Project button.

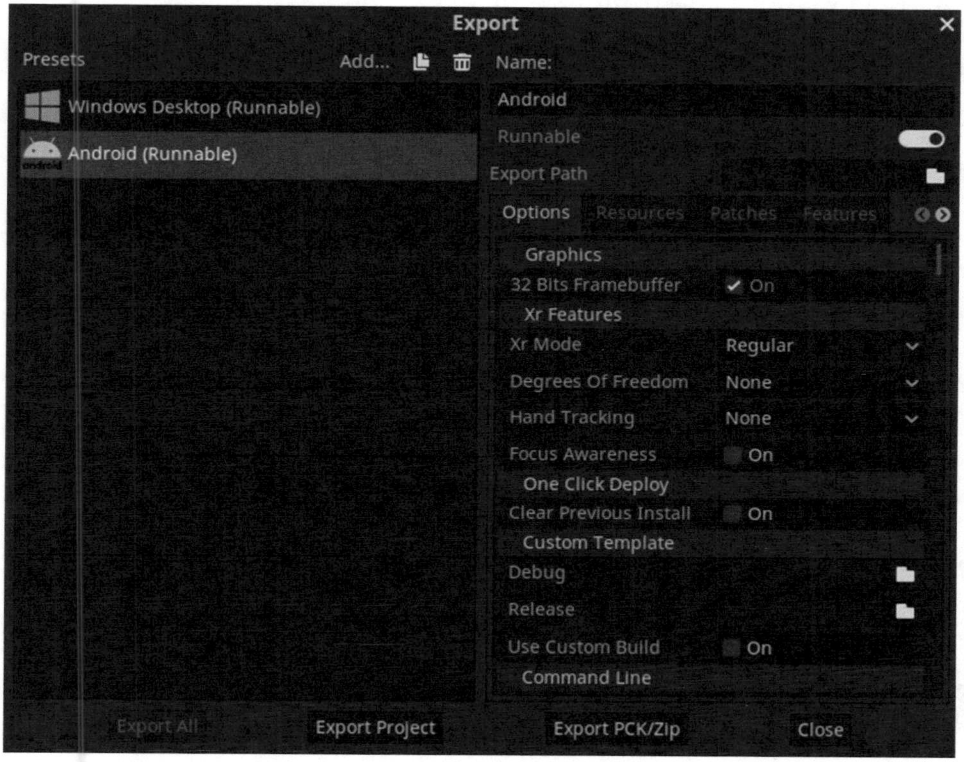

Figure 10-30. *An Android export preset is added to the Export window*

10. In the Save a File window that opens, navigate to the path where you want to save the game, and enter the name of your game in the File field, as shown in Figure 10-31. Make sure that Export with Debug is not enabled during your final export.

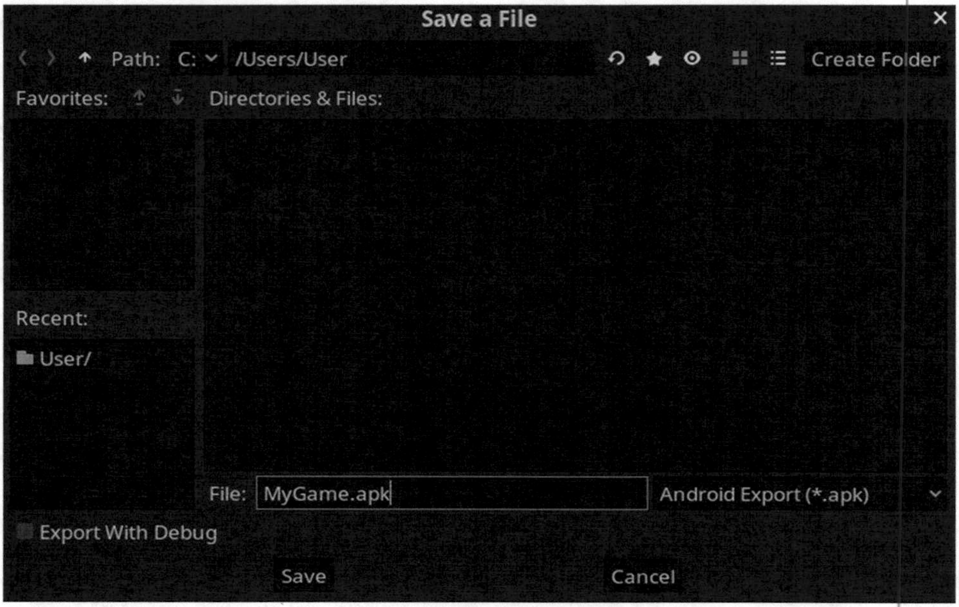

Figure 10-31. *Specifying the path and name of the Android export*

11. Once you click the Save button, the game APK will be created at the path specified.

12. Connect your Android mobile phone to your computer using a USB cable, and copy the game APK file (e.g., MyGame.apk) into your phone.

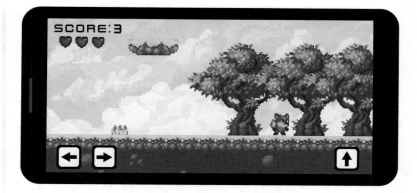

Figure 10-32. *Author's depiction of the game being played on a mobile phone*

13. You can now click the app on your phone to install it. Since this app is not from a verified source on the Google Play Store, you might get a warning asking you to confirm whether you want to install the app (you need to enable installation from a third-party source). Click Install Anyway to install your app and start playing on your mobile phone!

Exporting to Browser (HTML)

Follow these steps:

1. Click the Project tab at the top of the interface, and navigate to Project ➤ Export to open the Export window.

2. Click the Add button and select the HTML5 option. This creates an HTML5 preset, as shown in Figure 10-33. If you have already created presets for other platforms, such as Windows Desktop and Android, they will be present in the Presets list.

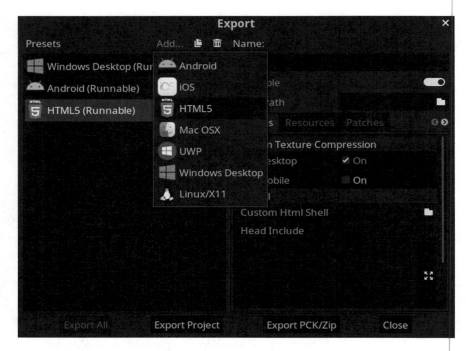

Figure 10-33. *Adding an HTML5 export preset*

Note   Make sure that you've downloaded the Export templates, as explained previously. If you haven't done so, navigate to Editor ➤ Manage Export Templates, and then click the Download Button to install the export templates.

---

3. We can change different features related to this export by changing the properties on the right side of the Export window.

4. Click the Export Project button, and the Save a File window will open. Create a new folder under the path where you want to save the exported game, and then navigate to the path. Name the file index.html, as shown in Figure 10-34, and then click the Save button.

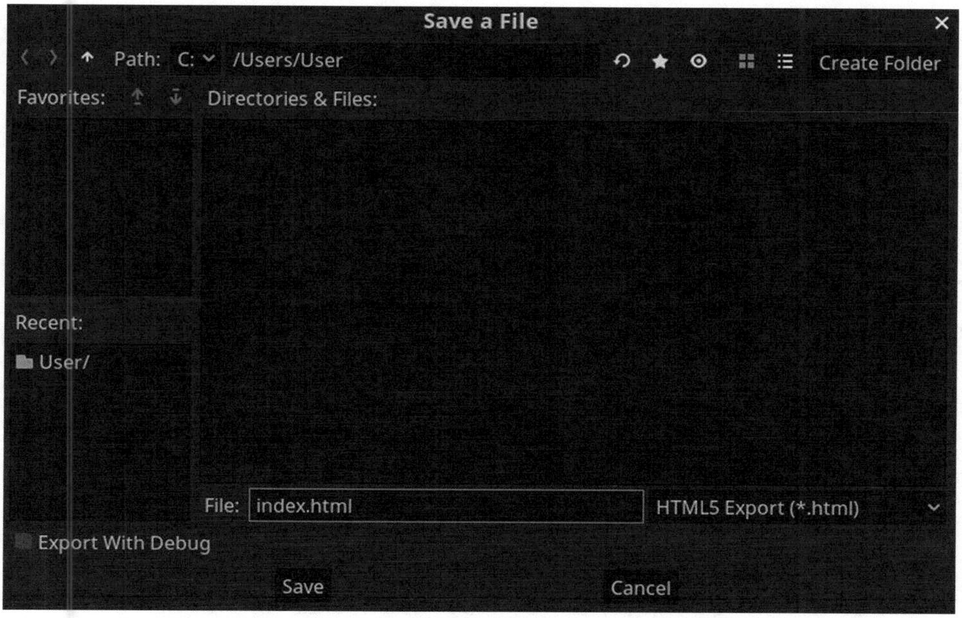

Figure 10-34. *Specifying the path and naming the HTML5 export*

Note   For uploading your browser file to Itch.io, you will need to save it as
`Index.html`.

---

5.   Now, open the folder where you saved the file on your computer.
      You'll notice that six different files have been created in this folder,
      one of them being `index.html`.

6.   We need to create a zip files containing all these files. Select all the
      files, right-click, and under 7-Zip click "Add to archive," as shown
      in Figure 10-35. If you don't have 7-Zip, you can download it for
      free from `https://www.7-zip.org/download.html` or use any
      other software for creating the zip file.

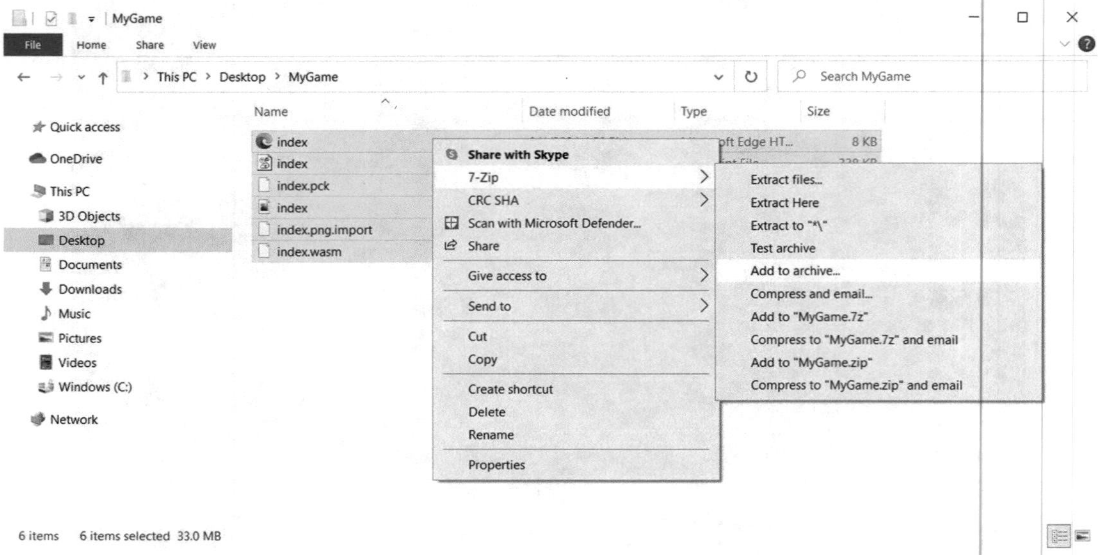

Figure 10-35. *Creating a zip folder for the browser files*

> 7. In the Add to Archive window that opens, change the Archive format
> to zip, and then click the OK button. A compressed folder called
> MyGame.zip is created and is ready to be uploaded on a website!

Publishing Your Game

There are tons of different websites or platforms that you can publish and sell your game
on, with some of them being paid and some free. Examples include Steam, Itch.io, Game
Jolt, Google Play, and the Apple Store, among others. Each website or platform has its
own set of requirements, and some require you to pay a certain amount to publish your
game or share a part of the profit that your game makes with them. We'll take a look at
how to publish your game on a platform that is completely free to publish and sell your
game on: Itch.io.

Itch.io

As we saw in previous chapter, Itch.io is a website that has a variety of indie games
and game assets (free as well as paid). It even hosts themed game jams, where you can
submit your games for competitions. It's a great place for indie-game developers to
publish their game. Let's take a look at how to do just that.

1. Create an account on Itch.io (`https://itch.io`).

2. Once your account is created, head over to your Creator Dashboard, as shown in Figure 10-36, and then click "Create new project."

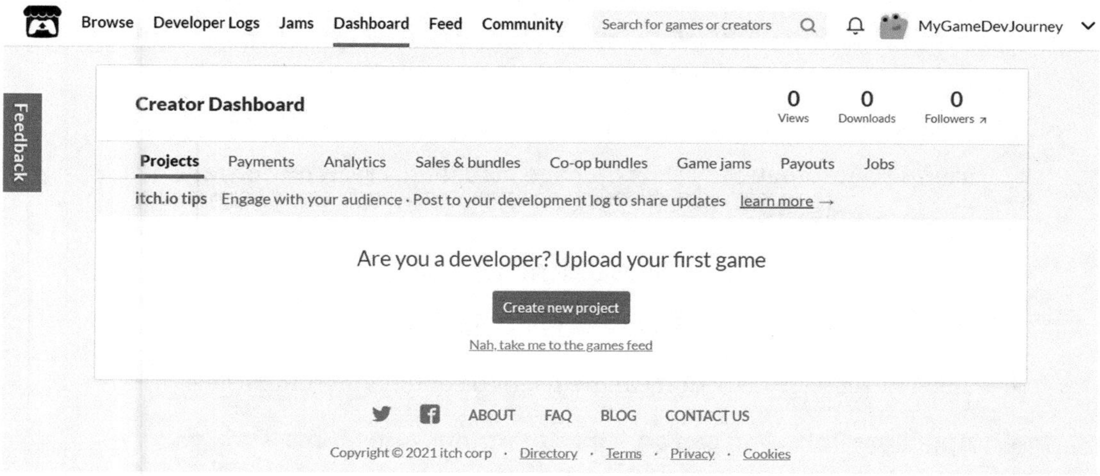

Figure 10-36. *Creator dashboard of Itch.io*

A page opens where you can enter various details of your game, such as the following:

- Title of your game

- Project URL.

- Description or tagline.

- Classification: Select Games, since we are uploading a game.

- Kind of Project: Choose HTML, since we are uploading an HTML file. This will allow the game to be played in the browser. If you set this to Downloadable, then your game files will need to be downloaded by the player, and the game cannot be played in the browser in this case.

- Release Status.

- Pricing: This needs to be separately set up on your Itch.io account for you to be able to accept payments for your game.

- Uploads: This is where you'll be uploading your game files. To upload your game files, click the Upload Files button, and then navigate to and select your zipped game folder. Once the folder is uploaded, select the "This file will be played in the browser" option.

- Embed Options: Select Embed in page, select Manually set size, and in the Viewport dimensions, set the Width and Height to be equal to the dimensions of your game.

- Frame options: You can select various options such as Mobile friendly, Automatically start on page load, Fullscreen button, and Enable scrollbars.

- Description: Enter a few lines describing your game.

- Genre: Select Action, Adventure, Platformer, Strategy, etc.

- Tags: Enter keywords that can be used to search for your game.

- App Store links: You can add links to various App Stores if you've uploaded your game there as well.

- Community: You can add a Comments section or even a community page called a *discussion board* to get feedback from the players of your game.

- Visibility & access: Set it to Draft and save the page, and then set it to Public to release your game to the Itch.io community. If you set to Restricted, then only those with a link to your game page can view and play your game.

You can also upload a cover image, a video trailer, and screenshots of your game at the top of your new project page.

Note   You can check the dimensions of your game in the Godot interface by navigating to Project ➤ Project Settings ➤ General ➤ Display ➤ Window.

Now, click the Save button at the bottom of the page, and click the View Page button. Now, a page will open with a button called "Run game." Click the button to start playing in the browser! You can always update your game files and upload them anytime to the same project from the dashboard.

TRY IT!

Export and Publish

1. Export your game to PC (Windows), mobile (Android), and browser (HTML5).

2. Explore various options for publishing and monetizing your game.

3. Publish your game!

Exporting Tips

Here are some quick tips that can make it easier to export your game:

- If there is an issue with exporting your game, copy all the files that are in your project, and paste it in a new, empty Godot project (using the Windows File Explorer). Give the new project a different name than the first one, and try to export again.

- The same Godot project can be opened in different versions of Godot, and changes made in one version are reflected when you open the project in another one. Do note that projects created in newer versions of Godot may not work correctly when you try to open them in older versions of the engine. On the other hand, projects created in older versions generally work fine in newer versions of Godot.

- When exporting your game, make sure to adjust the Project Settings (Display) such as:

  - Dimensions of the game (width and height)

  - Borderless or bordered game screen

  - Resizable or fixed-sized game screen

- Full-screen mode

- Orientation: landscape or portrait

- Stretch mode

Monetizing Your Game

Websites that let you publish indie games such as Steam and Itch.io usually have the option of selling your game. Apart from that, there are various other ways that your game can earn money:

- *In-game currency*: You can introduce an in-game currency that the player can use for buying extra lives, character customization items, extra skills, and in-game consumables.

- *Premium content*: You can set certain content in your game to be "premium" such as a new character, new outfits, or even extra game levels, which are locked unless the player buys them through in-app purchases.

- *Advertisements*: A lot of free-to-play apps on the Google Play store use in-app advertisements to generate revenue. You can link your game to certain videos or websites of advertising agencies that will pay you every time the player clicks the links leading to them. You can offer a small reward for watching videos or downloading other games or apps.

- *Merchandising*: This method may need quite a bit of investment on your side. Once your game earns a certain amount of revenue, you can invest in creating merchandise related to your game that people can buy in real life.

What's Next?

After going through all the chapters in this book, I hope that you've gained the confidence to create and publish your first 2D platformer in Godot! Although it may seem that we are at the end of our journey, this is just the beginning. Godot has numerous features that you can explore such as post-processing effects, lighting and illumination, support for augmented and virtual reality integration, and a whole new system for making 3D games, I hope that you're excited about what's ahead. Here are some ideas to tickle your brain:

- Adding multiple game levels to your game, each with an increasing level of difficulty.

- Spawning different types of enemies randomly throughout your game.

- Creating and adding more elements to your game world such as springboards for higher player jumps, power-ups that give the player more skills/lives, ladders that the player can climb, and secret areas in the game that the player can explore for greater rewards.

- A game screen for controlling the game settings such as the music volume, level difficulty, choice of character, and character outfits.

Key Takeaways

In this chapter, we learned how to upgrade our game by adding more features such as adding a global variable system, enemy shooting, and touchscreen buttons. We walked through the steps for exporting our game to various platforms such as mobile (Android), PC (Windows), and browser (HTML5). We saw the different places where we can publish and monetize the game and were introduced to a few ideas that we can explore further as a game developer.

Index

© Maithili Dhule 2022
M. Dhule, *Beginning Game Development with Godot*, https://doi.org/10.1007/978-1-4842-7455-2

H, I, J

K

L

M

N, O

P, Q

Printed in the United States
by Baker & Taylor Publisher Services